# Raise the Bar

## Real World Solutions for a Troubled Profession

**Lawrence J. Fox, Editor**

**Foreword by Brad D. Brian**

ABA
Defending Liberty
Pursuing Justice

FIRST
CHAIR
·PRESS·

Cover design by ABA Publishing.



Printed in the United States of America

10 09 08 07 5 4 3 2 1

**Library of Congress Cataloging-in-Publication Data**

Raise the bar / edited by Lawrence J. Fox. — 1st ed.
p. cm.
Includes index.
ISBN 978-1-59031-879-9
1. Lawyers—United States. 2. Practice of law—United States. 3. Law offices—United States. 4. Legal ethics—United States. I. Fox, Lawrence J., 1943–

KF297.R35 2007
174'.30973—dc22

2007028266-9

Discounts are available for books ordered in bulk. Special consideration is given to state bars, CLE programs, and other bar-related organizations. Inquire at Book Publishing, ABA Publishing, American Bar Association, 321 North Clark Street, Chicago, Illinois 60610-4714.

www.ababooks.org

# TABLE OF CONTENTS

**Foreword** vii

**About the Editor** xi

**Introduction** xiii

**Part I: The Billable Hour** **1**

1 Our Gilded Cage
*By Scott Turow* 3

2 End Billable Hour Goals . . . Now
*By Lawrence J. Fox* 15

**Part II: The Law Firm** **31**

3 A Pig in a Poke? The Uncertain Advantages of Very Large and Highly Leveraged Law Firms in America
*By Michael H. Trotter* 33

4 Organizational Perspectives on Raising the Bar: Five Tentative Solutions
*By Robert L. Nelson* 53

5 Law Firms as Great Places to Work
*By Dr. Scott Cawood* 69

**Part III: Being Honest** **85**

6 A View from Outside the Law Firms
*By Bruce D. Collins* 87

7 The Death of Partnership: Can We End the Trend?
*By Lawrence J. Fox* 103

**Part IV: The Work** **111**

8 A New Path to Excellence: Balanced Hours 101
*By Cynthia Thomas Calvert and Natalie M. Hiott-Levine* 113

9 Solving the Legal World's Problems: A Sole Practitioner's Perspective
*By Roland Baggott* 137

**Part V: Associates and Mentoring** **165**

10 Mentoring: Alive and Well?
*By Louise A. LaMothe* 167

11 There's No Turning Back: Five Practical Ways to Motivate the New Breed of Associates
*By Coke Morgan Stewart* 183

12 Developing Young Lawyers
*By Dean Zipser* 199

**Part VI: Serving the Wider World** **215**

13 Pro Bono: More Than a Professional Responsibility
*By Joanne Martin and Stephen Daniels* 217

14 Let's Start a Ripple: Building Diversity in the Legal Profession
*By: Kay H. Hodge* 237

15 Should We Mandate Doing Well by Doing Good?
*By Lawrence J. Fox* 251

16 The Statesman Lawyer: An Oxymoron?
*By Robert N. Sayler* 257

17 Service to the Bar
*By Robert Grey, Jr.* 265

**Part VII: Valediction** **271**

18 The City Upon the Hill
*By Michael E. Tigar* 273

**Index** **291**

# FOREWORD

Why are so many lawyers unhappy? I'm not; I've loved the practice of law. But as a recent Chair of the ABA Section of Litigation, I came to see how lucky I've been. For too many, professional life has failed to live up to the dreams of those who chose a life in the law.

The essays in this book, by some of the most thoughtful lawyers working today, explore the gap between aspiration and experience.

Much in the life of the law has changed. The hours; the instant communications that leave lawyers on-call even when off-duty; the tremendous growth of litigation and transactions in both scale and complexity; the literal explosion of electronic data in the national and world economies: all have changed the world in which we practice law.

I initially thought the unhappiness of lawyers would have a generational flavor, reflecting different expectations and experiences, as well as the changing demographics of law school graduates. But I was wrong about that, and much else. An ABA Section of Litigation project, known as "Raise the Bar," held a series of focus groups and face-to-face meetings for lawyers and other professionals of every age, gender, and race. We found the sources and nature of unhappiness among lawyers to be almost universal.

First, lawyers at every level complained to us about the transformation of the legal practice from a *profession* to a *business.* While per partner profit statistics indicate that lawyers have reaped large financial rewards from this transformation, those rewards have come at a price: more hours, less loyalty, increased tension among colleagues, reduced time for pro bono work and public service, and greater disruption of family and personal lives.

Second, lawyers across the spectrum complained about the reduction in hands-on experiences. Increasing complexity of cases and transactions means that more lawyers spend more time as parts of teams gathering and sorting information—and less time with clients or in court, arguing motions or trying cases.

This problem can't be evaded; it must be faced. Lawyers throughout history have needed information to do what they must do. In the age of information, however, we are constantly at peril of being overwhelmed. Neither Clarence Darrow nor Perry Mason could have gathered, let alone reviewed, a million documents. Today, we can put a million documents on a computer and carry it with us wherever we go. That can be a powerful tool, but it is an oppressive one nonetheless.

Whatever the cause, lawyers are leaving the profession in droves. Others remain in the profession, but are unhappy with their careers and in some cases their lives. Worse yet, many college graduates are choosing not to pursue legal careers at all.

These problems have their roots in larger changes in the world around us—the world that we as lawyers must enter and serve. It is nice to dream of by-gone times, but are there solutions to what ails us in the here and now?

That is the question we set out to answer in the Raise the Bar project. Through focus groups and meetings—and with the assistance of professionals from outside the legal field—we came up with some recommendations. We hope they can help restore some of the age-old satisfactions from a life as a lawyer in our society.

This book is the culmination of this project. After describing problems plaguing lawyers today, the essays identify specific recommendations for increasing lawyers' satisfaction with their careers—enhancing mentoring roles in law firms, eliminating billable hour requirements, increasing pro bono and trial opportunities, and breaking up a career with a few years in government, a non-profit institution, or even a different legal specialty or community.

None is a panacea. Some will suit some lawyers better than others. I am particularly concerned with increasing the opportunities for lawyers to try cases before juries, because that lies so near the heart of my own reasons for becoming a lawyer. But all these ideas merit consideration, whether you are pondering your own career or hoping to help younger lawyers with theirs. You will have to judge for yourself what might work best for you.

For many lawyers, the practice has been financially rewarding. But for most of us, that was not the original draw. We *decided* to become lawyers because of the allure of other ideas and ideals: justice, fairness, equality, opportunity, service. We liked the idea of helping or championing a person, a cause, an idea. If we could do that, and do it well, then with or without financial rewards the life of the law would be good indeed. The essays in this book suggest that, if we give these defining ideals a place in the shaping of our careers, we could be a happier and more justly admirable lot.

Brad D. Brian
Los Angeles, 2007

# ABOUT THE EDITOR

Lawrence J. Fox is a partner at Drinker Biddle & Reath in Philadelphia, PA. He focuses his practice on corporate and securities litigation, as well as advising for corporations and private law partnerships on ethics issues and disputes. He has twice served on the firm's board of managing partners and has chaired the firm's Professional Responsibility Committee. He received his B.A. and J.D. from the University of Pennsylvania.

Mr. Fox was instrumental in the creation of the ABA Commission on the Evaluation of the Rules of Professional Conduct (Ethics 2000), on which he also served. He has also served as chair of the ABA Standing Committee on Ethics and Professional Responsibility and the Planning Committee for the annual ABA National Conference on Professional Responsibility; chair of the ABA Section of Litigation; chair of the ABA Section Officers Conference; and chair of the ABA Post-Conviction Death Penalty Representation Project. He was the 2005 recipient of the ABA Pro Bono Publico Award, and the 2007 recipient of the Michael Franck Professional Responsibility Award.

Mr. Fox is the author of *Legal Tender: A Lawyers' Guide to Professional Dilemmas* and co-author of *Traversing the Ethical Minefield: Problems, Law, and Professional Responsibility; Red Flags: A Lawyer's Handbook on Legal Ethics;* and *Your Lawyer: A User's Guide* with professor Susan R. Martyn.

Mr. Fox has lectured on ethics and litigation issues at over 35 law schools, teaches legal ethics at the University of Pennsylvania, and has taught legal ethics at Harvard and Cornell.

# INTRODUCTION

Brad Brian, Chairman of the ABA Section of Litigation for bar year 2005–2006, approached his new responsibilities with the gusto, vision and optimism only a true advocate could muster. Take on the Justice Department's dim view of the attorney-client privilege? Done. Address the human rights crisis in Darfur? Done. Oh, and not by the way, let's cure the great ills of our profession as reflected, Brad observed, in the generation gap between the new generation X and Y lawyers, on the one hand, and those like this writer, whom Brad politely described as "seasoned" lawyers, on the other.

Thus was launched one of Brad's major initiatives, co-chaired by Yuri Mikulka and yours truly, with an imaginative and dedicated task force that included the Section's remarkable staff director Patsy Engelhard; her invaluable assistant, Karen Kasparaitis; Brad's field commander, the whip-cracking, Andra Greene; and Karen Williams, Aimee Moore, and Coke Stewart.

We began, as do so many discussions addressing the malaise in the profession, by meeting among ourselves, rehashing and bemoaning the usual ills that we thought were reflected in the generational divide. From this grew the idea that Yuri and I each convene a focus group of lawyers in each age cohort to formalize our task force's investigation into the problems we were charged to address. So, in the heat of an Atlanta August in windowless conference rooms at the ABA Annual Meeting, each "generation" met for several transcribed hours of conversation. When the results of these meetings were digested three important ideas emerged.

First, we decided that thinking about these matters in terms of generational divide was not necessarily correct and, in any event, was not helpful. The truth was, everyone on either side of our constructed divide saw the problems in much the same way and seemed equally committed to addressing them.

Second (and this one was my epiphany), in gathering the seasoned lawyers, individuals who had great responsibility in their respective law firms, one could not help but be struck by the way in which all of these issues were ones that were attributed to so-called outside forces. In short, these leaders of law firms, including me, did not want to take any responsibility—none whatsoever—for what had occurred on their (my) watch. Blame for the American Lawyer, economic forces, and impossible clients was universal. Blame for the management of that great institution—the modern American law firm—was non-existent.

Third, we recognized that long ago the profession had literally exhausted itself in examining the topic of the wrongs that beset the profession. What was needed was a focus on solutions. We needed to refresh old ideas and imagine new ones that addressed the problems, since decrying them, a project the profession had raised to a high art form, was getting us nowhere.

Armed with these three insights we changed the name of the project to Raise the Bar (no relation, none whatsoever, to a campaign to sell cell phones) and we sponsored four major conferences to bring together important opinion leaders to help us seek solutions. We invited young lawyers, seasoned lawyers, a group we labeled sandwich lawyers (the hard-charging young profit-driven partners both young and old lawyers had labeled part of the problem), in-house counsel, academics (including non-lawyer professionals), representatives from Price Waterhouse, the media, and others.

The brainstorming worked. Multiple ideas emerged. One was the book you are holding in your hands. We are proud to present this volume bringing together eighteen chapters from sixteen authors from a vast range of backgrounds to offer the profession the essays you will find here. Each was given only one instruction, the exact same one that has animated this entire endeavor: write about solutions that our profession can embrace. And we hope you conclude that these generous authors have fulfilled the mandate in a splendid way.

Permit me to whet your appetite for each chapter.

The famous novelist and trial lawyer Scott Turow shares his trenchant observations about the use of billable hour requirements and why they should be abandoned as inconsistent with best interest of clients and the lawyers on whom they are imposed.

This author, inspired by the speech Mr. Turow gave to the ABA Section of Litigation in 2004 that Mr. Turow has turned into the chapter you find here, wrote a second article that specifically addresses the evils that would be eliminated if these minimum billable hour requirements and bonuses for achievement of even higher billable hour "accomplishments" were jettisoned in favor of less certain, more nuanced evaluation of the contribution and compensation of lawyers, emphasizing those professional activities that are not billable but are critical to the health of firms, the profession, and society.

Michael H. Trotter, a partner in Atlanta at Kilpatrick Stockton, LLP, has added to a distinguished legal career astute observations on the business of law firms, including the well-received *Profit and the Practice of Law: What's Happened to the Legal Profession*. Here he offers readers of this volume proof that neither size nor leverage, two impediments to raising the bar, are necessary for a law firm to be successful.

Robert Nelson, the brilliant Director of the American Bar Foundation and an eminent sociologist who is also a lawyer, provides our readers with a comprehensive menu of possible solutions, the kind of outpouring of imagination one could only elicit from a fecund mind like Bob's.

One of the most exciting ideas to come out of the Raise the Bar Project was some way for law firms to benchmark their achievements in this area. Scott Cawood, former President of ModernThink, offers our readers an excellent description of how a Best Law Firm initiative might work.

Bruce Collins addresses us from an interesting perch. Although he has never worked at a firm, his role as in-house counsel for C-Span and his hobby of mentoring many who are considering careers in the law has provided him a perspective on what ails us and how we can improve. His surprising conclusion is a double-barreled recommendation that we tell those who are thinking about the practice of law the unvarnished truth of what they might expect and (here comes the real surprise) we encourage many that the practice of law is not for them.

This author suggests in "The Death of Partnership" that debunking the professional myths of who will make partner and what partnership means may go a long way toward creating realistic expectations and avoiding disappointments that contribute to the professional malaise.

Two leaders of the Project for Attorney Retention, Cynthia Thomas Calvert and Natalie M. Hiott-Levine, outline a new path to excellence for law firms in developing not just lip service but real dedication to a balanced hour program that can bring sanity and success to law firm life.

Roland Baggot delivers to our readers a short autobiography that is so introspective and compelling it deserves a careful read. Only when the reader gets to the end will one understand the credibility that should attach to Roland's suggested solutions, arising as they do from his poignant, heartfelt, and often disquieting unvarnished look at his relatively brief but rich career at the bar. One wants to know what Roland's chapter will look like when it is vastly expanded with ten years' more of his experiences.

Louise LaMothe, a former Chair of the ABA Litigation Section and star litigator at Irell & Manella, now is a valued mediator who pioneered the concept of mentoring for woman lawyers in the glass-ceiling-breaking early years of women's rise to prominence in the profession. Louise passes on her tips for making mentoring a keystone of any program that addresses our issues.

Coke Morgan Stewart, a lawyer turned consultant to law firms, directs our attention to the motivation of young lawyers, explaining in a wonderfully lucid and insightful way how the younger generation approaches big firm practice in ways that bear little resemblance to what may have been the case (or is our distorted memory) of the good old days, demanding that law firms rethink many of the old approaches.

Dean Zipser participated in one of our Raise the Bar conferences and lent to our endeavors a call for more rigorous and dedicated mentoring and training for young lawyers. It is an endeavor, Dean reminds us in his important essay, that demands hard work, tenacity and imagination by both those offering the services and those receiving them, if the effort is to make a difference.

Joanne Martin and Stephen Daniels, Professor Nelson's learned colleagues at the American Bar Foundation, have turned their far more extensive and rigorous research to the world of lawyers providing pro bono services to deliver a prescription for the profession that cries out for implementation: a vast expansion of the breadth and commitment by law firm lawyers to the provision of pro bono services inspired by the catalogue of opportunities they have identified.

Kay Hodge, a leading Boston lawyer and former Chair of the American Bar Association's Commission on Racial and Ethnic Diversity, not only reminds us of why diversity programs will contribute to raising the bar, but also provides us with real-world solutions to an issue that has bedeviled the American law firm for decades: how to recruit, retain, and promote lawyers who reflect the ever-increasing diversity of our clients.

This author's final contribution is a chapter that asks the question why, amidst such financial success, do so many law firms contribute so little to pro bono services? Perhaps, as this author suggests, mandating pro bono yields not an oxymoron, but rather a solution.

Robert Sayler, a statesman himself, whose career has bridged our professional world from Covington & Burling to the law school of the University of Virginia, tells us how the search for lawyer statesmen and women—lawyers who value the roles of diplomat, wise counselor, amd thoughtful partner—can ameliorate many of our profession's ills.

The elegant Robert Grey, Jr., past President of the ABA and a public speaker whose felicitous style and thoughtful content can captivate a room (even a room of egotistic lawyers), accepted Raise the Bar's invitation to provide our readers with the compelling arguments why lawyers must support organized bar activities and how that participation can lend a richness to a lawyer's professional life that can help overcome the purposelessness so many feel in a world of billable hour demands, being on call 24/7, worring about making partner, lack of training, and often less-than-meaningful client work. Robert's career is Exhibit A for his argument, even if he is too modest to acknowledge it.

Every human being is unique but no one is more unique than the silver-tongued Michael Tigar, professor, trial lawyer, defender of great causes, raconteur, classics scholar, and visionary, all of which skills are exhibited in huge portions in Michael's towering exegesis on the profession's difficulties and how they can be overcome. Michael's "closing argument" is as elegant a disquisition as one could imagine and why your editor made his remarks the last voice from whom we hear.

Lawrence J. Fox

# PART I

# The Billable Hour

# CHAPTER 1

# Our Gilded Cage

**By Scott Turow**

All of us who make our livings as litigators have stood up in court from time to time recognizing that we are on the verge of saying something regrettable, and thus stifling an internal objection along the lines of, "Your Honor, I'd like to strike my next question."

And I admit that I offer these observations with some trepidation. I have many friends in our profession, and I hope I can still say that after they've read this. But I have too much respect for my colleagues not to speak from the heart.

For a few years now, I have been asking myself a question that I wanted to share with all of you. It started three summers ago, when my wife and I were driving my two older kids to the airport. The academic year was about to resume. The younger child, my son, was returning to college; the older, my daughter, to law school.

"Say," I heard my son ask his sister in the back seat, "what do you think you'll do when you get done with law school?"

My daughter expressed some uncertainty but ended up answering, "I think I'll become a litigator."

I nearly hit the brakes.

"Oh," I heard myself moan, "don't be a litigator."

My advice to my daughter had the usual effect, another demonstration of Newton's Third Law, the one about equal and opposite reactions, a rule which also applies to parental advice. Before the academic year was over, my daughter had enrolled in a legal clinic and tried her first—and second—lawsuits. It was those experiences, rather than anything she heard from me, that led her away from the courtroom.

But I, candidly, was shocked by my own reaction. Because for the last twenty years I have chosen to continue my occasional role as a litigator, despite having the option not to do so, thanks to my literary career. I have always believed that I've had a charmed life as a courtroom lawyer. When I left law school, I could not imagine becoming anything other than a litigator. The courtroom was where the law was made, where the fundamental struggle to fit the law to facts took place. The people writing contracts were, in my youthful view, not much different from consultants. Although I have learned to love and appreciate hundreds of transactional lawyers in the years since, I notice, in looking over my novels, that I have not yet had a hero who is any other kind of a lawyer but a litigator. My protagonists have been prosecutors, criminal defense lawyers, a judge, a tort lawyer, a commercial litigator—even journalists. But no deal guys—or gals. In the restricted zone of my imagination, it's the litigators who are the real thing.

Anton Valukas, one of the United States Attorneys for whom I worked in the Northern District of Illinois while I was a federal prosecutor, once remarked to a national publication that "Scott Turow stands in the top ten percent of obsessive-compulsives." Truth, as they say, is an absolute defense. And the tendencies Tony remarked upon have often left me inflicting untold pain on myself, especially as I have prepared for trial.

But overall, I like reviewing my own personal highlight reel as a trial lawyer: Conviction of the sitting attorney general of this state. A role in connection with Operation Greylord, the project that sent to the penitentiary a dozen and a half of corrupt state court judges and more than fifty of the lawyers who had paid them off. Several great civil trials in private practice, including one involving defense systems and Middle Eastern potentates which I still can't talk about in public. And a number of extraordinary pro bono engagements, including one that helped pave the way to freedom for a man who had spent years on death row, for a murder committed by somebody else. I mean it when I say I wouldn't trade any of it.

So why is it—given the satisfaction I've taken from being a litigator, a calling that my wife would tell you I've flat-out loved—that some piece of my heart shrieked out in opposition to the idea of my child doing the same thing? That's the question I have been asking myself for a while now, and which I want to reflect on here.

I believe what motivated my outcry, in a few words, is that I think it would be hard for someone starting today to have it as good as I have had it. The ratio of pain to pride has grown too high. And the contemporary environment has become much less congenial to aspects of the lawyering craft that deeply pleased me. We all hear the complaints from our colleagues, especially the men and women in my age range who have been doing this now for decades. For too many litigators, our life increasingly is a highly-paid serfdom—a cage of relentless hours, ruthless opponents, constant deadlines, and merciless inefficiencies.

In saying these things, I have the freedom of being a stranger in a strange land. I am still a litigator, but one who has practiced part-time for years now, and who has the liberty to look at our world more as a frequent visitor than a full-time habitué. That may make me more objective. Or perhaps too quick to criticize. In any event, I realize that what I'm about to say doesn't apply to everybody listening—but enough of us, I hope, that it's worth venturing.

By now it's obvious that the U.S. Supreme Court's decision in 1977 in *Bates v. Arizona,* which invalidated on first amendment grounds the long-time bars on lawyers advertising, was in retrospect the opening cannon shot that essentially set off the competitive war in our profession. In doing so, it did no favor to lawyers' lifestyles. The free flow of information about who is making what that soon followed, courtesy of Steve Brill and his publication *The American Lawyer,* ushered in the big firm star system, in which rainmakers rule, because they are the lawyers who can most easily set up shop elsewhere. The threat posed by that mobility in turn has cued the struggle in every firm to ensure that incomes remain high, especially at the top of the pyramid. Nor do we, in the bar, have any right to complain. The fierce competition that now characterizes the business of being a lawyer is exactly what the market requires. No matter how much we'd like it to be otherwise, lawyers can't claim any privilege to live by different rules from everybody else in our economy.

But I still believe that lawyers in general, and litigators in particular, are yet to confront the realistic limits of that competitive environment. And in this regard there is no more vicious culprit than the practice of basing our fees solely on the time spent on a matter. Dollars times hours sounds like a formula for fairness. What could be more equitable than basing a fee on how long and hard a litigator worked to resolve a matter? But as a system, it's a prison. When you are selling your time, there are only three ways to make more money—higher rates, longer hours, and more leverage. As the years have gone on, the push has continued on all three of those fronts.

Let me be clear: I don't think there is anything wrong with lawyers making money. There is a unique satisfaction in representing somebody well and being rewarded for it in a manner commensurate with the effort and skill required. I am not engaged here in a jeremiad aimed at getting litigators to join in vows of poverty, or even to agree to make less. I believe enough in the free market to know that if what we ask our clients to pay us wasn't worth it to them, they wouldn't continue to do it. But my concern is with the externalized effects of the system we are currently following.

Consider, for example, the consequences of dollars times hours for those entering the profession. When I left the government to go into private practice in 1986, the hours expectation for young lawyers was 1750 or 1800 hours a year in the large firms in Chicago. Today it's 2000, 2100, even 2200 hours. And the only real outer boundary is that there are 24 hours in a day—and 168 in a week. Increasingly, if we allow time for trivialities like eating, sleeping, and loving other people, it is clear, as a simple matter of arithmetic, that we are getting close to the absolute limit of how far this system can take us economically.

More tellingly, the prospects for success for lawyers have markedly diminished over the years. Virtually all firms today make fewer partners and take a longer time to do it. And the smaller you make the eye of the needle, the more young lawyers arrive on the job as uncommitted nomads, at the best, acquiring skills they'll take elsewhere, at the worst, cynically trying to pile up money before the axe falls. But both states of mind alienate them somewhat from the workplace, the colleagues they work with and the clients they serve.

Worst of all, however, is that when somebody is working 2200 hours a year, they have less chance to pursue the professional experiences that nourish a lawyer's soul. Lawyers of all stripes can and should offer their services for free to the needy, but I find it hard to imagine more satisfying work than pro bono litigation. That is because when you give the poor and powerless access to a just forum there is a triumph, no matter what the outcome in a case. Those who have lived without now stand on a more equal footing with their antagonists. The lawyer who is involved in doing that learns an invaluable lesson about the power and goodness that is inherent in being a lawyer.

I don't know many young lawyers who leave law schools without dreams of becoming pro bono princes and princesses, nor is there a dream of youth that seems to die faster. I am familiar with the efforts made in my own firm to counteract the effect of a billing system that discourages pro bono work. We give young lawyers some billable credit for pro bono time, and also have a full-time pro bono partner who works hard to engage the firm's lawyers in these projects. And we are hardly alone in the profession—many other firms make similar efforts. These are noble gestures. And ones fully worth undertaking. But it's still a little like King Canute ordering the sea to roll backwards. As long as it's dollars times hours times partners, we know that the tide will always rise.

The day I arrived at Sonnenschein Nath & Rosenthal in the fall of 1986, there was a notice in the daily bulletin that in those antique days was still printed on paper and distributed by hand to every lawyer's desk. The only item I recall said something like this: "Lawyers Against Nuclear War Will Be Organizing In Conference Room D." It was signed by Bernard Nath, whose name remains on the door even today, although Bernie is now a blessed memory. Bernie was a titan, a counselor of renown to business clients. He was fabled at the firm for the cheapness of the hotels he favored when he was traveling on the client's dime, and for the pro bono work he did throughout his life that literally changed the landscape of Chicago.

I think of my old friend Jerry Solovy, duly honored by the American Bar Association Section of Litigation the day I first gave a version of these observations to that group. Jerry has had a magnificent career as counselor and courtroom representative of the mighty, but he has also been a stunning force for progress in countless pro bono cases. For lawyers like Bernie or Jerry, the practice of law was and has been seamless, where fee-paying work and pro-bono work have stood side by side, the entrée and dessert of legal life, that went to make a satisfying whole.

I know that Bernie—and I think this may be true of Jerry—started out in a world where a lawyer sent a client a bill at the end of a matter that said simply "For Services Rendered" and gave an amount. I cannot imagine how the young lawyers of today who are entering the profession with the hours monster breathing down their necks will possibly develop a view of the opportunities and responsibilities of practice that are as round as the one that led Bernie or Jerry to have careers of such extraordinary distinction.

Let me again make it clear that I am not calling for lawyers to band together to abandon hourly billing. The antitrust division of the Justice Department would be likely to have something to say about that, and well they should. But I am hoping that lawyers, especially litigators, will more often be bold enough to consider offering clients alternative billing arrangements. And I hope clients will be bold enough to accept them.

That by itself is a mouthful. Many years ago now, I went shopping for a lawyer in Hollywood to represent me in the dealings that I have been fortunate to have with movie and television producers in connection with my books. Naturally, I asked each of the lawyers I spoke to about his or her hourly rate. One attorney answered, "We don't bill hourly. We use the fair fee method."

Then I asked, "Pray tell what is that?"

"Well," he said. "We do the work and at the end we get together and agree about what's a fair fee." This sounded to me like an invitation to jump without knowing whether there was water in the pool. "Trust me" is not a persuasive motto. A solid economic relationship ought to start out with both sides understanding the scope of the engagement.

I know that there aren't many lawyers who haven't reflected at length about what I am discussing, and I also realize that many of them are better at business than I am. One reason that dollars times hours continues to prevail is because it's hard to devise a fair alternative. Columbus setting out from Spain, destined, in some minds, to sail off the end of the earth, probably had a better idea what he was headed for than either a lawyer or a client at the inception of a piece of litigation. Whatever alternative arrangements are made have to be flexible enough to adapt to changing knowledge and the unexpected. It will take some education and experimentation on both sides. But I think we have reached the point where that is virtually required.

The fact is that the widespread practice of billing by the hours exists almost in defiance of the principles that are supposed to guide our profession.

The Model Rules of the American Bar Association address attorneys' fees in Rule 1.5 and suggest that all the following are the guidelines by which to measure the reasonableness of what we charge:

1. the time and labor required, the novelty and difficulty of the questions involved, and the skill requisite to perform the legal service properly;
2. the likelihood, if apparent to the client, that the acceptance of the particular employment will preclude other employment by the lawyer;
3. the fee customarily charged in the locality for similar legal services;
4. the amount involved and the results obtained;
5. the time limitations imposed by the client or by the circumstances;
6. the nature and length of the professional relationship with the client;
7. the experience, reputation, and ability of the lawyer or lawyers performing the services; and
8. whether the fee is fixed or contingent.

Only one of the named factors speaks directly to the time spent on the legal task, and yet, despite the fact the guiding ethical rule of our profession encourages lawyers to look to other factors, dollars times hours remains, so to speak, the near universal standard of commercial litigation.

This is in some way a segue to my principal argument on this subject. At the end of the day, my greatest concern is not merely that dollars times hours is bad for the lives of lawyers—even though it demonstrably is—but that it's worse for clients, bad for the attorney-client relationship, and bad for the image of our profession. Simply put, I have never been at ease with the ethical dilemmas that the dollars times hours regime poses, especially for litigators. And in this regard, I think my views depart from what is commonly acknowledged (including, I hasten to add, by disciplinary authorities, who of course have not disallowed the current system.)

But from the time I left the U.S. Attorney's Office and entered private practice to today, I have been unable to figure out how our accepted concepts of conflict of interest can possibly accommodate a system where the lawyer's economic interests and the client's are so diametrically opposed. Looking again to the model rules, the general provision on conflicts of interest, Rule 1.7, provides in part that, "A lawyer shall not represent a client if the representation of that client *may* be materially limited by . . . the lawyer's own interests, unless:

1. the lawyer reasonably believes the representation will not be adversely affected, and
2. the client consents after disclosure."

I ask you to ponder for just a few minutes about whether that rule can really be fulfilled by hourly-based fees.

It is fair to assume, of course, that sophisticated clients are fully aware of the hazards of being billed by the hour. But we all know that conflict waivers require more than fair assumptions. When was the last time anybody here really sat down and actually explicitly set forth the problems of this system for a client, the way we do with other conflicts? Who ever says to a client that my billing system on its face rewards me at your expense for slow problem-solving, duplication of effort, feather-bedding the work force, and compulsiveness—not to mention fuzzy math. Does anybody ever tell a client what the rule seemingly requires, "I want you to understand that I'm going to bill you on a basis in which the frank economic incentives favor prolonging rather than shortening the litigation for which you've hired me." The truth is that even to imagine that conversation would almost necessarily require the lawyer to be prepared to offer the client an alternative.

I understand some of the counter-weights to what I have just said. There is more than a little merit to the idea that the market will reward the efficient lawyer, who labors to hold down her fee in the recognition that it will lead to further engagements. And of course just like the vast, vast majority of self-respecting practitioners, I can say with conviction that I have never consciously ordered work or labored longer for the sake of increasing my bills. I think that litigators who send out bills are generally as stunned as their clients by the way time piles up.

But before we can say that this is proof of the rule's other prong—that the lawyer reasonably believes the representation will not be materially affected—I think we must look a little further. How many times have you heard a lawyer speak mournfully of the case that settled rather than going to trial, with the resulting detrimental impact on that lawyer's economic fortunes? More tellingly, who among us can say that they've never accused the lawyer on the other side of "running the meter"—of doing unnecessary discovery, filing frivolous motions, or foot-dragging before engaging in meaningful settlement talks—all in order to pad his fee. And that's not just to make excuses to the client. When we say it, we mean it. Looking at the lawyer on the other side of the versus, we can see clearly how the temptation to earn more might impact a representation. If we can see the effects of the dollars-times-hours system so clearly when we look across the courtroom, how can we be so fully confident about ourselves?

Personally, I doubt that greed is the principal motivation for the overwhelming majority in our profession, including my opponents. First and foremost lawyers want to believe they have done their utmost for their clients—and it would be a rare attorney indeed who took much satisfaction out of thinking of himself as well-paid but incompetent or undedicated. Like every other conflict issue, the problem is one of appearances and temptations. But how can anyone ever know exactly why certain marginal tasks were undertaken? The truth is that anybody who has ever investigated a case or prepared to try one knows that there is no limit to the potential issues, the avenues for investigations, the questions to be researched, or the variable scenarios that the courtroom might offer. Dollars times hours subtly influences lawyers not to ask themselves what's most probable. It offers scant rewards for discipline.

The more often lawyers find themselves engaged in wheel-spinning, in running out ground balls rather than focusing on the strike zone, the more isolated they feel from the principal goals of the profession, which will always be doing justice. But again it's the effect on the lawyer-client relationship which I think is the principal problem.

And as a result of hourly billing, the fee collecting process has grown far more fractious between lawyer and client over the years. There are now law firms which specialize in disputing other firms' bills—and in-house nudniks who demand copious details and then flyspeck them. Other clients search for means, whether it's strict litigation budgeting or task-value billing, to put a finger in the dike. But what does it do to the environment of our profession, to our perception of ourselves, and our clients' perceptions of us, that we are locked into a system in which clients are saying from the beginning of the relationship, I can't really trust you to be fair to me? And if there is even a grain of truth to that characterization, how reasonable is it to believe that our representations have not been materially affected?

Perhaps a dozen years ago, I talked to the ABA about the image of the legal profession. What I said, in essence, is that America is ambivalent about lawyers. They are impressed with our knowledge and the power that knowledge gives us, and jealous of it as well. They see us as too often self-seeking, manipulative, and greedy. We all know that this is not a balanced picture. Every time I hear about a DNA exoneration on radio or TV, I wait vainly to hear what I know is the rest of the story—about the lawyers, usually an army of them, who worked for years, generally for free, to give that prisoner back his liberty. The story of the lawyer doing good because he or she is committed to doing good is not one of the narrative themes American media is fond of presenting, because it's not something the public wants to hear.

But recognizing how far behind the eight-ball we remain in the eyes of the public, should we really continue to engage in billing practices that even our clients, who know us best, have been telling us inspire distrust?

Let me emphasize that I do not think that hourly billing is the only culprit in why litigators' lives can sometimes be unpleasant. Being a litigator is simply a hard job. You cannot run litigation without deadlines, and deadlines mean stress. Trials are win-or-lose propositions which frequently ask for everything from our adrenal systems. And there are massive inefficiencies that are beyond our control without cooperation from the judiciary. For years, I have yearned for some systemic improvement that would prevent settling cases only on the eve of trial, a practice whose untoward effects ripple throughout the entire system, whether it's playing havoc with judges' calendars, increasing fees unnecessarily, or leaving litigators in a purgatory where they never know for sure if they're going to the mound or back to the bullpen.

But if I had only one wish for our profession from the proverbial genie, I would want us to move toward something better than dollars times hours. We have created a zero sum game where we are literally selling our lives, not just our time. We are fostering an environment that doesn't provide the right incentives for young lawyers to live out the ideals of the profession. And we are feeding misperceptions of our intentions as lawyers that most crucially go to disrupt our relationships with our clients. Somehow, people as smart and dedicated as we are can do better.

# CHAPTER 2

# End Billable Hour Goals . . . Now[1]

**By Lawrence J. Fox**

We are delighted you have selected Austen Dental Services for all your dental needs. We look forward to providing you with high-quality, cost-effective services. Our team of talented young dentists are highly motivated to give you outstanding services not only by virtue of their professional commitment to you, but also because the very best of them will be offered partnership in our great organization. To that end, we are sure you will be pleased to learn that we will charge for our services on an hourly basis. To demonstrate their dedication, we require our young dentists to record at least 2,000 billable hours per year, with bonuses if the dentist should achieve benchmarks of hourly dedication beyond 2,000.

* * *

Hourly billing has been with the legal profession a very long time. The evolution from on-line bills "for professional services" to billing on the basis of precise calculation of time began when clients, particularly those with in-house counsel, as well as insurance companies that hire lawyers to represent insureds, looked for greater accountability and precision in the way they were charged for lawyer services. What started as an innovation grudgingly accepted by law firms soon became the gold standard, applied almost universally to this day, despite numerous objections and staunch advocates in favor of alternative billing methods.

From accepting hourly billing, it was not very long before the tracking of time became not only a basis for preparing invoices but also a welcomed, even celebrated, management tool. Raise the hourly rate $5 or $10 and the revenue went right to the bottom line. Get each lawyer to add one billable hour per month, per week, or per day, and you achieved the same results. Review time accounting records and you could rank order not just associates, but all lawyers, in terms of their commitment to the enterprise. Lawyers went from being professionals evaluated on their excellence to being full-time equivalent timekeepers ("FTE's") evaluated on the basis of numbers. Differences among lawyers' billable hours became the source of much grinding of teeth. If only Caldwell & Moore could move the fifth quintile of timekeepers up to the fourth, the firm's profits would soar. If every lawyer's hours were above average, the possibilities were unlimited. And what started as an effort at simply drawing comparisons slowly evolved into a method of punishing, at first, associates whose billable hours were below average, and then, partners whose low billable hours translated into their being perceived as "unproductive." That perception may even have provided reason enough to urge these slackers, who had grown up and become members of the firm in a different era, to look elsewhere for future employment.

The next step in the march of the billable hour was the adoption by firms of billable hour goals—just like those describing so many affirmative action initiatives. And not, heaven forefend, to be confused with billable hour quotas or requirements. Just a gentle nudge directed at all lawyers that the firm had expectations. But it was not long before these goals became much more than that. Firms told their lawyers, especially the associates, that the firms would provide bonuses to those lawyers whose billable hour production exceeded certain thresholds, perhaps $25,000 for 2,000 hours, another $10,000 for the next 200 and so on, bonuses cascading without limit. It is these billable hour requirements, with both their attendant bonuses and the unspoken but inevitable negative effects of failing to meet the firm's expectations, that prompt this ethical rumination, addressing the question of whether what we are doing with billable hours violates principles of professional responsibility, if not the professional responsibility rules themselves.

## Lawyers Are Good People

Let me start by observing that I firmly believe that most lawyers are honest in keeping track of their time and conscientious in undertaking tasks that are consistent with their clients' best interests. I do not believe the profession is engaged in wholesale fraud. But it does not require a finding of rampant criminal conduct to conclude that billable hour goals raise important ethical issues. Nor are the professional responsibility implications of billable hour quotas and bonuses the only reasons why law firms should cease this practice and cease it now.

## The Conflict—Compounded

Though hourly billing is universally employed, and has many characteristics that recommend it, hourly billing certainly has one huge ethical deficit. The client has a very real interest in limiting the client's legal fees; the lawyers get rewarded, at least in the short run, for an increased number of hours. In short, hourly billing is a great incentive for the lawyer to undertake more tasks and to complete them more slowly, perhaps contrary to the interests of the client.

The imposition of specific goals, quotas, or requirements for billable hours by law firms only heightens this conflict and, as the fictional disclosure in the preface to this article makes clear, they are hard to justify as serving any legitimate client interest. Simply ask yourself how you would feel if your dentist made that disclosure to you before you underwent a painful root canal. While the pain the young dentist might be inclined to prolong to add to her hour total may be more stinging than any a lawyer can inflict, any incentive to inflict pain on clients by delaying resolution of their matters or increasing their fees is something our profession should stamp out, not encourage.

## Distortions

Think about the distortions that are introduced by this system. The affected lawyers are always asking two questions: What are my hours? What goal can I achieve? As the year drags on the lawyer either falls behind the goal or realizes that yet a higher goal (and its resulting additional bonuses) is achievable. Either way the obsession with these statistics only grows. Assignments change, on the downside, from being opportunities for service to clients to way stations on the path to keeping one's job and, on the upside, to "earning" bonuses. These new job opportunities are not evaluated on the basis of the lawyer's interests or likely experiences (can I take a deposition? argue a motion? meet a client?) but on how many hours the matter will add to the associate's annual hour harvest.

Think also about the likely effect of this system on the recording of time. In the brave new world of lawyer time accounting, hours are measured in tenths (a mere six minutes), an absurd construct that was designed to avoid overcharging of clients by the earlier use of quarter-hour billing. In fact, however, it has placed virtually every lawyer in America in a position in which he or she is guilty of multiple mini-frauds every day. If one really kept track of every hour every work day in six-minute increments, that is, in fact, all one would have time to do. Stop watch or chess clock at the ready, lawyers probably could keep track of their time in tenths, but unless one were fortunate enough to be in a long deposition, on trial, or at a closing, "keeping track of time," not substantive work, would be the task entry on the lawyer's billing sheets. And for the typical lawyer who waits until the end of the day to record time, accuracy to a tenth of an hour is an impossible assignment (was it twenty-four minutes or thirty?).

Given this reality—that when most lawyers put down their time they are doing so based on estimates—the question arises whether it is likely that the presence of billable hour punishments and rewards has any distortive effect on how these estimates are made. Do we suppose that estimates high and estimates low are essentially equivalent, making the use of estimates mere harmless error that comes out in the wash? Or do we think that the special incentives built into the system by billable hour rewards might, just might, encourage lawyers to estimate and record on the high side the number of six-minute increments dedicated to any given task?

This distortive effect is undoubtedly compounded as the associate contemplates the day of reckoning: the end of the fiscal year. Am I close to the minimum requirement? To getting the next available bonus? If so, can I find some more work? Stretch out what I have? Or "borrow" work that I know I'll be doing next year? I'll just record extra time doing document review now and then do it for free come January.

Or what if I am already over and can't get close to the next higher goal? I'll work hard now, but not enter my time into the system. Then when January comes my "banked" November and December time will give me a big head start in 2007. Nothing wrong with that, both fictitious lawyers easily rationalize, as they game a system whose absurdities are manifest.

All of which says nothing about the unspeakable possibilities. Short on hours? Need a few to achieve the minimum requirement? The next highest goal? Who can really say all the research for this memorandum only required three hours? I'll just read a few more cases to make sure I've got it right. Or see if there are any law review articles on point. Or maybe I can draft a memorandum to the client. Write a few letters. Prepare a memo to the file documenting my work. I am just being careful, precise, conscientious, avoiding malpractice—all admirable goals worthy of nothing but high praise.

And then there is the most unspeakable effect of all. No one follows me around. No one really knows how much time I spent reviewing these documents in a lonely warehouse. Yet since I worked so efficiently isn't it fair to record an extra hour or two? No, not an even hour. How about 1.3 hours? Or that last memorandum took two point four hours but was worth so much more. What an insight I had! It's clearly worth, shall we say, 8.6? Or while I traveled for, and billed Client A, I was working on Client B's matters. Shouldn't they both pay for my six-hour flight to L.A.? Twelve added billable hours credited to my account.

Yes, we hate to admit it, but even among the legal profession are those who would work extra slowly or record phantom hours, hours not dedicated to the client's matters, but hours nonetheless "earned," hours the lawyer is entitled to record to reflect the efficiency or excellence of the work that was performed, rationalizations that permit the surreptitious rewriting of a billable hours retainer agreement to include new qualitative terms that always result in an uptick in the bill, but that no one gets around to confirming with the client.

## Bad Policy

Even if billable hours were scrupulously and honestly kept for only those tasks efficiently performed and essential to serving the best interests of the client, it still would be the wrong way to award bonuses to associates for a number of different reasons.

The purpose of having a billable hour requirement is to make sure every high-paid associate is dedicated to hard work. Caldwell & Moore doesn't want to continue to employ those who don't "earn" their $125,000 per annum first year salary. And it is undoubtedly true that some associates may not actively seek out work, may leave early or arrive late, are never available when the legitimate demands of the practice require extraordinary efforts, even all-nighters and seven days per week commitment. Nor do I suggest for a moment that law firms may not design a program to ferret them out and either reform their conduct or terminate their employment.

But, because it fails to distinguish among very different situations, establishing a billable hour requirement is a hamhanded way of accomplishing this goal. While it is true Caldwell & Moore should want to reward hard work, lack of hours may not be the associate's fault. The ready, willing and able associate may be assigned to a department that does not generate the outsized tasks (interminable depositions or endless closings) that generate the high hours. Or by virtue of the assignment luck of the draw, the associate may not have been given the "opportunity" to spend hundreds of billable hours staring at a computer screen reviewing documents for attorney-client and attorney work product privilege. Or an associate may need to be on a reduced schedule to care for a child or an elderly parent or simply to maintain some balance in his or her life. Being put in this position by necessity or choice, it would be totally fair to conclude that the affected associate is not eligible for a billable hour bonus, but when that is the only basis on which associate bonuses are awarded, the firm has missed a chance to reward real talent for other meritorious accomplishments.

Put simply, looking at a chart of associate annual hours does provide a method of awarding bonuses with apparent precision, but its simplicity of application belies the fact that not all similar billable hour statistics reflect similar situations—or anything close to it. For that reason, it is critical that the firm embarked on such a billable hour reward and punishment enterprise must go behind the stark numbers on the computer printout to understand why the numbers are what they are, whether they reflect sloth or some failure on the part of the firm to provide sufficient work, allocate work fairly, or otherwise give the affected associate appropriate opportunities. A failure to take this nuanced approach, while surely reducing administrative time, breeds resentment among the associate corps, directed at both their "fortunate" colleagues pocketing the extra bonuses and the partners who use such a mechanical measure for allocating rewards.

The use of billable hour bonuses also only focuses on one narrow dimension of an associate's total performance. Think for a moment about the questionnaire we know Caldwell & Moore uses to evaluate associates. It certainly asks questions about the associate's ability to research and write, to be responsive, to deal with clients, to follow instructions, to accept increasing responsibility, to take the initiative, and to succeed at myriad other activities. Yet when it comes to bonuses, Caldwell & Moore only rewards associates on the basis of billable hours. Where is the bonus for the brilliant brief, the riveting oral argument, the call the associate got directly from the client with new business for the firm, the imaginative idea that saved the client thousands of dollars? To make judgments like these certainly takes more familiarity with what associates are doing and how they are doing it than to look at the billable hour chart, but surely Caldwell & Moore owes its associates the awarding of bonuses (if any there shall be) on qualitative factors at least as much (I would say far more) as it does on raw billable hour totals. Far more important, Caldwell & Moore owes its clients the knowledge that when the client's law firm rewards its professionals for work done on behalf of the firm's clients, it values excellence, imagination, cost-savings, efficiencies, and speed at least as much (again, I would say far more) as it values the accumulation of hour upon hour of professional services. In fact, should not clients be assured that if Caldwell & Moore is going to reward the achievement of billable hour thresholds, those rewards will be granted only if the hours are not just calculated but also evaluated for their necessity and competence?

Think for a moment, moreover, about what a billable hour reward and punishment system says about where the law firm's real values are. The hiring literature, the firm Web site, the summer associate presentations all may talk about a balanced life. Many firms have enshrined the work-life balance in their mission statement. But the true firm commitment to that concept is found, not in what the firm says, but in what it does. And what it does when it engraves its devotion to high billable hours in a billable hour reward and punishment system is to tell associates that the rhetoric of work-life balance is just so many eloquent but meaningless words. The real message—the one that counts—is that Caldwell & Moore is a sweat shop and the more you sweat the more you will be rewarded with bonuses now and with the fruits of the bonus-striving of associates later if you bill enough hours to become a partner.

## Does It Count?

No. The answer to the question is no. Does [fill in the blank non-billable activity] count as billable hours for purposes of bonuses? That is the question out of every naïve associate's mouth. The sophisticated already know—whatever the activity, no matter how important to the health of the firm or the good of the poor—it doesn't really count. Hiring, pro bono, bar association work, writing an article, attending a CLE. Oh, sure, some firms pay lip service to permitting these hours dedicated to these frill endeavors to "count." But remember we are talking about billable hour goals. And that is because ever higher billable hours are what Caldwell & Moore is trying to achieve. So every time it agrees to "count" something that is not a billable hour as if it were, Caldwell & Moore might end up saying a given associate has met the minimum goal or even earned a bonus. But the firm does so with its collective fingers crossed, with more than a little reluctance, with a grudging admission that to do otherwise in public would be unseemly. Yet any associate who thinks these non-billable hours really count in the same way real billable, likely-to-yield-$200-or-more-dollars-per-hour, hours count was born yesterday. If it were otherwise, the firm would never have instituted such a unitary bonus system in the first place.

## The Solution

In fact, all of these activities must count. In the long run, Caldwell & Moore will succeed only if its lawyers dedicate themselves with real quality time to hiring and retaining the very best talent, training the firm's lawyers to perform at the highest professional level, mentoring associates to become partners, developing a real diversity program that recruits, retains, and promotes women and minorities. Moreover, the profession of law will survive only if lawyers—including Caldwell & Moore lawyers—dedicate themselves to pro bono, bar association work, continuing legal education, and the greater civic good of the community.

But, instead of making these "non-productive" hours count in a billable hour bonus system, the entire rewards and punishments for the billable hours method should be jettisoned in favor of a system of rewards and punishments that rewards excellence, innovation, imagination, savings for the client, pro bono dedication, bar association commitment, hiring, mentoring and training, diversity, and all of the other characteristics that yield a rich fulfilling professional life.

Consider the following mythical memo:

**TO: All Associates**
**FROM: Management Committee, Caldwell & Moore**
**RE: Compensation**

The Managing Partners of Caldwell & Moore have spent the last year studying the way in which we compensate and provide bonuses to our associates. As a result, we are announcing effective as of the beginning of the firm's next fiscal year a new basis on which our associates will be rewarded for outstanding achievement.

### Salaries

Effective July 1, 2006, our starting salary will be $135,000 for all full-time associates. Base salaries for associates in years two through six will increase by $10,000 and in years seven and eight by $15,000 each year.

### Elimination of Billable Hour Bonuses

At the same time, we are eliminating any bonus system based solely on billable hours. We recognize that such a system is not only inconsistent with our commitment to our clients, but also both an unfair way of compensating associates and inconsistent with our desire to encourage some of the non-billable activities our firm and our profession must value.

This does not mean we do not expect hard work from our associates. Caldwell & Moore is a business in a competitive marketplace. We pay competitive salaries and expect every associate to be committed to earning such generous compensation. Indeed, bonuses will be awarded to those associates who make an extraordinary commitment in terms of time. It is simply that in the future these bonuses will not be tied automatically to the achievement of any given number of billable hours and will only be granted in light of a number of other factors described more fully below.

### The Bonus System

Bonuses can be earned by all but first-year associates. Bonuses will be rewarded at the sole discretion of the firm in amounts that will be significant, but without regard to any formula.

### Professional Services

With respect to work for clients, associates may earn bonuses not only for the number of hours dedicated, but also for the quality of the work and imaginative ideas that advance the interests of our clients. To consider the latter, we will be asking partners to make an evaluation of each associate's hours in terms of efficiency, diligence, and necessity, and to nominate for bonuses those associates whose initiatives saved clients money or whose ideas enhanced clients' likelihood of achieving their goals.

### Firm Activities

It is just as important for the firm to hire, retain, and promote a talented, diverse associate corps. To that end, bonuses will be rewarded for recruiting, training, and mentoring hours and initiatives in the same way as work on client matters. Similarly, service on the associates committee, if undertaken in a dedicated and effective way, may result in an award of a bonus to the associates involved.

### Pro Bono

In the past, the firm "counted" so many hours of pro bono. Beyond that level, the associate had to seek a waiver for the hours to count. We know this misled some associates into believing that pro bono really did not count, discouraging them from undertaking pro bono engagements. It is Caldwell & Moore's policy to encourage and support pro bono endeavors. The firm would like to achieve 100 percent participation by all of its lawyers at a level of 50 hours per year within the next three years. Meanwhile, the firm recognizes that pro bono engagements do not come in 50-hour assignment blocks. Henceforth, once an associate undertakes an approved pro bono matter for the firm, it will be treated like any other firm matter. Associates will be expected to dedicate all necessary time and effort to the matter. And associates can expect that in the evaluation of their commitment and hard work, the firm will count all of their pro bono hours—so long as they meet the same criteria of necessity and competence as all other hours—toward the awarding of any bonuses. Our pro bono clients are not second-class citizens, and we do not want any associate to feel that our compensation system is inconsistent with that principle.

### Bar Association and Other Civic Endeavors

Our lawyers' obligations do not end with commitment to clients—both paying and pro bono—and to the firm. Caldwell & Moore is a leader of the profession. We expect our lawyers to get involved in the organized bar by serving in leadership positions, writing articles and books, presenting at continuing legal education seminars. Similarly, our lawyers should serve as leaders of the larger community. School boards, houses of worship, charitable and arts organizations, and similar endeavors all will benefit from the leadership of Caldwell & Moore lawyers. You can expect to be evaluated on your participation in these activities and for bonuses for outstanding accomplishments in this area to be awarded in the same way as for other achievements.

### Work-Life Balance

While Caldwell & Moore expects extra effort from all of its lawyers, we recognize that the number of hours a lawyer is able to devote to all of the activities listed above varies widely because of the necessity of fulfilling even more important personal obligations, such as child-rearing or other family obligations. We also recognize that some of you have made lifestyle choices that are inconsistent with 2,000 or more hours per year of professional time. Though those circumstances or choices may mean that you will not earn bonuses for your number of hours, Caldwell & Moore wants to emphasize that you will still be eligible for bonuses for the quality of your work, your imagination and skill, and for the other firm activities should your qualitative performance warrant it.

**Business Generation**

Though it is rare for associates to bring in significant business, any business generated by an associate will be evaluated in terms of the revenues generated and the quality of the work for possible bonus awards. Far more important, associates will be evaluated in terms of the foundation they are laying during their associate years for business generation thereafter. Is the associate dealing well with clients, making a name for herself in her field, writing articles, appearing in CLEs, taking leadership in young lawyer divisions of the various bar associations, joining civic and charitable organizations, developing a marketable specialty? Professional life is a long journey, but the first seven years of the trip set the course for all that follows. The associate who does this in an outstanding way can expect to be considered for bonuses based on how he or she starts his or her professional journey.

* * * *

Having read the memorandum, the reader undoubtedly thinks I've been smoking a controlled substance. Admittedly, it is way too easy to craft such a memo when you do not have to consult eight other managing partners, a firm executive and chief financial officer, or 135 partners. But it does seem to me that, though my offering does not reflect the perfect antidote to billable hour punishments and rewards, nor the perfect solution to so many other ills in the modern law firm, it could open a dialogue not only on how this memorandum to associates should read, but also how the modern American law firm must change to raise the bar to the level of professional commitment, professional responsibility, and professional rewards the profession must offer, not just to associates, but to all lawyers.

## Anticipating the Critics

This diatribe has already drawn considerable dissent. Perhaps it will draw more. I certainly welcome the dialogue. But permit me to answer in advance a few of my critics.

It has been asserted that my concern about the recording of billable hours is slanderous, that I am accusing the profession of wholesale fraud. That is certainly not my intent. But we also cannot blind ourselves to four things. First, there have been far too many documented cases of billable hour abuse. From the case of the celebrated Chicago law firm partner billing over 6,022 hours in one year,[2] to Lisa Lerman's catalogue of over-billing, expense padding, and other criminal conduct by sixteen high-profile lawyers at prestigious *American Lawyer 200* law firms,[3] to think our profession is pristine is to ignore the facts. Second, I am much more focused on the subtle effects that billable hour quotas and rewards create then I am on out-and-out fraud. To suggest that these effects are not likely is to assume lawyers are not human beings, when we know all too well that they are. Third, even if lawyers were perfect, it is impossible to think that we are carrying the right message to our firm colleagues—when we employ billable hour requirements and provide billable hour bonuses—about the importance we place on non-billable activities. Fourth, and most important, we are a profession that owes all these duties to our clients; they are our raison d'etre, and how must they feel if they know this is the basis on which lawyers working on their matters are rewarded? Consider again the mythical three-hour root canal procedure to capture the point.

It has also been argued that associates really want to be rewarded this way; they like the certainty of knowing that if they put in exactly 2,103 hours they will achieve the 2,000 bonus and the 2,100 extra bonus. This argument proves my point. While there is so much associates hate about our billable hour culture, of course they do like certainty. Everyone likes certainty. And knowing that I've got a lock on an extra $15,000 so long as I spend New Year's Eve in front of a CRT reviewing documents for privilege-guaranteeing compensation that will pay for far more than my midnight champagne makes me feel warm and fuzzy all over. But the certainty that arises from no more than the writing down of a pre-stipulated number of hours is not a desired result. Rather an associate should know that his or her lawyers' hours will be evaluated for quantity for sure, but also for quality, for innovation, for benefit to the client; and that the associate's non-billable hours will be evaluated too, and then—no certainty here—the associate may get a bonus if this overall review yields the conclusion that the associate is entitled to a bonus. Is it subjective? To be sure. But we are lawyers, producing legal work, running law firms, preserving a threatened profession, and there is no way a lawyer's contribution to those goals should be evaluated in other than a qualitative, albeit subjective, way. Leave it to the production line employees installing windshields and rearview mirrors to get compensated by purely objective criteria.

Last, I have been confronted by those who say that far too many firms operate this way to change things now. Indeed, I have been accused of systematically seeking to change virtually the whole big firm business model.

To this I plead guilty. My experience with the Raise the Bar Project has convinced me of two things. First, our problems are profound and deeply troubling. Any enterprise that loses 78% of its new hires in the first three years is in a state of crisis. Second, we must change the way we do business other than incrementally if we are going to turn the ship of state around. Half-measures will not work. Maybe this idea will not either. But in our search for solutions we will have to develop ideas that change in some dramatic way the manner in which we do business, that overcome the litany of problems—too long to repeat here—that started the Section of Litigation to declare, enough of decrying the current state of affairs, let us find solutions, the goal of the project and this article.

## Endnotes

1. This article grew out of the author's work as Co-chair of the ABA Section of Litigation's Raise the Bar Project launched by Section Chair Brad Brian in 2004. This article was also the genesis for a Report and Recommendation that the Section of Litigation successfully presented to the American Bar Association House of Delegates in August 2006 in

Hawaii. Because the Section of Litigation leadership is far more diplomatic than the author, the Report and Recommendation did not take such a strident view toward minimum billable hours, while still urging the profession, nonetheless, to mend its ways.

2. *Chapman & Cutler Axes 17 Firm Staff*, CHICAGO DAILY LAW BULLETIN, MARCH 22, 1995.

3. Lisa G. Lerman, *Blue-Chip Bilking: Regulation of Billing and Expense Fraud by Lawyers*, 12 GEO. J. ETHICS 205 (1999); *see Bill Padding Happens*, LEGAL TIMES, Oct. 18, 2004.

# PART II

# The Law Firm

# CHAPTER 3

# A Pig in a Poke? The Uncertain Advantages of Very Large and Highly Leveraged Law Firms in America

**By Michael H. Trotter**

The growth in size of the major law firms in America and their increased utilization of and reliance upon leverage are the most significant changes that have negatively affected working conditions in the legal profession over the last 50 years. Greatly increased size and leverage (in the form of more associates, non-equity partners, staff attorneys, contract attorneys, and legal assistants) have transformed organizations that were small and amiable professional partnerships in the first half of the 20th Century into very large and generally impersonal business organizations in the early years of the 21st Century.

Publicly available information suggests that in 1950 throughout the United States most of the larger business practice firms were very small in comparison to today's firms, and most had fewer associates than partners. (By "business practice firms" I mean what are sometimes referred to as "corporate firms"—firms that primarily represent larger business enterprises and their officers, directors, and controlling shareholders.)

How much larger are law firms in America in 2004 than they were in 1950s? The largest law firm in the country in 1960 (Shearman, Sterling & Wright) had 125 lawyers. At that time there were only three firms in New York City with as many as 100 lawyers and only seventeen other firms in the United States with more than 50 lawyers. By 2004 the largest law firm in America had 2,992 lawyers. The smallest of the firms on the AmLaw 200 list had 110 lawyers. Major business practice law firms today are vastly larger than they were 55 years ago, and most are much more highly leveraged.

The following chart compares the 1950 size and leverage of a number of well-known American law firms to the size and leverage of these same firms (some augmented by mergers) in 2004. Unfortunately, many New York City firms, and some located elsewhere, did not disclose the number of their associates in the 1950 *Martindale-Hubbell Law Directory* (my principal source of information about the size of law firms at that time). For information about recent size and leverage I have relied upon *The American Lawyers'* AmLaw 100 and 200 Reports for the year 2004, as reported in 2005. The AmLaw 100 identifies the 100 firms headquartered in the USA with the largest gross revenues from legal work listed in the order of their gross revenues. The AmLaw 200 lists the next 100 firms based on their gross revenues. The term "AmLaw Two Hundred" is used herein to denote all of the 200 firms that appear on one or the other of the lists.

The chart shows the total lawyer personnel of each firm, if known, and below it the breakdown between equity partners and other non-equity lawyers. I have used the AmLaw definitions of equity partners and non-equity lawyers. The letter "P" identifies equity partners and the letters "NE" identify non-equity lawyer personnel. (Leverage has also been increased by the addition of billable non-lawyer personnel such as legal assistants and investigators, but this additional leverage is not reflected in the numbers below.) The letters "NA" are used when the information is not available because a firm did not disclose its number of non-equity lawyers (normally associates in 1950). In such cases it is not possible to determine the firm's leverage in 1950.

## CHART REFLECTING GROWTH IN SIZE AND LEVERAGE

| | 1950 | | 2004 | |
|---|---|---|---|---|
| FIRM | SIZE | LEVERAGE | SIZE | LEVERAGE |
| **NYC** | | | | |
| Cahill Gordon | NA | | 242 | |
| | 9 P–NA | NA | 60 P–182 NE | 3.03 |
| Cravath | NA | | 389 | |
| | 21 P–NA | NA | 79 P–310 NE | 3.92 |
| Davis Polk | NA | | 538 | |
| | 25 P–NA | NA | 145 P–393 NE | 2.71 |
| Debevoise | 29 | | 536 | |
| | 12 P–17 NE | 1.42 | 125P–411NE | 3.29 |
| Milbank Tweed | NA | | 480 | |
| | 27 P–NA | NA | 107P–373NE | 3.49 |
| Patterson Belknap | 15 | | 163 | |
| | 7 P–8 NE | 1.14 | 55 P–108 NE | 1.96 |
| Shearman & Sterling | NA | | 963 | |
| | 31 P–NA | NA | 207 P–756 NE | 3.65 |
| Simpson Thacher | NA | | 632 | |
| | 21 P–NA | NA | 152 P–480 NE | 3.15 |
| Skadden Arps | 6 | | 1,554 | |
| | 4 P–2 NE | .5 | 361 P–1193 NE | 3.30 |
| Strook Stroock | 14 | | 331 | |
| | 8 P–6 NE | .75 | 100 P–231 NE | 2.31 |
| Sullivan & Cromwell | NA | | 589 | |
| | 22 P–NA | NA | 156 P–433 NE | 2.78 |
| Weil Gotshal | 19 | | 1,080 | |
| | 9 P–10 NE | 1.11 | 184 P–896 NE | 4.87 |
| White & Case | NA | | 1,685 | |
| | 27 P–NA | NA | 247 P–1,438 NE | 5.82 |

*(continued)*

| FIRM | 1950 SIZE | 1950 LEVERAGE | 2004 SIZE | 2004 LEVERAGE |
|---|---|---|---|---|
| **Atlanta** | | | | |
| Alston | 12 | | 664 | |
| | 9 P–3 NE | .33 | 151 P–513 NE | 3.40 |
| Kilpatrick Stockton | 11 | | 442 | |
| | 6 P–5 NE | .83 | 126 P–316 NE | 2.51 |
| King & Spalding | 10 | | 707 | |
| | 9P–1 NE | .11 | 148P–559 NE | 3.78 |
| Powell Goldstein | 8 | | 265 | |
| | 6 P–2 NE | .33 | 76 P–189 NE | 2.49 |
| Sutherland | 9 | | 352 | |
| | 7 P–2 NE | .29 | 108 P–244 NE | 2.26 |
| **Chicago** | | | | |
| Bell Boyd | 27 | | 207 | |
| | 16 P–11 NE | .69 | 64 P–143 NE | 2.23 |
| Kirkland | 40 | | 1,258 | |
| | 22 P–18 NE | .82 | 409 P–849 NE | 2.10 |
| Winston Strawn | 28 | | 793 | |
| | 15 P–13 NE | .87 | 179 P–614 NE | 3.4 |
| **Los Angeles** | | | | |
| Gibson Dunn | 33 | | 745 | |
| | 17 P–16 NE | .94 | 245 P–500 NE | 2.04 |
| Latham | 10 | | 1,502 | |
| | 6 P–4 NE | .67 | 387 P–1,115 NE | 2.88 |
| O'Melveny | 44 | | 910 | |
| | 15 P–29 NE | 1.93 | 231 P–697 NE | 2.94 |
| **Texas** | | | | |
| Andrews Kurth | 24 | | 394 | |
| | 13 P–11 NE | .85 | 145P–249NE | 1.72 |
| Baker, Botts | 52 | | 643 | |
| | 16 P–36 NE | 2.25 | 222 P–421 NE | 1.90 |
| Fulbright | 42 | | 831 | |
| | 16 P–26 NE | 1.63 | 330 P–501 NE | 1.52 |
| Thompson, Knight | 24 | | 320 | |
| | 13 P–11 NE | .85 | 100 P–220 NE | 2.2 |
| Vinson Elkins | 65 | | 661 | |
| | 20 P–45 NE | 2.25 | 226 P–435 NE | 1.92 |

As is obvious from the chart, most of the firms listed had grown by at least 1,000 percent and some a great deal more. Some of the New York firms, having been among the largest firms in the country in 1950 and having since followed different strategies from most other major firms, have not grown as much.

Leverage ratios increased for most of the firms in the range of 100 to 200 percent, although several firms in Texas with unusually high ratios in 1950 have seen their ratios decline.

These changes in size and leverage resulted in fundamental changes in the dynamics of the major business practice firms in America that significantly altered working conditions in these firms. As a result, they became very different sorts of organizations than they had been in the middle of the 20th century.

A-100 lawyer "very large firm" in 1950 would not make the AmLaw Two Hundred today. The ideas of what is a "large" law firm and what is a "highly leveraged" firm have changed as a result of the tremendous growth in size of major business practice law firms and the tremendous increase in the leverage utilized by these firms. For the purposes of this discussion I am treating major law firms with fewer than 300 lawyers today as "small firms," firms with between 301 and 500 lawyers as "medium" firms, and firms with over 500 lawyers as "large firms." Those firms with more than 1,000 are treated as "very large firms." Based on this classification of the firms listed in the 2004 AmLaw Two Hundred, there were 11 very large firms and an additional 51 large firms, 68 medium firms, and 70 small ones. There were only three AmLaw 100 firms with fewer than 300 lawyers, but there were 67 such firms in the Second Hundred. The smallest firm on either list had 110. The largest firm in the Second Hundred had 410 lawyers. Consequently, none of the Second Hundred firms would be classified as large firms.

## Why Growth and Leverage Increased in the 1960s

Before discussing the impact of increased size and leverage on the organizational, operational, and financial dynamics of major business practice law firms, it is important to understand how such growth in size and leverage began during the 1960s. Most law firms did not make a conscious decision to grow in size or to increase their leverage—growth came about because of the tremendous growth in worldwide economic activity and an increase in governmental regulation.

As a result there was a significant increase in the amount of legal work to be done, but there were not enough lawyers in practice or students in law school to serve the growing needs of the major firms' clients. This shortage of lawyers was a result, in part, of the surge of economic growth, and in part a result of stagnation in the size of the legal profession for almost 30 years after the start of the Depression. In addition, the lateral movement of partners or associates from one firm to another was frowned upon and rarely occurred prior to the 1970s. Consequently, the only way a firm could provide the additional services needed by its growing clientele was to work the lawyers it had harder and to hire at the entry level more new associates to be developed as quickly as possible. During the 1960s and early 1970s, if major business practice firms were to grow in size they had to do so primarily by the addition of new associates fresh from law school.

First-year enrollment in accredited law schools in the United States had declined from 19,532 in 1948 to 13,111 in 1953. Enrollment then started back up, recovering to 15,607 in 1960. In order to meet the demand for additional lawyers, first-year enrollment more than doubled to 34,289 in 1970, and then increased gradually over the next 20 years to reach 44,104 in 1990. As a result of the low level of enrollment in the 1950s and early 1960s there was a shortage of lawyers to meet the increasing needs of business clients.

These circumstances created exceptional opportunities for law school graduates in the 1960s. Good students from top law schools were greeted with several job offers from major firms, rapidly increasing compensation, and the high-percentage prospect of a partnership within 5 or 6 years. In 1960, starting compensation in Atlanta was $3,600 a year and in New York City it was $6,000. Starting salaries in New York increased in increments during the 1960s, moving from $10,500 to $15,000 in 1968 as a result of the famous decision by Cravath in one fell swoop to raise starting salaries significantly. Associate compensation in Atlanta also moved in increments influenced by New York City salaries to reach $14,000 a year in 1969, an increase of approximately 300 percent in the decade.

I started with the Alston firm in June of 1962, left for 6 months of Army Reserve training, and returned to the firm in April of 1963. Before I became a partner in 1968, I had been the principal responsible attorney on at least one major public securities offering and had worked as second in command under a single partner on several other securities offerings and acquisitions. There was a lot of good, challenging work to be done. Young associates with ability and confidence handled major transactions and got great on-the-job training working directly with senior partners on the firm's most important matters, as well as on every other legal engagement undertaken by the firm.

The revenues produced in the 1960s by this higher level of activity and the swelling ranks of associates (with few older associates in the pipeline to become partners) resulted in higher compensation for the partners. Growth and the resulting leverage drove profitability, rather than the desire for profitability driving leverage and growth. Growth was both necessary and profitable. With sufficient new business to support more lawyers and higher associate-partner ratios, many firms continued to grow and prosper by enlarging their workforce of young associates. In the process, for most major firms associate leverage was slowly but steadily increasing.

Because so many new associates were hired during the 1960s and such a high percentage of them became partners, most of the major firms were faced in the 1970s with hiring even more associates in order to maintain their existing partner compensation levels. However, during the early 1970s the dynamics of the profession changed quickly and in a new direction. The Vietnam War began to siphon off both law school graduates and college graduates who otherwise would have gone to law school. The growth in the supply of new lawyers slowed, and many of the major firms lowered their hiring standards in order to employ the numbers of lawyers that the growing volume of work required. Partners at most of the major firms began to realize that they could not maintain, much less increase, the higher levels of compensation to which they had become accustomed unless 1) fewer associates became partners, 2) the firms maintained or increased the higher levels of leverage that had developed naturally during the 1960s and 3) in order to do so they lowered their hiring standards.

Firms that had not been keeping time and billing by the hour began to do so, and in the process became more aware of the impact of billable hours on their financial well-being. Some partners began to look at some of their new associates as "cannon fodder" rather than as future partners. As compensation increased, law schools began to attract more students who were interested in earning substantial incomes and, in due course, there was an increase in the number of young lawyers who were highly motivated by money.

## Why and How Has Increased Size Affected Working Conditions in the Major Law Firm?

As a result of all of these factors, the working environment and relationships in many major firms began to change significantly, and over time the personnel dynamics of these firms bore less and less resemblance to what they had been in the 1950s and 60s. Gone were the days when every lawyer knew every other lawyer in his firm and most of the staff as well. Indeed, many of us do not know the names of all of our partners these days. Gone were the days of the "firm family" when every lawyer also knew the spouses, and often the children, of the other lawyers—when new lawyers and their spouses were drawn into a tight-knit community of firm clients, friends, and relationships.

It was inevitable as law firms grew in size that it would become increasingly difficult for the lawyers to know well all the folks with whom they worked and to take a personal interest in their lives. Because it is very difficult in a firm with more than 100 lawyers for the firm leaders to know firsthand the professional skills of each lawyer, it became necessary to rely on information that could be easily quantified, standardized, and communicated, like hours billed, fees collected, clients attracted, and similar statistical measures. Consequently, the relationship between a firm and its lawyers becomes less personal and more numbers oriented.

It is more difficult to care about someone you do not know in a distant office than it is to care about someone you see every day and know personally. It is harder to forgive a brusque response to a question when you do not know about the personal difficulties with which the brusque person may be dealing. In short, very large organizations are inevitably more impersonal organizations than smaller ones.

At the same time the prospect of a career-long relationship with one's firm also slipped away. Increased associate leverage meant that firms would have to grow faster and larger while the percentage of associates becoming partners was reduced. Even those few associates who became partners were much more likely than in the past to see their firm as a way station for a lateral move to another firm or to an in-house position.

Increased numbers also tended to put more layers of lawyers between the senior partners and the younger lawyers. As a result, the firm managers obtained their view of many of their lawyers from the impressions and words of intermediaries, and through quantifiable information. Most senior partners will choose to invest their limited time in lawyers who are likely to remain with the firm in the years ahead. Today, even in small firms (as I have defined them), it is difficult for the more senior partners to develop relationships with any associates. They have to work hard to get to know their partners. Yet I know that most associates would rather be in a firm where they personally knew and worked with the senior lawyers than in one where they did not.

Large size may also increase financial risks. Partners in large firms are more likely to end up on the wrong end of a malpractice suit filed against the firm on account of the work of a partner in a distant city whom most of them may not know personally. It has become necessary for large firms to put into place procedures and safeguards to protect against rogue partners, or financially distressed ones. As a result, intra-partnership relationships become more structured and formal. In much smaller firms, personal observation and relationships may make such problems easier to spot and to fix.

Of course, larger firms require more office space, more computers and copying machines, a larger line of credit, and more support staff, many of whom are specialized and highly compensated. Consequently, the decision to add non-equity lawyers is also a decision to add office space, equipment, and additional support personnel, all of which must be paid for with even more legal work that must be developed by the partners. As firms grow larger, the percentage of the revenues generated from their legal work that passes to the partners as profits tends to decline. In other words, it is necessary to generate substantial additional amounts of legal work simply to pay the overhead of larger firms.

Ultimately some lawyers must supervise the support staff and pass judgment on the new lease and space design, or at least supervise the person who is directly responsible for all of this effort. A lot of lawyers who signed on to practice law find themselves doing a lot of things other than that. In due course, the need to maintain one's production of billable hours generally trumps everything else. However, since the "everything else" does not just go away, it must be added to what is already a long and demanding schedule of billable work. Simply put, a lot more time and effort are required to run a "large" firm than a "small" one, and growth in size has contributed to the demanding working conditions faced by major firm lawyers today.

## How Does Firm Size Affect Client Service?

I doubt that law firm size is an important issue for the clients of most AmLaw Two Hundred firms. For those companies without corporate counsel, dealing with a firm large enough to serve all of the clients' needs may be something of a blessing. However, most clients utilizing AmLaw Two Hundred firms have employed full-time corporate counsel and many have large staffs of lawyers working in-house. For these larger clients the advantages of employing large outside firms are limited. Most corporate general counsels select to do their work the best-qualified lawyers at the best price regardless of firm size.

Many corporate legal departments have substantially reduced the number of outside firms with which they deal. In general, the effect of this policy for the surviving firms has been an increase in the amount of work of the type that they were already providing, rather than an expansion of the types of legal services provided by their firms. The fact that some major firms offer a complete range of legal services (that they are able to provide because they have so many lawyers) is not an important factor in the selection of outside counsel to provide a particular service. Indeed, most corporate counsel would prefer not to concentrate the work of their company in one or a few outside firms.

## Why and How Has Increased Leverage Affected the Working Conditions in Major Law Firms?

***For partners*** the increase in leverage has increased the amount of work they do and has changed what they do. As the ratio of associates to partners increased the number of associates who had to be recruited increased, and the time and attention required in that effort went up while the number of partners involved in the process did not grow at the same pace. If a firm wanted to maintain the same quality of associates, then the time and work required for that effort had to be even greater. Many firms hired non-lawyer personnel to manage a substantial part of their recruiting effort. While this practice has saved partner and associate time for billable work, it has made recruiting of the best prospects more difficult, and has distanced the more senior lawyers from their newer lawyers at a critical juncture: the beginning of their legal careers.

Once a larger number of associates had been hired it is necessary to train them and to supervise their work. While there may be some efficiencies of scale, experience tells us that the effort becomes increasingly difficult as the numbers increase relative to the number of partners. It is more difficult to motivate partners to devote time and effort to the development of associates when the odds are very low that associates will remain with the firm in any capacity. Time is too scarce and valuable to waste on a transitory asset. (It should be noted, however, that in firms with non-equity partners, many of such lawyers have sufficient knowledge and experience to effectively train and supervise the work of younger lawyers.)

The challenge of providing effective training is even greater if the quality of the associates recruited declines, which may have occurred if for no other reason than the number of law graduates in recent years has remained stagnant in the face of raising demand. However, not only has the number of graduates remained the same in recent years, but also the size of the pool from which law students are drawn has decreased. For the 1990–91 school year, 152,685 prospective law students took the LSAT. The number of test takers declined to 103,990 for the 1997–98 school year. The number has since recovered to 145,258 for school year 2004–05. The odds are good, given these numbers, that the overall quality of the pool has declined, in part because of the legal profession's notorious reputation for difficult working conditions.

Of course, rather than seeking to improve working conditions, the profession has generally responded to the problems of its reputation by raising pay, while at the same time insisting on even more demanding working conditions. As a result of raising the production expected of the associates, partners have to find additional work to support such additional production and to review the additional work, therefore making their firms even less attractive places for both themselves and associates.

When leverage is increased by hiring more associates, it is necessary for the partners to find additional legal work with which to occupy and train all of the expensive new associates that have been hired and to occupy them usefully for even more hours. When leverage was low, partners only had to find enough work to keep themselves fully occupied and some additional work to occupy most of one associate's time.

Finding and securing such large amounts of new business while trying to keep up with rapidly developing law in your field and managing your practice is a tremendous challenge. Many partners have been unable to do so, and as a consequence have seen their positions downgraded to non-equity status or even eliminated. Many partners prefer practicing law to marketing, and find the increased responsibilities debilitating.

Some of the time that in the past an equity partner would have spent with his or her family, on community affairs, or on recreation and relaxation is now used to cultivate existing and potential clients and client referral sources. The creation of new non-equity lawyer categories (including non-equity partners) is in part a recognition that some partners are much better at finding work than others and, since the generation of substantial new business is necessary to the survival of large and highly leveraged firms, those partners who can bring in the work are becoming the equity partners for whom everyone else works, adversely affecting the relationships among the "partners."

Remember also that much of the new work that each major firm needs to support its leverage is work that is suitable for young and inexperienced lawyers. How could the nature of the work performed by major business practice firms change so that a much higher percentage of the work they do today is suitable for young and inexperienced lawyers than was the case 50 years ago? How have so many major business practice firms managed to add so many lawyers and work so many of them so long and hard in light of the growth in number of in-house lawyers and legal assistants? The changes that have occurred to generate this work are a subject for another day. Suffice it to say that these changes have transformed the job of many partners to marketers and to reviewers and editors of the work product of other lawyers rather than the producers of the work product themselves despite the fact that so many vastly prefer creating to marketing, reviewing, and editing.

As the numbers of categories of lawyers at some firms have increased, the level of respect among lawyers in the same firms has diminished. Fifty years ago in most firms no lawyer who was not thought to be on track to become a partner was permitted to remain for long. Today many firms have several "ranks" of permanent "non-commissioned officers" in the form of non-equity partners, counsel, staff attorneys, and some senior associates. Many of these more senior lawyers who have not been admitted to the partnership are viewed by their partner colleagues (and by associates) as failures, retained for the economic benefits they can bestow and the experienced help they can provide. It's not necessarily a bad life, but it is short on prestige and it certainly doesn't pay as well as being a partner.

In order to avoid the debilitating effects of multiple classes of lawyers, many of the most successful firms have only equity partners on one hand, and associates on the other. Of the 37 firms in the AmLaw 100 with 2004 Profits Per Partner in excess of $1,000,000, 14 had only one class of partner. Many of the firms producing the highest Value Per Partner had only one class of partner.

***For associates***, higher leverage means, as a general rule, that they get less training and supervision than they would have received at a less leveraged firm. It also is likely that they get less meaningful and challenging work because in most firms the partners cannot generate enough of that sort of work to keep everyone happily occupied. As already noted, it also means that they have less of a personal relationship with senior lawyers in their firm and, as a result, less bonding occurs. Greater effort by the senior lawyers cannot solve the problem because time is an essential and limited ingredient. There is no way a partner can do a better and more effective job overseeing two or more associates than he or she could if overseeing only one.

Perhaps of greatest importance for associates, as leverage is increased the opportunity to advance within a firm must ultimately be reduced. This affects a firm's ability to recruit and retain the best law school graduates. Because the odds are better that an associate with the lower leveraged firm will remain with the firm, the partners in such firms should be more able and willing to make the effort necessary to train their associates well, and because there are fewer associates to train relative to the number of partners, the partners can more easily accomplish the task and do a better job in the process. Also, the lower ratio increases the chances that an associate will get challenging work earlier in his or her career. All of these factors work together to make life in the lower-leveraged firm more attractive for associates.

If you were a new law school graduate, which firm would you rather work for if more than one offered you the same starting salary and good work—a smaller firm with a relatively low leverage ratio or larger one with a relatively high leverage ratio? To be sure there are a few exceptional larger firms that are growing very rapidly and therefore can also offer better work and a better chance for advancement than other large firms, but such firms are rarely among the AmLaw Two Hundred—how could they not be?

## How Does Lower Leverage Benefit Clients?

It is axiomatic that more experienced lawyers will perform a higher percentage of the legal work provided by lower-leveraged law firms. Seasoned lawyers should provide more cost-effective services than less experienced lawyers. They should be better able to put issues into context and to get more quickly to the relevant point. The hourly rate difference between what most firms charge for starting associates and what they charge for their top partners is about 3 to 1. There is very little in the practice of law that a lawyer with significant experience cannot do more than three times better and more efficiently than a new recruit.

Far fewer of today's young lawyers become partners than was the case 50 years ago. As a result, much of a firm's and its clients' investment in training these young lawyers is lost. In the process, the client has paid for a lawyer to become familiar with its business and its legal issues, and then lost the benefit of that investment because of its law firm's internal management and financial policies (unless, of course, the client hires some of these lawyers as many do). The client is then called upon to bear the cost of educating another young lawyer about its business and its legal issues. This is an inefficient process for both clients and law firms.

The lower-leveraged firm also fits the needs of clients with corporate counsel better than the higher-leveraged model. Most large and many medium-sized clients have a corporate counsel staff that provide the day-to-day services required by their client, as well as many more specialized services. Increasingly, in-house lawyers need to talk with experts on particular issues, rather than to send entire projects to outside counsel.

When they call on outside counsel, clients often need an answer, if not immediately, then in a few hours. Increasingly clients are not interested in having associates research issues, and write long memos to be then edited by more senior lawyers and then passed on to the client. Many do not have time to read such memos or care to do so. They want a good, quick answer to their question from a recognized expert. Inexperienced lawyers are incapable of giving such advice. Clients generally are well served by reduced leverage, which results in their making less use of relatively overpriced associate time and more use of relatively under-priced partner time.

## Can Significant Professional and Financial Success Be Achieved by Smaller and Less Leveraged Law Firms?

Given the many disadvantages of larger and more highly leveraged law firms, why have so many major business practice firms opted to become large and highly leveraged firms? Is large size necessary to achieve significant profitability? Is high leverage necessary to achieve significant profitability?

The accompanying chart, drawn from the AmLaw Two Hundred information for the calendar year 2004 released in 2005, lists the top 20 firms in Profits Per Partner, their size, and their leverage ratios. Added to the top twenty are a few other firms with interesting statistics that were further down on the list.

The ratios of equity partners to other lawyers is based on the AmLaw Two Hundred information for 2004 and the ***American Lawyer*** definitions of equity partners and non-equity lawyers. The chart also shows the total number of lawyers and equity partners. My method of presenting the leverage ratios is to show the number of non-equity lawyers per equity partner.

| Firm | Profits Per Partner | Size | Leverage Ratio |
|---|---|---|---|
| 1) Wachtell | $3,500,000 | 197 | 1.46 to 1 |
| 2) Boies Schiller | 2,600,000 | 180 | 6.50 to 1 |
| 3) Cahill Gordon | 2,455,000 | 242 | 3.03 to 1 |
| 4) Sullivan & Cromwell | 2,350,000 | 589 | 2.78 to 1 |
| 5) Simpson Thacher | 2,330,000 | 632 | 3.16 to 1 |
| 6) Cravath | 2,205,000 | 389 | 3.92 to 1 |
| 7) Paul Weiss | 2,155,000 | 480 | 3.66 to 1 |
| 8) Cadwalader | 2,110,000 | 486 | 5.23 to 1 |

*(continued)*

| Firm | Profits Per Partner | Size | Leverage Ratio |
|---|---|---|---|
| 9) Davis Polk | 2,005,000 | 538 | 2.71 to 1 |
| 10) Kirkland & Ellis | 1,975,000 | 897 | 4.37 to 1 |
| 11) Milbank Tweed | 1,900,000 | 480 | 3.49 to 1 |
| 12) Quinn Emanuel | 1,890,000 | 209 | 2.27 to 1 |
| 13) Schulte Roth | 1,815,000 | 354 | 3.99 to 1 |
| 14) Skadden | 1,735,000 | 1,554 | 3.30 to 1 |
| 15) Cleary Gottlieb | 1,715,000 | 844 | 4.02 to 1 |
| 16) Weil Gotshal | 1,700,000 | 1,080 | 4.87 to 1 |
| 17) Willkie Farr | 1,635,000 | 507 | 3.09 to 1 |
| 18) Irell & Manella | 1,530,000 | 208 | 1.57 to 1 |
| 19) Gibson, Dunn | 1,515,000 | 745 | 2.04 to 1 |
| 20) Debevoise | 1,510,000 | 536 | 3.29 to 1 |
| 23) McKee Nelson | 1,375,000 | 110 | 1.75 to 1 |
| 27) White & Case | 1,220,000 | 1,685 | 5.82 to 1 |
| 36) Bingham McCutchen | 1,150,000 | 790 | 6.38 to 1 |
| 43) Ropes & Gray | 1,060,000 | 501 | 1.75 to 1 |
| 45) Munger Tolles | 1,045,000 | 164 | .93 to 1 |

If there is a correlation between the size of the AmLaw Two Hundred firms and their profits per partner, it is that smaller is better. In 2004 Baker & McKenzie, the largest firm in the AmLaw Two Hundred, was 106th in Profitability Per Partner ("PPP"). Jones Day, the second-largest firm, was 88th. White & Case, the third-largest firm, was 27th, Skadden Arps, the fourth-largest firm, was 14th, and Latham & Watkins, the fifth-largest firm, was 22nd. Holland & Knight, the eighth-largest firm, was 163rd.

On the other hand, the three highest firms had fewer than 250 lawyers; firms #6, 7, and 8 on the list had fewer than 500 lawyers; three more had fewer than 635 lawyers; the largest and least profitable one of the group had 897 lawyers. Of the top 25 firms selected from the 2004 AmLaw Two Hundred as the "Value Leaders" (i.e. the firms that produce the most profits per lawyer), four of the top five firms had fewer than 250 lawyers. Ten out of the 25 firms had fewer than 250 lawyers, and 15 of the 25 firms had fewer than 500 lawyers. Only two firms with more than 1,000 lawyers made the list, in positions 18 and 19.

What is the correlation between high leverage and profitability? Of the top 25 firms on the Profits Per Partner list, three had leverage ratios of less than 2 to 1, two had ratios of less than 2.5 to 1, and five had ratios of less than 3 to 1. However, of the top 25 firms on the 2004 "Value Added" list, two had leverage ratios of less than 1 to 1 (#7 and #22), two more had leverage ratios of less than 1.5 to 1 (including Wachtell, the category leader), three more had leverage ratios of less than 2 to 1, and seven more had ratios of less than 3 to 1. One had a ratio of 6.5 to 1 (in 11th place) and one had a ratio of 5.23 to 1 (in 25th place).

It is perfectly clear that relatively small firms with lower leverage ratios can earn high Profits Per Partner, can create a lot of "Value Added," and can perform economically as well as or better than most large or medium-sized firms. Wachtell is first in Profits Per Partner, and first in Value Added Per Lawyer, while being one of the smallest and least leveraged firms in the AmLaw Two Hundred. Third on the Value Added list is Cahill, Gordon, followed in fourth place by Irell & Manella and then by Quinn Emanuel. Cahill has 242 lawyers and leverage of 3.03 to 1, Irell & Manella has 208 lawyers and leverage of 1.57 to 1, and Quinn Emanuel has 209 lawyers and leverage of 2.27 to 1. In seventh place is Munger Tolles with 164 lawyers and leverage of .93 to 1.

There are 9 law firms listed in the AmLaw Two Hundred for 2004 with leverage ratios of less than 1 to 1. Munger Tolles is the only firm with a leverage ratio of less than 1 to 1 among the 50 AmLaw Two Hundred firms with Profits Per Partner exceeding $1 million in 2004. There are 24 firms on the 200 list with a leverage ratio between 1 to 1 and 1.5 to 1, including such well-known and highly profitable firms as Wachtell Lipton ($3,500,000 PPP), Williams & Connolly ($870,000 PPP), Robbins Kaplan ($820,000 PPP), Jenner & Block ($660,000 PPP), and Chapman and Cutler ($565,000 PPP).

There are an additional 36 firms on the AmLaw Two Hundred operating with a leverage ratio between 1.50 to 1 and 2 to 1, including highly profitable firms like Irell & Manella ($1,530,000 PPP), McKee Nelson ($1,375,000 PPP), Ropes & Gray ($1,060,000), Vinson & Elkins ($895,000 PPP), Baker Botts ($865,000 PPP), Arnold & Porter ($830,000 PPP) and Covington & Burling ($825,000 PPP).

The difference in a leverage ratio of 1 to 1 compared to a ratio of 2 to 1, or 3 to 1 may not sound like much, but the financial and cultural advantages of a lower ratio can be enormous. A firm that is able to generate competitive profits per partner with a lower leverage ratio has a big advantage over more leveraged competitors with the same PPP. These advantages exist in terms of firm dynamics and culture, cost-effective service to clients, intra-firm lawyer relationships, required marketing effort, working conditions, stress, administrative costs, recruiting, and training.

How can any firm produce Profits Per Partner of more than $1 million a year with fewer than 250 lawyers and a leverage ratio of less than 2 to 1? Five American firms managed to do it in 2004. I suspect that they were able to do so by attracting superior talent, providing high-quality training, and by creating a close-knit working environment in which all of the firm's lawyers felt they were making a contribution and were being challenged by their work. An additional critical ingredient, if the firm aspires to a very high level of financial success, is the development of a very high level of expertise in most of its areas of practice. Within this sort of legal working environment the lawyers in such firms at all levels often enjoy working hard and are well paid for the effort.

I also suspect that these firms are sought out by clients who have especially challenging problems that require legal advice from established experts with outstanding records of success on behalf of their clients. And such clients are more than willing to pay the price of such counsel.

There are successful alternatives to the big firm–high-leverage model: the hardworking smaller and lower-leveraged firm. The equity partners of smaller and lower-leveraged firms have fewer young and inexperienced lawyers to recruit and to supervise. The amount of new business each has to find is less. As a result, more of the partner's working day can be devoted to the practice of law, and less to marketing and administration. Therefore, the partners in a smaller, lower-leveraged firm may be able to generate more economic value while devoting less total time to the enterprise (or to generating higher levels of income from the same total effort). In addition, the lower-leveraged firm requires less rent and administrative overhead, which should result in a higher percentage of each dollar earned flowing through as partner compensation. For these and the other reasons noted, the partners of smaller and less leveraged firms have many advantages.

Many smaller firms with relatively low leverage ratios are providing great compensation for their lawyers while creating a better working environment for all of their lawyers, and providing better value to their clients. However, smaller size and lower leverage alone cannot produce the highest levels of compensation unless they are accompanied by a deserved reputation for effective application of knowledge in particular areas of practice, and for those firms in the adversarial practice, a unusually strong record of success in the courts or in arbitration. Obviously, small size and low leverage do not assure financial success. The financially successful firm must also offer outstanding service, a great record of success in their work on behalf of clients, and superior expertise.

Consequently, not every firm can make this smaller sized–lower leveraged model work with outstanding financial results. It would also be very difficult, financially and culturally, for a firm that has operated for a long time as a large higher-leveraged firm to convert to a smaller lower-leveraged firm. Small size and low leverage are not for everybody, but we can see that they are working very well for a number of major American firms, their lawyers, and their clients. In addition, I believe there are a substantial number of firms too small to be listed in the AmLaw Two Hundred that are successfully pursuing a smaller size–lower leverage strategy. We have several such firms in Atlanta, and I know that some have preferred to stay with their current arrangements, passing up the opportunity to become part of one or another of the larger firms.

Every firm that is thinking about growing in size and increasing its leverage, before pursuing such a course of action, needs to think seriously about the issues raised by this chapter. Greater size and leverage not only do not guarantee financial success, but they can undermine much that makes the practice of law attractive in the first place. While many smaller (or much smaller) firms do not enjoy the financial success of the top-performing firms, they do more than well enough, and their partners and other lawyers find that the total return on their efforts, quality of life considered, offers to them a better result than a million-dollar income in a larger and highly leveraged firm. I think that a lot of firms that elected to merge and/or aggressively grow in size and leverage over the past 15 years will find that their efforts would have been better directed toward improving the quality of their knowledge, personnel, training, and practice. Time, of course, will tell.

# CHAPTER 4

# Organizational Perspectives on Raising the Bar: Five Tentative Solutions

**By Robert L. Nelson**

The problems that have been identified by the Raising the Bar initiative appear difficult to redress because they may be embedded in the very business structure of large law firms engaged in litigation. No law firm would advocate on the basis of professional values for the patterns that are seen as troubling: lack of mentoring, lack of training, lack of trial experience, declining loyalty at the associate and the partnership ranks, reducing opportunities for pro bono work, excessive demands for billed hours, and excessive entry-level salaries. Indeed, I suspect that if we asked the managing partners of law firms about how their firms were dealing with these issues, they would either deny that they are serious problems in their firm or assert that they are produced by market forces beyond the control of any one firm.

In this essay I analyze the organizational conditions in large law firms that may facilitate or resist efforts to achieve the professional values that the Raising the Bar initiative seeks to encourage. As a shorthand, I refer to these goals as "core professional values." In keeping with the purpose of this volume, I couple my analysis of organizational actors with proposed solutions.

Efforts to better realize core professional values could be led by actors within the law firm organization (firm leadership, other partners, or associates) or from outside the law firm (from recruits, clients, the organized bar, or consultants and management scholars). I organize the discussion around internal and external sources of organizational change.

For the sake of argument, I will assume that the problems listed above are real, even if they rest on subjective evaluations and may be difficult to demonstrate empirically. It is sometimes the case that scholars and commentators paint an exaggerated image of problems within the legal profession. Claims about widespread dissatisfaction among lawyers is a good example (see Heinz et al. 2005). When the claims are rigorously examined through proper survey methods, we find the vast majority of lawyers are satisfied or very satisfied with their jobs. A skeptic might also ask for evidence to prove the gravity of the problems asserted above.

## Internal Sources of Change

**Firm Leaders.** It may seem ridiculous to ask whether the leaders of law firms might become agents for positive change in their organizations, for certainly they must bear the responsibility for the current state of affairs. Yet for many reasons, the leaders of law firms may be presiding over organizational practices that have effects they do not consciously embrace and feel powerless to change.

Possible reasons may include:

1. Limited power in a collegial organization. Despite the movement in most large law firms to specialized management structures (Heinz et al. 2005, Galanter and Palay 1991, Lazega 2001), with a management committee and

professional administrator, the management of large law firms do not possess the same kind of authority over their partners and associates as corporate management does over subordinates. This complicates the managerial task of developing systems that simultaneously meet work demands, revenue goals, and the professional goals of training and mentoring. Some firm policies may be easier to define and implement (e.g. billable hour targets) than the "softer" goals of encouraging mentoring or public service.

2. Avoiding systemic responses to professional concerns. A related problem is that law firm leadership may choose informal approaches to professional concerns rather than defining certain problems as systemic in nature, and requiring a systemic response. As law firms have grown in size, this is a recurrent tension (Nelson 1988). They no longer can rely on face-to-face interaction for coordination, but often are reluctant to develop formal systems to meet professional goals. An earlier study of the ethical issues that arise in the discovery practices of large law firms, also sponsored by the Litigation Section, found similar tendencies in the ethics area (Nelson 1998).
3. Unconscious signaling. Without being aware of it, firms may communicate that they do not really value training associates. For example, many law firms, rather than deploy the firm's own top litigators for this purpose, bring in law school clinicians to run trial practice sessions for new associates. Many practical reasons may favor such an arrangement, yet such an approach limits direct training of associates by the firm's own partners.
4. Failing to state the professional values that are part of the employment relationships that make up the firm.

The leadership of firms may fail to think through the professional values they want to include as part of the exchange relationships on which the partnership is based. What are they prepared to offer partners and associates in terms of stable employment, training, opportunities for professional development, opportunities for pro bono work, and public service? If the employment relationship primarily is defined in economic terms, such as salary in return for billings, then it is predictable that the parties will relate to each other primarily on these dimensions.

**Proposed Solution:** Firm leadership must articulate positive professional values and develop mechanisms for their realization. If firm leaders value mentoring, training, loyalty, experience, judgment, and community service they must state those as goals for the organization and develop policies that will help to achieve those goals.

**Partners.** The meaning of partnership in large law firms has undergone significant change in recent years, from a form of life tenure in the "golden era" of law firms to today's environment in which partners may be "pushed off the iceberg," are paid according to "eat what you kill" formulas, and are divided into various categories of equity and non-equity partners (Galanter and Palay 1991). In this milieu, it may be more difficult for partners to assert professional values, because these values appear to run counter to the now dominant economic theory of firm management. Also in a larger, more complex organization, it is more difficult to be heard. A partner cannot simply rise at a partnership meeting and make a speech endorsing core professional values and hope to have much effect (if ever that was the case). To shape the organizational practices that affect core professional values in today's large law firms will require significant political effort and organization.

Partners hold varying degrees of power and influence in their firms vis-à-vis firm leaders. Yet collectively no large law firm can function effectively without the enthusiastic engagement of the partnership tier. This gives partners an opportunity to urge their firms to organize their practices in ways that realize the ideals envisioned by Raising the Bar. Partners also may make demands on the law firm that cut against these ideals. By demanding more income, partners may push the firm to focus on dollars and billable hours. Moreover, unless partners are willing to act as mentors or to conduct in-house training or to facilitate pro bono efforts by associates, the firm will not achieve these goals.

Some of the changes in partnership policies that have been adopted by firms in an effort to increase profitability may be counterproductive. A fascinating analysis of law firm profitability by William Henderson suggests that two-tier partnerships may in fact be less profitable than single-tier partnerships (forthcoming). Gilson and Mnookin (1985) argued in the mid-1980's that lockstep compensation approaches would lead to more profitable partnerships than marginal productivity approaches. I do not mean to imply that one partnership form is more or less consistent with core professional values. I simply mean to point out that some traditional organizational practices may prove to be economically more successful, at the same time that they preserve organization tradition.

**Proposed Solution:** Partners in law firms should urge their leadership and colleagues to embrace core professional values and should act to advance those values in their own sphere of practice.

**Associates.** Many of the concerns of the Raising the Bar initiative revolve around the relationship between associates and large law firms. Indeed a number of paradoxes are apparent in this relationship. The American Bar Foundation's study, After the JD, which is tracking the entering bar class of 2000 for the first 10 years of their careers, provides unique data on this paradox (Dinovitzer et al. 2004). Although AJD respondents had been out of law school less than three years, already one third had changed jobs once (not including judicial clerkships) and 18% had changed jobs twice. Interestingly, the associates in large law firms (100 lawyers or more) had exhibited the fewest number of job moves. However, 55% of associates in law firms over 250 lawyers responded that they intended to change jobs within the next 2 years. Moreover, that same group of associates, who had the highest pay among their cohort (a median income above $140,000 per year), were also the least likely to say they were happy with their decision to become a lawyer. The best and the brightest of the profession, the graduates of elite law schools, were less committed to their careers as lawyers than other members of the profession.

In a forthcoming paper, Dinovitzer and Garth (forthcoming) analyze the dimensions of career satisfaction among the AJD respondents. They find that associates working in large law firms are unhappy with many aspects of their worklives: the recognition they receive for their work, their relationships with colleagues, their control over the work, job security, the intrinsic interest they find in their work, the social significance of their work, workplace diversity, and opportunities for pro bono work.

Yet they are drawn to "the power track" in the firm. That is, they are attracted to the money they earn and their opportunities for advancement.

These are the unhappy terms of the exchange between associates and law firms. Associates are required to bill extraordinarily high numbers of hours; firms are required to pay high salaries to attract associate labor which they can control in ways that are unsatisfying for associates. Neither party is happy with some aspects of the bargain; but neither party is willing or able to change the terms.

Associates and recruits may have more power than they realize to redefine the terms of their employment with law firms. At the very least they should ask for explicit and honest disclosure of firm policies on work expectations, training, mentoring, and pro bono opportunities. They should be skeptical if firms are not willing to discuss their approach to hours expectations and compensation. And if associates are serious about reducing work hours, they may need to look seriously at firms that offer different packages of work demands and compensation. Once associates join a firm and learn about its work culture, they can attempt to organize as a group to discuss with firm leaders the terms of their work and compensation.

**Proposed Solution:** Associates should demand clarity from law firms about firm policies that affect core professional values, should organize within law firms to engage in constructive dialogue with firm leaders about the tradeoffs between billable hour requirements and compensation, and should be prepared to vote with their feet if the bargain the firm is prepared to offer does not comport with their view of core professional values.

* * * * *

There may be more common ground between leaders, partners, and associates in the pursuit of core professional values in large law firms than the parties realize. Firms may fear that by developing explicit policies on efforts to realize core values—and engaging in the discussions necessary to articulate those goals and the mechanisms for pursuing them in a professional organization—that they may undermine the very collegiality they value. Nor is it the case that there is "one" solution to these tensions that will succeed in all law firms. The three major internal actors in firms need to work within their law firm's distinctive culture and distinctive political structure to critically assess what they can achieve to raise the bar.

## External Sources of Change

**Recruits.** During the recruiting process, law firms must project an image of the organization that will attract needed talent and personpower out of law schools. My discussion of associates applies to potential recruits. Recruits may possess more influence on law firms than they realize, although individuals must have the courage to ask questions of law firms that matter to them. And recruits must ask enough individuals at different levels of law firms to determine whether they are receiving realistic information. Potential employers are likely to respect this kind of intelligence and self-confidence. They are the same traits they look for in partners.

In the 1960s, large law firms of those days were confronted with recruits who came to law school with a zealous commitment to social change. Law students demanded that they be allowed to engage in significant pro bono activity. Many law firms accommodated to those demands by allowing more pro bono activity than previously had been the case (Heinz and Laumann 1982, Powell 1979).

In the current period, we find that young associates are more politically conservative than the lawyers who entered law firms in the 1960s, many of whom now govern large law firms. In this environment, we find that large law firms have institutionalized the commitment to pro bono activity (Daniels and Martin 2005), even though we also know from the After the JD study that young associates tend to be dissatisfied with the opportunities available for pro bono work (Dinovitzer et al. 2004). We also know from After the JD that the graduates of elite law schools have career options outside the law, which may tempt them away from law practice.

These patterns suggest that today the matchmaking process between recruits and law firms is more complicated than in previous eras. Law firms cannot assume what is important for their recruits. The reverse holds as well. The hope of Raise the Bar is that core professional values are articulated as part of those expectations.

**Proposed Solution:** During the recruiting process, potential recruits should ask law firms about their commitment to core professional values and the policies they have enacted to achieve them. Law students, both individually and through student groups, should encourage law firms to make meaningful information about such issues available and develop methods for cross-validating such information, through in-depth interviews with young alumni, alumni surveys, and so forth.

**Law Schools.** One ally for both law firms and recruits during the recruiting process is law schools, the site of much placement activity. Law schools already have established procedures that discourage recruiters from engaging in discrimination in the interviewing process. Law schools, law firms, and law students have much to gain from obtaining a better match between recruits and employers. If the graduates of particular law schools do not "stick" in particular law firms, it may diminish the prospects for future graduates in that law firm. Similarly, if a law firm develops a negative reputation in a law school, it may damage its recruiting efforts there.

Law school placement offices might usefully coach law students on how to ask the difficult questions about an employer's commitment to core professional values that I suggested above. Placement officials, in their particular labor market, but also in their national organizations (such as the National Association for Law Placement), can raise the consciousness of employers about the importance of core professional values.

**Proposed Solution:** Law schools should educate law students to be better consumers of information about the commitment of legal employers to core professional values. Law school placement officials should work to elevate awareness by legal employers about the importance of addressing policies relating to core professional values during the recruitment process.

**Competition among Employers.** If legal employers and recruits make policies on core values an identifiable aspect of hiring and retention decisions, market forces can work to advance core professional values. Scholars of professional firms often have speculated about whether law firms can step off the forced march to higher billable hours requirements, higher partnership profits, and higher entry-level salaries for associates by offering "lifestyle" tradeoffs (Galanter and Palay 1991). The issue has been particularly salient around questions of part-time work for women of childbearing years (see Epstein et al. 1999).

The answer amongst large law firms is uncertain at best. Judging by the statistics generated by systematic surveys of lawyers, in Chicago (Heinz et al. 2005), Toronto (Kay and Hagan 1999), and the After the JD national sample (Dinovitzer et al. 2004), we see a continuation of the same patterns of tension between work demands and preferences for spending time with (indeed having) a family. It is true that a law firm that breaks from the pack to offer more flexibility in hours or a different balance of mentoring/training and compensation, will be difficult to detect even in a large sample. It is beyond the scope of this article to systematically review journalistic reports. The recent *National Law Journal* issue on law firm recruiting contained an article entitled "Training Becomes a Recruiting Lure" (Howard and Marshall, May 1, 2006). Law firms with distinctive policies probably do exist. The question is whether innovative firms have begun to change the overall environment of organizational practices that relate to the core professional values.

Where we see differences in hours worked, amount of control over work, and work-family tensions is across segments of the profession—including differences across sectors of practice (solo, small law firm, government, inside counsel, nonprofit) and geographic markets. Women continue to gravitate out of large law firm practice to government or corporate counsel work over the course of the careers; those who stay in law firms defer marriage and childbearing until making partner (Hull and Nelson 2000; Reichman and Sterling 2002). Very few lawyers work in law firms where men took paternity leave, but all public defenders and legal services lawyers worked in offices where at least one person had taken such a leave (Heinz et al. 2005, p. 126). And we see in the After the JD sample very significant differences in hours worked across practice settings. Associates in law firms over 250 lawyers average more than 52 hours per week (and one third work more 60 hours per week), compared to 45 to 48 hours in government, legal services, and business contexts respectively (where 16% or fewer work more than 60 hours per week) (Dinovitzer et al. 2004, p. 36).

There are correspondingly large differences in income across these practice settings. The median salary for associates in large law firms is $140,000 compared to $63,000 in the federal government, $45,000 in state government, $40,100 in legal services and public defender offices, and $84,000 in Fortune 1,000 businesses (Dinovitzer et al. 2004, p. 43).

The differences in hours worked, practice setting, income, and satisfaction with the decision to become a lawyer also correspond to geographical differences. Respondents to the After the JD survey from nonmetropolitan areas, such as parts of Florida, Tennessee, Oklahoma, Indiana, Utah, and Oregon, work fewer hours on average, do not work in large law firms, and have lower earnings even when controlling for practice setting. Yet they also are far more likely to say they are satisfied with their decision to become a lawyer than their urban peers. Thus, while 60% of respondents from New York City said they were likely to leave their employer within 2 years, only one-third of respondents in non-metropolitan areas indicated such an intention to leave.

It appears from these data that there are major differences in work conditions relating to core professional values across practice settings and geographic areas, but not very much variation within types of law firms within geographic areas. The competition among legal employers seems to require that lawyers choose very significant tradeoffs in working conditions, rather than calibrated choices on these dimensions. The implication is that the market thus far has been a crude instrument in service of core professional values. Law firms and recruits would need to develop far more detailed information about the policies and practices that relate to core professional values, for there to be meaningful competition among legal employers in these terms.

**Proposed Solution:** Legal employers/providers should develop information about the policies that relate to core professional values for employees and clients that will foster competition in pursuit of the core values.

**Clients.** What role might the clients of law firms have in efforts to pursue core professional values? At least in the corporate sector, very often the client is herself a lawyer. That is, very often the official who retains and works with outside counsel is inside, corporate counsel (Nelson and Nielsen 2000). While one might think that this would make clients sympathetic to the efforts of law firms to balance core professional values and economic considerations, this is not necessarily the case. The Beyond

Ethics Project, the Litigation Section effort referred to previously, found that inside counsel often were openly hostile to the lament of outside law firms that they no longer could spend time training associates while working for clients.

> When we raised the complaint offered by outside counsel that they were under economic pressure from inside counsel to reduce costs, and that this had negative consequences for ethicality, civility, and training, inside counsel reacted bitterly. Clearly we had struck a raw nerve. Inside counsel rejected the notion that the new competitiveness in corporate legal services had any negative consequences, on ethics or anything else.... Worrying about changes in the large law firm is like worrying about the loss of the family farm. What is the point? (Nelson 1998, p. 802)

As this passage reveals, clients will not be persuaded that they should subsidize the pursuit of core professional values in law firms. Yet if clients appreciate the contribution that core professional values make to the representation of their interests, and if clients seek positive indications from law firms that they have policies in place to achieve those values, client demands can have a very significant effect. We already see this pattern in the arenas of diversity programs and pro bono projects. When significant clients of law firms indicate that they will value such efforts by law firms, law firms pursue such efforts aggressively (Leipold, May 1, 2006; Daniels and Martin 2005).

Corporate clients should be interested in policies that promote core professional values. Ultimately such policies will produce legal work and lawyer-client relationships that are more ethical, thoughtful, and efficient.

**Proposed Solution:** Law firms and their corporate clients should explicitly discuss their mutual interest in core professional values and examine how they can best be realized in each organization and in the law firm–client relationship.

**Bar Associations.** The organized bar, through initiatives like Raise the Bar, has played an active role in sponsoring efforts to advance core professional values. These have been especially important with respect to diversity and pro bono projects, where bar groups have challenged legal employers to establish concrete goals and measure progress towards them. As in these areas, it is unlikely that bar associations can come to agreement on mandatory provisions for enhancing core values, if indeed that were desirable. Yet it may be that bar associations, and specialized professional groups like the Litigation Section, can develop realistic best practice models for achieving core professional values that can become a standard within an organizational field. If those standards come to be seen as legitimate, they become a point of reference for all the actors inside and outside the law firm. Similar to efforts to establish and diffuse professionalism programs in law schools and attorney disciplinary systems, bar groups could take the lead in developing "raising the bar" programs among various groups and within legal employers. The target of these efforts should be the environments in which core professional values are on the line. The legal professions literature demonstrates that professional ideals are very much shaped in the legal workplace and in the specialized "communities" of practitioners who practice in the same field or before the same courts (Nelson and Trubek 1992, Mather, McEwen, and Maiman 2001). To be effective, bar groups must engage lawyers in these contexts.

**Proposed Solution:** Bar associations should promote "raise the bar" programs that attempt to articulate standards for the realization of core professional values in the association's sphere of influence and expertise.

**Consultants and Management Scholars.** As law firms have grown and become more complex, they increasingly have turned to consultants and other professionals to assist with recruiting, training, performance evaluation, and compensation. Organization theory has demonstrated that professionals can be influential carriers of innovations (DiMaggio and Powell 1983). If these consultants were committed to core professional values in the management models they brought to legal employers, it could have a dramatic effect on law practice.

We know relatively little about the effect that consultants have on large law firm practices, especially with respect to the core professional values. This is fertile ground for empirical research and theorizing. Casual observation suggests that there are no dominant approaches within law firm consulting, but rather an amalgam of adapted practices. Most consultants attempt to align the objectives of law firm leadership with managerial policies and practices. In that sense, consultants hold up a mirror to the very organizations to which they are providing services.

Relatively few management scholars work in the field of law firm management. Those who do tend to emphasize the distinctive character of professional organizations, including the difficulties of using corporate managerial approaches within them (Greenwood, Hinings, and Brown 1992). What these scholars report then is the tension between professional values and efforts to develop management systems that are more rational and efficient. It would be helpful if the management academy could provide more comprehensive analyses of the organizational models that exist in large law firms, and what the consequences of those various models are for core professional values.

**Proposed Solution:** Consultants should be brought into the conversation about what managerial practices best promote core professional values. More empirical research on the managerial practices that firms are using, with what consequences for core professional values, should be conducted.

## Conclusion

The Raising the Bar initiative has identified a set of concerns that resonate across the legal profession. The problems of lack of training, lack of mentoring, loss of loyalty within law firms, and excessive demands for billable hours, to name a few, have deep roots in the structure of modern day law practice. As a result, the problems will not be easily solved. The organizational analysis I have offered here provides an abbreviated inventory of the actors inside and outside corporate law firms who might play a role in redressing these issues, but who might also resist change.

While all these actors can affect the outcome of reform efforts, I think the pivotal actors in coming years will be the leadership of large law firms. They have the most power to control the organizational practices within law firms that relate to the professional values at stake. They are in a position to develop the business models that are the foundations of their law firms. Clients have immense influence on the law firms they do business with, but the partners who have client responsibility ultimately translate that influence into the law firm.

The Raising the Bar campaign represents an instance of institutional leadership from the organized bar. Significant as that effort is, it is fair to say that the leaders of law firms face a greater challenge. As they campaign for core professional values, they may well feel that the economic well-being of their firms, and thus of their own personal professional success, is at stake. They must not only convince their partners and associates of the need to give priority to professional values, they must convince potentially skeptical clients and an unforgiving marketplace for legal services.

## References

Daniels, Stephen, and Joanne Martin. 2005. Presentation at MidYear Meetings of American Bar Association, summarized in 16 *Researching Law* 4–6.

DiMaggio, Paul, and Walter Powell. 1983. "The Iron Cage Revisited: Institutional Isomorphism and Collective Rationality in Organizational Fields." *American Sociological Review* 48:147–60.

Dinovitzer, Ronit, Bryant G. Garth, Richard Sander, Joyce Sterling, and Gita Z. Wilder. 2004. *After the JD: First Results of a National Study of Legal Careers*. Washington and Chicago: NALP and American Bar Foundation.

Dinovitzer, Ronit, and Bryant G. Garth. Forthcoming. "Lawyer Satisfaction in the Process of Structuring Legal Careers." *Law and Society Review*.

Epstein, Cynthia Fuchs, Carroll Seron, Bonnie Oglensky, and Robert Saute. 1999. *Part-Time Paradox: Time, Professional Life, Family and Gender*. New York: Routledge.

Galanter, Marc, and Thomas Palay. 1991. *Tournament of Lawyers: The Transformation of the Big Law Firm*. Chicago: University of Chicago Press.

Gilson, Ronald, and Robert H. Mnookin. 1985. "Sharing Among the Human Capitalists: An Economic Inquiry into the Corporate Law Firm and How Partners Split Profits." *Stanford Law Review* 37:313–92.

Greenwood, Royston, C. R. Hinings, and John Brown. 1990. "P2 Form Strategic Management: Corporate Practices in Professional Services Firms." *Academy of Management Journal* 33: 725–55.

Heinz, John P., and Edward O. Laumann. 1982. *Chicago Lawyers: The Social Structure of the Bar*. New York: Russell Sage Foundation and American Bar Foundation.

Heinz, John P., and Robert L. Nelson, Rebecca L. Sandfur, and Edward O. Laumann. 2005. *Urban Lawyers: The New Social Structure of the Bar*. Chicago: University of Chicago Press.

Henderson, William. Forthcoming. "An Empirical Study of Single-Tier versus Two-Tier Partnerships in the Am Law 200," 84 *North Carolina Law Review*, (2006).

Howard, Bruce P., and Juli Wilson Marshall. 2006. "Training Becomes a Recruiting Lure." *National Law Journal*, May 1, 2006, R1, R25.

Hull, Kathleen E., and Robert L. Nelson. 2000. "Assimilation, Choice or Constraint? Testing Theories of Gender Differences in the Careers of Lawyers." *Social Forces* 79 (1): 229–64.

Kay, Fiona M., and John Hagan. 1998. "Raising the Bar: The Gender Stratification of Law Firm Capital." *American Sociological Review* 63:728–43.

______. 1999. "Cultivating Clients in the Competition for Partnership: Gender and the Organizational Restructuring of Law Firms." *Law and Society Review* 33 (3): 517–56.

Lazega, Emmanuel. 2001. *The Collegial Phenomenon: The Social Mechanisms of Cooperation among Peers in a Corporate Law Partnership.* Oxford: Oxford University Press.

Leipold, James G. 2006. "The Market for Lateral Hires Continues to Heat Up." *National Law Journal*, May 1, 2006, R1, R26.

Mather, Lynn, Craig A. McEwen, and Richard J. Maiman. 2001. *Divorce Lawyers at Work: Varieties of Professionalism in Practice.* New York: Oxford University Press.

Menkel-Meadow, Carrie. 1994. "Culture Clash in the Quality of Life in the Law: Changes in the Economics, Diversification and Organization of Lawyering." *Case Western Reserve Law Review* 44:621–63.

Nelson, Robert L. 1988. *Partners with Power: The Social Transformation of the Large Law Firm.* Berkeley and Los Angeles: University of California Press.

______. 1998. "The Discovery Process as a Circle of Blame: Institutional, Professional, and Socio-economic Factors That Contribute to Unreasonable, Inefficient, and Amoral Behavior in Corporate Litigation." *Fordham Law Review* 67:773–808.

Nelson, Robert L., and Laura Beth Nielsen. 2000. "Cops, Counsel and Entrepreneurs: Constructing the Role of Inside Counsel in Large Corporations." *Law and Society Review* 34 (2): 457–94.

Nelson, Robert L., and David M. Trubek. 1992. "Arenas of Professionalism: The Professional Ideologies of Lawyers in Context." Pp. 177–214 in Nelson, Robert L., David M. Trubek, and Rayman L. Solomon, eds. 1992. *Lawyers' Ideals/Lawyers' Practices: Transformations in the American Legal Profession.* Ithaca: Cornell University Press.

Powell, Michael J. 1979. "Anatomy of a Counter-Bar Association: The Chicago Council of Lawyers." *American Bar Foundation Research Journal* 4 (3): 501–41.

Reichman, Nancy J., and Joyce S. Sterling. 2002. "Recasting the Brass Ring: Deconstructing and Reconstructing Workplace Opportunities for Women Lawyers." *Capital University Law Review* 29 (1): 923–77.

# CHAPTER 5

# Law Firms as Great Places to Work

**By Dr. Scott Cawood**

Law firms are facing unprecedented changes in how they do business. Perhaps for the first time, they are finding they need to revisit and overhaul their historic traditions to become more modern, competitive businesses. This means refocusing on how they do business externally, but more critically, how they do business from within. In the wake of skyrocketing salaries and alarming attrition, firms must find fresh solutions in competing for clients, associates, and staff, but also at the same time be excellent lawyers.

No one ever promised that working for a high-powered, high-profit law firm would be a walk in the park! True, the legal profession offers an abundance of prestigious, top-paying jobs in cushy surroundings, but so often that comes at a staggering price—relentless stress, demanding partners, cutthroat colleagues, and long hours away from home. The pressures are unyielding for billable hours, and a 100-percent-plus focus on firm business is the norm, often at the expense of personal and family priorities. According to the American Bar Association, 75 percent of lawyers surveyed said they wouldn't want their children to follow in the footsteps of their profession.

The Raise the Bar Project, sponsored by ABA's Section of Litigation, has identified several critical issues facing the profession—issues that are reflected clearly, though not exclusively, in the larger law firms in America. The billable hour culture. Lack of mentoring. Lack of training. Lack of trial experience. Mind-numbing document reviews. Intrusive 24/7 technology and demand for availability. Unclear paths to partnership. Depreciation of the status of partner. Resentment over associate salaries. Lack of law firm loyalty among associates and partners. Unreasonable client demands. Difficulty in pursuing pro bono. Unhappy work places. The list goes on and on.

How can law firms continue to be profitable, while at the same time provide their people with happier, more satisfying, more balanced lives? Through its attorney focus group discussions, Raise the Bar found that the key is a flexible approach—and the recognition of competing demands on time.

"That's not to say that people no longer have to bill any hours or do client work," says Andra Greene, Raise the Bar Project co-chair. "We're in the business of serving clients. But there are ways that, through—for example—attention on development of lawyers, law firms can make the work environment a better one." Spending time mentoring and making people feel that the firm has an interest in their career, along with a transparent compensation system that ensures people understand what is rewarded, will also go a long way in creating a better work environment, Greene says.

With increased competition for recruiting and retaining top talent, law firms are beginning to treat their firms as businesses—understanding that the happier people are on their jobs, the better job they'll do for the firm in satisfying clients and in building the bottom line. "Certainly law firms need to be profitable," Green notes. "They're not going to cease being profitable, but the opportunities are there to combine a more satisfying experience for lawyers in the firm with profitability for the firm. And in fact, the case may be made that a law firm will be more profitable if its lawyers are satisfied with their careers and hence more productive. If you can lessen attrition, that certainly increases profitability."

## Living the Equation

A few firms are already living this equation. Five were included in *Fortune* magazine's 2006 list of the "100 Best Places to Work," with the following rankings: Alston & Bird, number 19; Perkins Coie, number 48; Nixon Peabody, number 49; Arnold & Porter, number 54; and Morrison & Foerster, number 88. The cultures of these five firms, which ultimately landed them on the list with such luminaries as Cisco Systems, American Express, Goldman Sachs, Ernst & Young, Microsoft, and Starbucks, share many common denominators. In this chapter, we look at the people practices of these organizations, with a focus on the two firms at the top of the list, Alston & Bird and Perkins Coie.

For the 115-year-old law firm Alston & Bird, it's "not just about billable hours," says Cathy Benton, chief people officer. With 700 attorneys, 1,500 total employees, and a turnover rate of less than 8 percent—well below the national average for law firms—A&B has the reputation of being a place where "the good people work." Just ask the many lawyers and other staff members who have migrated to A&B from other firms because of their attraction to the firm's people principles.

"You can be a great place to work *and* a profitable organization," Benton says. "But what makes the difference is you have happy employees who will really take care of your business." The fact that the firm hasn't had a layoff in its 115-year history underscores how much it values its people. The goal of this chapter is not to mandate that your firm be a "Great Place to Work." It's to have you consider the environment you'll need to foster greatness in your people—one that ultimately enables everyone in the firm to be, or support being, the best possible lawyer.

Seattle-based Perkins Coie, in operation since 1912 with 15 offices in the U.S. and China, prides itself on its people-centric practices. Darrin Emerick, chief personnel officer, says the firm focuses on engaging its employees, giving them a sense of purpose beyond their job, and being present to the needs of the whole person.

As law firms realize the battle is fierce for lawyers, staff, and clients, more and more are willing to invest heavily to "raise the bar" of excellence in providing a people-first work environment. In the age-old profit-versus-people dilemma, there is no one-size-fits-all remedy, yet these *Fortune* firms offer up many lessons:

**Cultivate a Culture of Fairness.** When employees believe they are treated unfairly, they are prone to disconnect from their organization and ultimately leave it. Being treated unfairly brings out the absolute worst in everyone—including partners. Before we were lawyers, we were people. At our core of being human, we believe fairness is our right, and we believe organizations and bosses are no exception.

When people perceive fairness and unfairness at work, they retaliate in all sorts of ways. They take things back—not just things from the supply closet, but they withhold ideas, perspectives, service to internal and external clients, and communication. They hold back on giving their best performance. They see opportunities and don't tell people about them. That withholding costs the organization at every level. Firms that still hold on to practices and policies that keep lawyers and staff at odds will always face a "we and they" mentality, something that is both costly and ineffective in the 21st century business model.

Great-Place-to-Work law firms have defined what fairness means for their people, their business partners, and their clients, and they have systems in place to ensure the fairest workplace possible. Great firms do not treat everyone the same, but they do have a spirit of equity that permeates every level of the firm. We encourage the motto, "If you give it to one group, why not give it to all?"

Alston & Bird's employees praise the firm for its culture of fairness—largely because the firm's systems and policies are transparent, says managing partner Ben F. Johnson III. An example is the firm's lawyer evaluation system. "When partners prepare written evaluations of the associates, the associates are invited to review them. They can sit down with the partner, challenge what they said, and talk it over." The same is true for partner evaluation. "Every partner knows that he or she can come to us and get an explanation of his or her compensation," Johnson explains. "Our people know they will be respected as important parts of the organization—and that they will advance in a system that they can readily understand."

A&B also strives to minimize distinctions between lawyers and staff. "Our human capital is the driving force behind our organization," says Cathy Benton. "So we emphasize how much we value every person in the organization, whatever position they hold in the firm."

Benton notes the firm has done much to break down the class structure inherent in many law firms. Two years ago, they opened up what was formerly the attorney dining room to everyone at the firm. Managing partner Johnson also holds a firmwide meeting at the end of each month to talk about the firm's business. "For most law firms, that kind of meeting would be just for attorneys," Benton explains. "Here, anyone can come."

To reinforce the value it puts on its staff, Perkins Coie sponsors a Staff Mentor Program. "All new employees are taken to lunch with up to four people, up to three times," Emerick explains. "They're then assigned a 'buddy' who becomes a mentor to help address concerns and guide them in making decisions." Similarly, the firm recently rolled out an Associate Mentor program, pairing partners with associates to help associates on their way to becoming partners.

San Francisco-based Morrison & Foerster, 114 years old with 19 offices worldwide, also emphasizes its lack of hierarchy. To ensure equality from the start, the firm puts a high premium on training and mentoring, as associates practice with, and learn from, experienced lawyers. For the first two years at the firm, each new associate is assigned an "Odyssey Partner" with whom they can have regular, specific, and personal interactions. Odyssey Partners offer mentoring and guidance in professional development, ensuring the firm is providing equal opportunities to all attorneys.

**Encourage Open, Honest, and Frequent Communication from Everyone in the Firm.** Firms that share their vision, goals, progress, and challenges openly—and frequently—enhance staff and associates' sense of ownership and belonging. They foster cultures where everyone, regardless of their role in their organization, is encouraged to speak directly with anyone else in the organization. This open-door policy ignites high trust because leaders are available to listen to employees informally, thus avoiding misunderstandings or a rumor mill in overdrive.

For Alston & Bird management, communication is a high priority. The firm takes extraordinary measures to keep all employees informed through a series of town meetings in its offices in Atlanta, Research Triangle, Charlotte, Washington, DC, and New

York. As the firm continues to grow through mergers, leaders realize it takes time to get comfortable with each other. Placing a high value on relationships is a critical component of making money in today's ever-challenging business environment. Even with the technology advances, nothing replaces good solid relationships and trust when it comes to deciding which lawyer to use for representation.

"We don't do employee surveys," Benton notes. "We'd rather sit down in small focus groups, find out what's on people's minds, and be as open as possible about what we can and can't do." Policies are tweaked only after listening to what staff have to say in these small-group settings.

Perkins Coie fosters a highly collaborative environment, according to Emerick. "From the managing partner to the entry-level employee, we have ongoing dialogues to see how decisions affect every person in the firm. These dialogues help us open up the communication channels and address any preconceived assumptions."

Nixon Peabody, with offices in Boston and Rochester, prides itself in its "inclusive culture," says Andrew Glincher, managing partner of the firm's Boston office. "We try to get feedback from everyone," Glincher notes in an interview in *Metropolitan Corporate Counsel*, "If people are too intimidated to speak to the managing partner directly, they can submit their ideas or recommendations anonymously. The point is that if people know that you take feedback seriously, they will take the time to give you feedback. We are a better firm for having a free flow of information, and it serves to insulate us from unpleasant surprises as we move forward."

Arnold & Porter, one of Washington, DC's, Big Three firms, has been praised for its "notable lack of cruelty" in how partners relate to their underlings. Says one insider, "Partners treat associates like people. They're friendly, but professional."

**Know Who You Are as a Firm, and Hire for That.** It's long been suggested that "people are the most important asset" in an organization. That's not entirely true. The biggest asset is actually the "right" people who can maximize contributions at all levels of the firm. Many good people can be in the wrong job or in the wrong time of their life to help an organization perform. Top talent is only top talent when they can excel and get things done in your firm.

Therefore, hiring the best is conditional on knowing who you are as an organization.

Those you hire who can do well inside your particular culture will be more apt to stay longer, understand the expectations more clearly, and decide for themselves how to spend their time growing the bottom line for the firm. They will also help to perpetuate the culture and strengthen your organization's efforts to deliver the best client services.

Alston & Bird looks for people who value teamwork, have a stellar work ethic, produce quality work, and are committed to service excellence. These characteristics are scrupulously screened for in the firm's interviewing and hiring process. "We hire tough and manage easy," says Chief People Officer Cathy Benton.

Following what it calls a Top Echelon—an acronym for its values—the firm provides values training in such areas as teamwork, openness, creativity, humor, and service excellence. "These are values we have written down and talk about daily," Benton says. "We strive to keep them always at the forefront."

Benton notes the Human Resource team publishes an online newsletter highlighting the "value of the day"—designed to get people together to ask questions and share best practices on how they handle a variety of situations. Then, for 10 minutes each day, the firm holds what it calls "T Time," short for Top Echelon Time. Here, employees get together in their own groups and talk about whatever the standard of service is for the day. According to Benton, these daily get-togethers build teamwork and reinforce the behaviors the firm values—which translates into how they want to serve every client.

In A&B's two mergers, values were a key part of merger discussions. "In considering another firm, it's not just about the book of business they bring," notes Benton. "It's just as important that they will fit with us culturally and their people practices are aligned with ours."

At A&B, cultural misfits are coached in the A&B values in an effort to nip inappropriate situations in the bud. "People may join us from another law firm, believing that the way of getting something done is by bullying—or what we consider mistreating somebody," Benton explains. "We don't do that here, and when we see that behavior, we're quick to bring it to light. If an employee—even a profitable partner—cannot or will not change their behavior, we will let them go." Morrison & Foerster holds diversity as a prime value of its culture and hiring practices. Throughout the organization, recruitment and retention of the best women and minority attorneys isn't just a goal; it's a given. With 26 percent of the firm's partners and associates lawyers of color, the firm ranks second in diversity among the nation's law firms. An active diversity task force creates programs that reinforce cultural awareness and inclusiveness.

Arnold & Porter fosters a culture supportive of lesbian, gay, bisexual, and transgendered (LGBT) employees. "We can say without equivocation that an individual's sexual orientation is not an issue at Arnold & Porter," the firm says. Its nondiscrimination policy specifically includes sexual orientation, gender identity, and HIV status, and the firm offers domestic partnership health benefits to all employees. As part of its hiring practices, at least one gay or lesbian attorney serves on the hiring committee.

Similarly, Nixon Peabody has been nationally recognized for creating a work environment where inclusiveness is respected and embraced. The firm recently received a 100 percent rating from the Human Rights Campaign Fund in its annual Corporate Equality Index. "Fostering a diverse and inclusive workplace is morally the right thing to do and it makes great business sense," says Harry P. Trueheart, Nixon Peabody chairman. Adds William Simpson, the firm's director of human resources, "From our experience, creating an environment where all employees can flourish increases employee satisfaction, which contributes to client satisfaction and financial results—and give us an advantage in recruiting and retaining top talent."

**Provide Opportunities to Give Back to the Community.** In every industry, people say over and over that what matters most to them in the workplace isn't money. It's meaning. Pay and benefits alone aren't enough to keep anyone of good caliber. Every person in your firm wants to feel good about themselves and about the work they're doing. Money becomes the highest priority only when meaning is missing. People count on their leaders to create the kind of workplace where they feel valued, appreciated, and part of something bigger than their job. This is true of every staff member or employee in your firm.

Think that your paralegals don't have the same ambition and drive that your partners do? Not so! Why would you have a different expectation level for your partners as you do your staff?

We must create firms where everyone is involved, included, and rewarded for delivering to clients the best lawyers—and the best service of lawyers.

With a culture characterized as caring and civic minded, Perkins Coie immerses its employees in pro bono activities. A Community Service Committee, designed to promote, support, and facilitate volunteerism, oversees programs for the firm's offices, teams, and individual employees.

"In some fields of work—such as health care or teaching—it's easy to connect people to the organization," Emerick says. "What could be more purposeful than saving lives or fostering knowledge? With law firms, the work product is often not as easy to tie to a wider cause. We strive to go above and beyond in providing community service opportunities that connect our people to the greater good."

Along with making charitable contributions to deserving organizations, facilitating United Way contributions through regular payroll deductions, and sponsoring major fund-raising events, the firm encourages attorneys and staff to participate in smaller community projects. Projects range from painting a day care center in a poor neighborhood to setting up apartments at a homeless shelter to spending the lunch hour volunteering with seniors. On many community service projects, Perkins Coie partners with clients. The firm also takes on pro bono cases. Pro bono time has reached as high as 27,000 hours a year, or an estimated $8 million dollars of donated work.

Pro bono work and community service are also a cornerstone of culture at Alston & Bird. The firm actively encourages service to others and involvement in the communities that support their lives and livelihood. Projects have ranged from volunteering to represent immigrant and refugee children in asylum proceedings to building a house for Habitat for Humanity. The firm has also made substantial donations to advancing community life, joining in 2006 with Atlanta competitor King & Spaldin in a $5 million gift to the Atlanta Symphony Orchestra.

"Although our firms are competitive on a day-to-day basis, we both believe in this project and what it will mean for education and arts and culture in Georgia," says managing partner Johnson.

Nixon Peabody set up a Pro Bono Committee and appointed a firmwide pro bono partner to oversee it activities. Attorneys and paralegals alike receive full billable hour credit for their pro bono work. Annually, it contributes at least an amount of time equal to 3 percent of the firm's totally billable hours, or 60 hours per attorney, to pro bono work. The firm has handled hundreds of cases, from death penalty appeals to denial of social security disability benefits to orders of protection, custody, and divorce for battered women. It also has a long history of involvement with a variety of human rights, civil rights, and battered women centers.

Arnold & Porter counts social responsibility among its key values. Its attorneys are encouraged to spend up to 15 percent of their time on pro bono work. In 2005, they contributed over 60,000 attorney pro bono hours, and associates volunteer for six-month stints at the Legal Aid Society.

Morrison & Foerster, too, has as a cornerstone of its culture a tradition that strongly encourages and values pro bono work. The firm's primary efforts have focused on children in poverty and school education issues, civil right and civil liberties cases, international human rights and political asylum, environmental concerns, access to justice, and housing issues. The firm has also set up a foundation that operates as a separate nonprofit organization for maximizing charitable resources. It applies the same quality standards to its pro bono work as it does to its billable engagements, and in determining compensation, pro bono work is evaluated equally with other client work. Volunteer opportunities for all employees are abundant, while a Community Service Day encourages staff to take a paid day off to pursue their own path in community assistance.

**Honor the Needs of the Whole Person.** Everyone in the firm needs to find the right mix of commitments to their jobs, their families and friends, their extracurricular pursuits, and themselves. Great-Place-to-Work law firms have learned to focus on their employees as human beings, rather than just human "doings," and to proactively encourage a quality life and a quality work-life.

Alston & Bird has gone through great lengths to show it respects each individual as a person and not just as an employee. To support family life, the firm opened a child-care facility near its main office in Atlanta and has pursued child-care initiatives in its other offices.

A highlight of A&B culture is a children's art wall in each of its five offices, showcasing the latest creations of employees' children. "Family is really important to us," says Benton. "A lot of organizations think you leave the family behind when you come to work. That's not realistic."

To further support the whole person, A&B also has several on-site perks, including massage therapy, a fitness facility, and a Weight Watchers group. The firm also offers its employees flexible hours, job share arrangements, referral bonuses, and three-month paid maternity leave.

In encouraging life outside of work, Perkins Coie lets its employees determine how much time they want to be on the job. Associates guarantee the number of hours they'll work in a year, and if they log over the designated amount, they're rewarded with a bonus. It's an extraordinary shift from the business model of billable hours to one of personal choice. Work-life balance is further fostered through flextime schedules, job sharing, and part-time employment.

Perkins Coie also offers a sabbatical program to its staff and attorneys. Exempt employees are eligible for a two-month paid sabbatical after 10 years, and nonexempt after 13 years. If they have additional personal time off (PTO) hours, they can be gone for up to three months. "People travel all over the world on their sabbaticals and do things they've never done before," Emerick explains. "It gives them an opportunity to rejuvenate themselves. When they return to work, they often write stories of their adventures, posted for all to share."

On the job, Perkins Coie brings people together informally through its brownbag lunch seminars to talk about issues of mutual interest. Discussions focus on whatever employees think is important, from how to save money to how to communicate tragedy to children, the subject of a series of brown bag lunches after 9/11.

Nixon Peabody has a PTO plan to accommodate scheduled and unscheduled requests. For employees who do not take unscheduled time off, the firm buys back their time at 120 percent—resulting often in substantial monetary rewards.

Arnold & Porter, dubbed "the firm with a heart," provides long-term nursing care to retired employees and was DC's first law firm to offer full-time on-site childcare. Employees who adopt a child automatically get three paid months off and up to $5,000 from the firm toward the cost of adopting a child. The firm also has a written policy providing part-time attorneys consideration for partnership. Program advisors—women partners who work part-time themselves—mentor part-time attorneys. "Having a part-time program has allowed us to retain people who otherwise might have left the firm, or the practice of law," says James Sandman, managing partner of Arnold & Porter.

**Show Appreciation.** Few law firms ever "overappreciate" their people. From handwritten thank-you notes for a job well done to awards and parties to special bonuses, Great-Place-to-Work law firms are finding ways to recognize, appreciate, and reward the individuals, teams, associates, staff members, and partners who ultimately secure and satisfy their clients.

Alston & Bird's end-of-month meetings serve not only as arenas to share information, but to thank employees. "In discussing firm business, our attorneys recognize every person who worked on each deal, from partners and associates to paralegals to secretaries—even the people who set up the conference room," says Benton. "Everybody is acknowledged for their part on the team."

Perkins Coie shows its appreciation through abundant incentives to its staff, including a 5 percent bonus at year-end, a 7.3 percent contribution to retirement accounts, and quarterly prize drawings. Recognition awards include roundtrip airline tickets and gift certificates.

"People participate in the drawings after they receive a thank you card," explains Emerick. "A colleague writes a story about a good deed they did at work or elsewhere. It's a great way for others to give them a public pat-on-the-back—as well as reward them tangibly for a job well done."

Arnold & Porter is known for celebrating its employees in unique ways. For example, every July, the firm celebrates "Gerry Warfield Day" in its Washington office. Featuring awards for staff employees, the event recognizes the firm's longest-serving staff member, a woman who handles office supplies and has been with the firm since 1956.

**Balance Work and Fun on the Job.** In many workplaces, fun is as important as profit—and law firms that are successful in creating great places to work really know how to have it!

Alston & Bird encourages robust social interaction among its employees. Firm-sponsored events include a Friday night happy hour, and associates have been known to spend a lot of time together after hours on weekends.

In cultivating a fun place to work, Perkins Coie has raised social events to a high art form. Along with ice cream socials and excursions to Seattle Mariners baseball games, the firm hosts a huge holiday party every December. It assigns its newest attorneys to a skit committee, or in PC parlance, "Skitcom." "The goal is to outdo the previous year," Emerick explains. "It's always a parody of a current event happening at the firm, in the U.S., or around the world."

One of the most memorable skits was a takeoff on a firm event, showcasing a change in flu shot providers. "People had to wait in line 25 minutes to get their shots," Emerick says. "It was a fiasco." So that year, the skit featured an attorney dressed as a nurse, doling out flu shots with a caulk gun.

Arnold & Porter hosts an array of employee get-togethers, for which participation is completely optional, from evening social hours and weekly pizza parties to events designed to foster strong working relationships and build life-long friendships.

The Rochester office of Nixon Peabody holds a summer-long Wacky Office Olympics, featuring such events as waterballoon basketball, pin-and-win, a putting green, and office chair races. The culminating event is a carnival-style dunk tank in the firm's courtyard. Employees come out in full force to sink their fellow co-workers—and raise funds for a local youth organization.

At Morrison & Foerster LLP—nicknamed "MoFo"—fun is an integral part of the firm's creed in its 19 offices worldwide. "While we take our work seriously, we remember not to take ourselves too seriously," the firm's Web site states. "We're reminded that a sense of humor helps us stay focused on the important things growing, while preserving the culture that has been a source of our strength."

## Benchmarking for Greatness

Being a "Great Place to Work" in today's white-hot competitive environment is no easy goal. It takes more than financial incentives. In the competition for talent, success will increasingly be measured by each firm's ability to claim, and support, its Greatness. Firms that are actualizing their Greatness know that the key to enriched profits is engaged people: employees at every level who enjoy what they are doing, have a good relationship with management and colleagues, and are treated as important contributors to the organization's success.

One idea continuously raised in Raise the Bar focus group discussions was the need for some kind of benchmark or scorecard that could measure how well law firms—both big and small—are addressing key issues in the quest for Greatness. Brad Brian, past chair of ABA's Section of Litigation, recommends a questionnaire and benchmarking process. "Law firms would volunteer to participate," says Brian. "They would then facilitate the receipt by their personnel at every level of a questionnaire seeking to elicit critical information about the law firm's performance on various aspects of its operation."

In the first part of the Raise the Bar program, firms would complete an inventory of their practices. The questionnaire data would be compiled and analyzed by an outside consultant and used as part of a national database of practices, programs, and policies that have been successfully implemented in firms worldwide. The data would be categorized into benchmarks, offering insight into such key areas as turnover, salary, associate development, and pro bono options.

In the second part of the Raise the Bar program, partners, associates, and staff members would be surveyed to get a benchmark of how firms are doing compared to their competitors. Again, no law firm would ever see another's data, but each firm would receive their own employees' data, along with a benchmark of how these data compare with firms of similar size, region, or practice area.

While there would be no information shared about any individual firm to other firms, each firm could get an independent evaluation of their workplace, consider areas for improvement, and better understand how their associates, partners, and staff feel about the firm's culture and work environment.

"This is no reason for those scoring lower to hang their collective heads in shame," says Brian. "No one—except the firms themselves—will know which firms applied. And no firm will know what score any other firm achieved." Each participating firm will simply know how it did in relation to other firms, without identifying the others, he explains.

Participating firms will then have an opportunity to Raise the Bar on their own performance and to answer the key questions they face. Are we providing training for our associates? Are we mentoring them? Do they know what's needed to become partners? Are they getting trial experience and, if so, how much? What are our billable hour requirements, if any? Does pro bono count? How much pro bono is right for us?

"Our hope," Brian says, "is that the competitive juices will start flowing and the firms will take the results of their standing and constructively employ the lessons learned to improve. We're not asking firms to give up income to achieve what may be perceived as 'warm and fuzzy' goals. The lesson of the Great Law Firm Program will be that profitability soars in Great Place to Work, and hidden costs, like the cost of associate turnover or the cost of staff malaise, are dramatically reduced."

# PART III

# Being Honest

# CHAPTER 6

# A View from Outside the Law Firms

**By Bruce D. Collins**

There are a lot of unhappy lawyers in this country and most of them seem to be working in law firms. There are many kinds of lawyers, and you don't have to be an associate or a partner in a law firm to be unhappy. But if recent surveys are to be believed, it helps. According to the social scientists a good number of the very smart, ambitious men and women who succeeded in law school and who now occupy good paying desk jobs in some of the nicest offices in white collar urban America are also so disenchanted with their lives they would not recommend a legal career to their own children. The problem has been around for a long time, but like most social phenomena it broke into the popular consciousness seemingly all at once. The miserable lawyer enslaved by the billable hour has now become a cliche.

None of this is new to me, as I expect it is not to anyone else who has been associated with the law business in one way or another over the last forty years, as I have. I certainly did not predict this state of affairs for the law firms. That would have required much more insight and prescience of me than I possess.

Instead, I was a witness to the slow evolution of law firm culture from my position on the outside. Although I've been a lawyer for twenty years, I never worked in a law firm. Yet, my legal career has been strongly influenced by what I've seen from outside the law firm culture.

My decision to become a lawyer was made when I was twelve years old, or thereabouts. As a curious Upstate New York child in the early Sixties, I'd been drawn to politics primarily, especially during the 1960 Kennedy-Nixon presidential race. As my level of sophistication on such things grew I realized politicians had to be employed while seeking public office and if I was going to be a politician I knew I would also need a paying job. The life of a lawyer seemed well-suited to my political ambitions.

It influenced my decision considerably that my father was a lawyer. His mostly one-man practice was the dominant career role model for me, and it seemed particularly apt because he was also a politician. Although at first he tended to lose the races he entered, I noticed that his job seemed to work around his political activities rather than the other way around. It was the same when he was elected to the county legislature later on. Without having ever had any meaningful exposure to any other kind of career such as business or engineering, I confidently concluded that lawyering was the trade that best suited my talents and my ultimate career goal.

Even though my father was essentially a one-man band, I was aware that most lawyers, especially the more financially successful ones, worked together in groups. This arrangement seemed much better than the solo practice of my father. I had clear memories of him leaving the house after dinner on evenings toward the end of each month to visit clients at their homes. He was collecting his fees. For some reason, I didn't think lawyers in law firms would have to do door-to-door bill collecting. My idea was that I would team up with a group of maybe five or six other guys (women lawyers then were simply not in the picture) whom I would most likely have met in law school; then we'd hang out a shingle together. I imagined this would take place in a mid-size city somewhere in Upstate, perhaps Syracuse, Rochester, or Buffalo, it didn't matter exactly which mid-size city as long as it had enough business to support us all and it wasn't New York City.

With impressions of law practice formed by my father's experience and by TV shows like *The Defenders* and *Perry Mason,* I thought the expectations I had were realistic and attainable. Central to my view of a small firm practice was that my colleagues and I would have shared views of how to practice law and how to balance the requirements of work against the needs of the rest of our lives. While my fantasies (and that's what they turned out to be) never seemed to identify what kind of law we, or I, would be practicing, they did include very clear ideas of how we fellow lawyers could help each other out. For example, if after a couple years at my own firm I wanted to run for the state legislature, I was confident I would be able to cut back on my legal work during the campaign, letting my colleagues pick up the slack, which they would certainly, and cheerfully do. This they would do because each of them could expect similar support from me and the others for his particular need, whatever it may turn out to be. Maybe one of my partners would want to sail around the world before he was 40. I was confident we in the firm would be able to help him make that happen, all the while practicing law profitably and harmoniously.

With that idyllic view of law firm practice in my head, I continued to succeed academically, as I knew I must, in high school and in college. I did succeed, but politics delayed my chance to impress any law school admissions officer when, at age 23, I went almost immediately from undergraduate school to a successful congressional campaign. Perhaps because the new congressman was only two years older than I was, I found myself with a substantive job on Capitol Hill in Washington, DC. Law school would have to wait, and it did until I was 29 years old.

In the 17 years between the time I decided to be a lawyer and the day I entered law school my view of law firm practice was no longer idyllic. In fact, by that time I did not want to have anything to do with it. My adult perspective was less naive and more informed by experience than was my childhood view, certainly, but my very clear sense was that the profession had changed more than I had. Having worked during my twenties on the campaign trail and on Capitol Hill with many types of mostly young lawyers, including some who had been my undergraduate classmates, I had a close-up view of their work lives.

As hard as I worked as a political operative, a legislative staffer, and a lobbyist, my lawyer friends in the firms always burned more midnight oil than I did, and it seemed to me they tended to do it alone and under pressure. In contrast, although my work days were also long, they also tended to involve other people and I usually had some choice in what I did. Moreover, my colleagues' partners weren't pitching in to help, as my childhood fantasy of small law firm life would have had them doing. Their work seemed utterly different from what I had imagined a lawyer's life to be.

Without being able to prove it, I am convinced my childhood fantasy or at least a version of it actually existed for many lawyers at one time, even for some practicing in the larger cities. I am also convinced that at least by 1980 all traces of it were gone. By the time I entered law school that year the practice of law had become the business of law, and it no longer had any appeal to me. Fortunately, there turned out to be many other ways to profitably apply legal training in a challenging and interesting career in Washington, DC. I entered night law school confident I'd find one of them. Six years later, having taken a leave of absence for the 1984 presidential election campaign, I finished law school and passed the bar. The very next day I became in-house counsel for my employer. I never had a single interview with a law firm recruiter, and I never worked in a law firm.

Still, after twenty years as a general counsel and as a friend to many lawyers for longer than that, I've been able to peek behind the law firm curtain. I have even been invited into the inner sanctum a few times. What I saw there convinced me I had made the right choice for me.

In the mid-90s I think my name must have appeared on a new list of general counsel because within the course of only a few weeks I received several letters from lawyers looking for work at C-SPAN. A pattern among the letters quickly emerged. Each applicant had been working for at least a few years at a mid-size or a large firm, and was on a partnership track. The applicant was successful at the firm, but had recently come to conclude that at this point in his or her career a move to an in-house position seemed to be an attractive option. Some even mentioned the appeal of working for a nonprofit organization (C-SPAN is a tax-exempt nonprofit). Each letter included a resume, of course, and a request to be considered for any openings on my staff I might have.

After receiving about a dozen of these, I wondered if in my recent reading of the legal literature I had missed news of a major downsizing in the downtown firms in Washington. I hadn't. And the letters kept coming in a slow, steady stream. Surely, something was afoot, but I didn't know what. My response was to meet these mostly young attorneys and have a chat. As expected, each of them returned my call promptly, probably anticipating a solid lead on a job. I quickly explained to each applicant that although I was calling in response to his letter I did not have a job opening. Instead, I was interested in learning why he (or she) wanted to quit a law firm job so early in a career, and would he be willing to meet me to talk about that?

Every one of the eight lawyers I called quickly agreed. Maybe a few didn't really believe I had no job opening and instead thought they were being confronted with a new kind of recruiting trick with which they were perfectly willing to play along. I suggested breakfast meetings in a restaurant in my building. An early morning meeting would be less disruptive to each applicant's workday and would also attract less notice, which would be relevant to a young associate or partner who might not be eager to be seen meeting with a general counsel who was not a client of the firm. So began my education over the course of the next six weeks about life for young lawyers in a big DC law firm.

Each breakfast meeting began the same way. I thanked my guest for taking the time to meet with me. I said again that I did not have any job opening to fill and did not want to mislead my guest into thinking otherwise. Every one of them seemed to understand the rather odd situation perfectly, and in fact, it seemed to me, to be eager to begin the exercise. So I asked my question: "Why do you want to leave your current position at the firm to work in-house?" The answers were all different, but essentially all the same.

One young man spoke of how he had worked for nearly a year, including nights and weekends, on a business litigation case. The transaction at issue was complicated. He invested many hours mastering its details and devising legal theories in support of his client's position. Even as he kept putting off social events with his girlfriend, which he did not want to do, he was proud of his work, knowing that he was giving his client the best legal representation he knew how to give. He was also billing good hours for the firm and learning a lot about managing a big case, even if he was not the lead lawyer on it. The case actually went to trial before a jury, which he regarded as an unexpected bonus because he was able to assist at trial. In short, he said, his whole life was consumed by the case and he looked forward to the payoff at the end of the line. The end came in a verdict against his client.

Of course, he was disappointed, but as a professional he knew that losing the case was always a possibility. He found an odd satisfaction in the definitive nature of a loss at trial rather than the fuzzier outcome of a settlement where from the point of view of the litigator personality there is neither winner nor loser.

But his disappointment paled against the reaction he had to his client's comment upon hearing the verdict. The client, for whom he had sweated bullets during late nights and over weekends, and for whom he had given up a social life, turned to an aide and said simply, "Well, write the check." That was it. No thanks to his lawyers, and not even any particular angst over having lost a big case and a chunk of money along with it.

This was the moment of my breakfast mate's disturbing insight. He realized in that moment that not only had he spent a good part of the past year of his life fighting to prevent "one rich man from taking money from another rich man," but also that he was facing an entire career of doing the same thing over and over year after year. As lucrative as such a career might be for him, he told me, he just could not see himself spending his life moving money back and forth between rich people. He wanted to do something more fulfilling than that with his legal training and his life. That's why several other general counsel and I received his letter.

A few weeks later I had breakfast with another applicant, a woman associate in her early thirties. Hers was another litigation story. She had done vast amounts of drudge work on a case under the close supervision of a partner who kept her away from the client. While digging through literally thousands of pages of documents alone in a series of small, usually windowless rooms around the city, she became an expert on the case and came to know more about the client and his business than did her partner. She spoke of how just before each of the partner's meetings with the client she would brief him on the case to bring him up to speed; yet she was not invited to the meeting. In fact, she was never introduced to the client even when the case went to trial.

On the day of trial she had expected to sit at the counsel table alongside her partner in court and was stunned to realize she had been relegated to sitting behind the bar as if she were merely an observer of the case rather than an expert on it. As the day wore on she realized just how invisible her role was expected to be, despite the tremendous personal and professional investment she had in the events unfolding in front of her. And, like my earlier breakfast guest, she looked into her future at the firm and saw only more of the same. Unless she got out.

All of the lawyers I had breakfast with impressed me with their academic credentials, their personal presence, their confidence in their skills and their success (up to that point) in their respective law firms. Although I could have been snookered by a glib manipulator covering up for poor performance, I don't think I was. This was a group of sincere professionals who were confronting serious issues about their decision to pursue the practice of law as a career. It obviously had not yet measured up to their expectations and none of them, based on their experience thus far, believed it ever would in the law firm setting. Not one of them entering a law firm was completely naive about the workloads they would face or the unique pressures of the billable hour. They had worked hard all their academic careers and they expected to keep doing so, particularly in the early years of their first real jobs. Yet, these talented people who had succeeded in everything in their lives up to this point, hit a wall when they got to the day-to-day practice of law. If the long hours did not wear them down, the deadly dull work of document review did. Or the impossible demands of a supervising partner who also seemed always under the gun. Or the lack of any contact with clients. Or being slotted into one narrow area of legal practice. All of it took a toll on these still-young careers to the point they began to look for a way out.

My sample of lawyers was a self-selecting one, I know. I did not have breakfast with lawyers who were perfectly content. They were not the ones writing me letters asking for a job. And from my sample I did not conclude that law firm work cannot be fulfilling professionally and personally for many lawyers, and maybe even most lawyers. Rather, I concluded that too many young people entering the profession are making at least one of two serious errors in judgment. The first error is a failure to understand what work life is like in a big law firm. Despite the broad awareness among law students of how challenging their first jobs out of school are going to be, they can be excused their shock when confronted with the harsh reality that law firm life does not come with regularly scheduled breaks for exams or vacations. Life in theory is always better than in reality. The law firms do themselves no favors on this point when they organize summer associate programs that give law students the impression that life at the host firm is a series of lunches, dinners, and shows interrupted by occasional visits to the office. Even the least savvy recruit is aware that the summer experience is largely fantasy, but the experience still does nothing to prepare future lawyers for the reality of the long haul at a law firm. My sense is that the law schools do not do a very good job of it either.

The second error in judgment is more fundamental. It is the misjudgment of oneself. If all your career decisions are made based on somebody else's expectations—your parents, for example—the chances you will be in a job that satisfies you are very slim indeed. There are plenty of lawyers who went to law school for reasons having absolutely nothing to do with their high regard for the law or with themselves. They went because they scored unexpectedly high on the LSAT during a round of senior year graduate school exams, and figured they should be lawyers. Others saw law school as a means of breaking into a lucrative career in law. Others failed to get into medical school. Some went just to delay making a career decision for a few more years. And some went to please the folks. The result has been a lot of talented, smart people headed toward a legal career that does not have a chance of satisfying them because nothing about it has anything to do with who they are as individuals.

My series of breakfast meetings were very helpful to me in understanding what was going on in the law business. Some of my suspicions about law firm life were confirmed, but as bad as some of the stories were that I heard, I had expected worse. It seems things weren't as bad as I thought they'd be. And I was encouraged by the optimism of these young lawyers that they would be able to find satisfying employment without having to leave the profession entirely. This small group had the courage to act on their perhaps newfound self knowledge that they simply were not cut out for the kind of legal work they were doing. I was impressed with their decisiveness and willingness to overcome the sometimes powerful inertia of simply having a job, and a very well-paying job at that, to find another at very likely a lower pay level.

At the time I did not fully appreciate the influence these breakfast sessions had on me. Only after recalling them later did I understand how the personal testimonies of these lawyers had given me the ability to speak with confidence to others who sought my advice about entering law school and the legal profession. They gave me the vocabulary to speak credibly about law firm life, with which I had no direct experience, and they reminded me why I made the career choices I did.

Over the years I adopted a practice I have come to refer to somewhat inaccurately, as it turns out, as "talking them out of law school." As the general counsel at my company I am regularly approached by younger employees and summer interns to discuss their interest in law school and the kind of lawyering I do. I never turn down a chance to talk to them because I know how influential such talks can be on someone testing out options, and because I think my perspective is one they are not likely to get from anyone else. Usually, the conversation starts with my visitor telling me she wants to study law and could I talk about what it's like in law school. My response is not what she expects. I ask, "What is it you like to do?" Once she understands I'm not asking what kind of law she wants to practice, but rather what is it she actually likes to do with her time, which is to say with her life, only then does the conversation get interesting. I get all kinds of answers. Modern dance. Mathematics. Astronomy. Jazz. History. Fiction writing. Engineering. Law, even. I know we're getting somewhere when the conversation gets animated and my visitor starts to tell me something about her real interest, whatever it may be, that she thinks I don't know. And I usually don't. That's when I ask my next question. "Do you think law school will help you do that?"

Most times the question just lies there unanswered for a moment. The question seems out of place because she hadn't expected to be brought back to the subject of law just then. It is the moment when my point becomes clear because her answer is usually an obvious, "no." But, being the smart career oriented person that she is, she tries to avoid this turn away from law school talk by making a distinction between her career choice and her outside interests. Clearly, I am told, there is a distinction between the two. They really aren't connected.

My response is always to ask, simply and in I hope a non-challenging way, "Wouldn't it be nice to have a career in which you get paid for doing what you like to do?" My question sometimes brings out the pragmatist in my visitor who promptly discounts my pie-in-the-sky view by asserting that, yes, that would be nice but it just isn't the way the world works. Other times I get a thoughtful nod and a willingness to think outside the law school box she'd put herself in. That's when I will launch into an honest description of law school training and the demands it requires, including cost and time. I do this because it is usually new information about a tentatively held career goal, maybe enough to dislodge that goal. My view is that if my straightforward discussion of the realities of law school can make her desire to go to law school evaporate, then both she and the profession are much better off.

But not everyone is dissuaded at that point. If not, I shift gears to ask if she has any idea of a lawyer's typical workday. What tasks does a lawyer perform on a regular basis? How much time is spent reading, or writing, or researching, or persuading, or in meetings, or filling out forms, or in court, or waiting, or traveling? And so forth. I answer all of them, making the important point that the answers vary considerably depending on the type of lawyer you want to be. This leads to a discussion of the many different kinds of lawyers out there. We quickly get past the idea that the only way to be a lawyer is to join a firm and bill by the hour.

In all of these meetings I talk positively of the value of the training one gets in law school. In addition to learning how business works through the study of contracts and real property, you really do learn to think, as they say, like a lawyer. I make the point that graduating from law school does not mean you have to take the bar exam. There are many other lines of work for which a law degree has value. Some of my visitors are intrigued by this idea and seem to add it to their list of career options.

These are not short talks. It takes time to get a 20-year-old student to step outside the role of polite inquisitor of an older figure like me, especially when sitting in my office in the middle of my workday. It is only after my visitor loosens up and realizes I have a genuine interest in how he or she is thinking about a career that real information comes out. I begin each talk without any real intention of talking anybody out of going to law school. It's just that so often under my questioning it becomes clear to both of us that law school may not be the right choice for that person.

No decisions are made on the spot. Rather, it is more often the case that for the first time the student is getting good information about law school and the actual practice of law, and it was not what she expected. Some actually seem relieved to hear a lawyer suggest the law might not be right for them, almost as if a burden had been lifted from them. Others, of course, are perfectly suited for a career in law. They are self-aware and they have a pretty good idea of what they're getting into.

Frankly, I don't care if I talk somebody into or out of becoming a lawyer. My great concern is that those who actually spend the time and money in law school and who then sign up for law firm life are also the ones who are suited for it from the beginning. As the profession well knows, the cost in misused lives is too great for it to be otherwise.

If I have any goal at all, it would be to reduce the ranks of what I call the hyphenated lawyer. This refers to the usually mid-career lawyer who finally admits to himself he would rather be doing something else, but who also feels he cannot afford to make a career change. He makes too much money as a lawyer to quit, and he has serious obligations to his partners, his family, and the holders of his mortgage. So he tries to merge his legal career with a usually long-neglected personal interest such as writing, agronomy, finance, the environment, music, or anything else. He becomes a lawyer-novelist, a lawyer–financial consultant, a lawyer-musician. Sometimes the merger works out because the lawyer is only satisfying a personal interest that really does not arise above the status of a hobby. But other times the hyphenated lawyer is desperately trying to find an outlet for the true calling he ignored when he applied to law school. It is the rare business-minded law firm that will tolerate a seriously hyphenated lawyer for very long.

My view, from the outside, is that the profession as a whole and certainly the individuals involved would be much better off if the future hyphenated lawyers could be identified early. Law firms would not have to contend with essentially mid-career dropouts, and society and the economy would be rewarded with more talented and ambitious people who would contribute the whole of their knowledge and energies to areas of work and life that would otherwise have been drained away in a law office. The benefits of such early intervention are too great all the way around not to be attempted. That's why when a young man drops out after the first year of law school he should be congratulated rather than censured or made to feel a failure. It takes courage to admit to oneself, much less to reveal to parents and peers, that the tremendous investment in getting admitted to and then spending a year in law school has been for naught. The courage is founded in a self-knowledge that was not easily arrived at, and it deserves our recognition and praise. Otherwise, we feed the very forces that send so many bright and ambitious young people onto the wrong path.

As a nonprofit general counsel my encounters with law firm culture have come in a variety of ways. One of the unexpected encounters is a phenomenon known as the "big firm refugee." Most nonprofit general counsel understand the heavy freight that term carries. It describes the burnt-out lawyers from big law firms who apply for and often get challenging and rewarding legal jobs in nonprofit organizations. It also describes a good number of nonprofit general counsel themselves.

The phenomenon is not new and it is widespread. It is a boon to the nonprofit sector, and it is an indicator of a serious problem confronting the big law firms. As managing partners maintain an unremitting pressure to keep profits per partner up, many of their colleagues chafe at the real effects the need to bill more hours has on the quality of their lives.

In the meantime nonprofits continue to be the beneficiaries. Among my nonprofit general counsel colleagues the subject of big firm refugees in our midst sparked a lively and thoughtful discussion. One told of two lawyers on her staff who had ditched billable hour life despite their high incomes and professional success in law firms. She said one had just made partner before quitting to come to her shop and take a fifty percent pay cut. She suspected he had held out at the firm only long enough to make partner and pay off his law school loans. The other, an associate, was happy to make the move for one-third less than she had been making.

There was no gloating in this talk. Everyone agreed the refugees were excellent additions to their staffs because private practice in a big firm provides excellent training, experience, and discipline. Yet, one general counsel acknowledged that as good as the legal work might be, he picked up what he called an "atmosphere of fear" during his visits to the offices of some of the big firms he hired occasionally. Around the table heads nodded in agreement, sadly, I thought, at this rather harsh observation.

Some of them were certainly thinking of their own experiences in private practice before they made their moves in-house to nonprofit organizations. Even so, none regretted their stints at the big firms. They had good experiences and training, after all. But they also felt they had dodged a career bullet by getting out early—before too many compromises had been made. And there was a genuine concern for the profession itself—that despite the wealth of talent it attracts, it has not yet figured out how to serve its clients without eating so many of its young.

There are signs of progress, one of which is this book. It is the result of the efforts of many leaders in the profession, including managing partners who believe it is possible to achieve a balance between work and outside life for their partners and associates while still serving clients profitably. They have many possible solutions in mind and they understand that some will work better than others. Some will amount to mere tweaking of employment policies and others will attempt to change whole cultures of well-established firms. No doubt some will engender strong opposition. Others will be adopted, and eventually there will be change.

I am tempted to say, as the expression goes, "I don't have a dog in this hunt." As an in-house lawyer, and as a lawyer for a nonprofit organization at that, I am about as far away from the big law firm experience as you can get and still be in the law business. Yet, the law firm experience matters to lawyers like me. At the very least, as general counsel who from time to time hire the firms, we would rather have fully engaged and professionally satisfied lawyers working on our issues. And, as members of the legal profession we have an interest in its standing and credibility in society. We are also professionals with highly relevant career experiences that can be extremely valuable to young people who are thinking about becoming lawyers. As outsiders we are not going to have much, if any, influence on law firm culture and business practices. But as members of the profession we can add our support to those more directly involved in them. And we certainly can have a role in counseling students and other young people (or, perhaps not-so-young people) considering a career in law.

That is where the outsider's view is as credible as anyone else's in a profession-wide effort to "Raise the Bar" within the law firms. All of us have been through law school and we all have legal jobs of some kind. Some of us may even be so-called big firm refugees of one type or another. Regardless, we are regularly approached by young people seeking guidance on legal careers just as much as any other lawyers are. We can serve the profession as a whole by taking the time with these young lawyer wannabes to give them a good understanding of what it means to be a lawyer today. These talks should not be focused on "talking them out of law school;" rather, they should be focused on the unique talents and interests of the person we are talking to. We can tell him or her what we know about the law, then discuss whether it seems like a good career fit. The real contribution from us comes not simply from making the appointments, but from making the extra effort to engender real introspection on the part of our young candidates.

This simple approach is no doubt already being taken by many of us, but perhaps not with the health of the profession as a whole in mind so much as just the fate of the young person in front of us at the moment. That is a laudable perspective and an important one, but the addition of a profession-wide perspective would assist in efforts to Raise the Bar. It is important to steer good people into the law, and it is just as important to steer them into the right legal job once they get there. But it is also important to steer other good people away from the law if they don't seem suited to it. Think of it as a kind of career counseling triage.

In a triage setting a medical professional, usually in a war or disaster zone, ranks the severity of the wounds of the incoming patients. The ones whose lives are most likely to be saved by immediate treatment are sent in first. The second group's wounds can wait. The third group is deemed beyond help. It is a difficult process, considering the consequences, but many of the choices are easy to make because they are so obvious. The result is the most effective use of limited resources. The legal profession could benefit from the same kind of screening process at the front end.

We can spot the obvious cases, as Garry Trudeau did so creatively in his "Doonesbury" comic strip many years ago when he depicted the characters during their law school years. Trudeau often drew a quiet law library scene or a study group session when one young man would spontaneously erupt with the loud and unprompted exclamation, "God! I love the law!!!" then eagerly turn his attention back to his books. The other characters rolled their eyes and continued on about their business. We want that guy in law school. He's the easy choice. If "Doonesbury" had another law student character who kept muttering, "What the hell does this Rule Against Perpetuities got to do with my life?" we might have wished that guy had been steered in another direction. And most important, he might have wished the same thing five or ten years later.

The profession will be doing a lot of things, big and small, to improve itself. Studies, consultants, surveys, conferences, retreats, and many other techniques will be used to good effect toward that improvement. In the meantime, some of us outsiders can be useful with a bit of talking with the incoming. Talk is cheap sometimes, but it can also be extremely valuable.

# CHAPTER 7

# The Death of Partnership: Can We End the Trend?

**By Lawrence J. Fox**

## The Myths

Is it time to be honest? Haven't law firms gotten away for far too long with far too much fraud in the inducement to let it go unremedied? Don't we owe everyone honest disclosure of what we are doing? Won't candor, if not make things better, at least cure one demoralizing problem the profession faces: dismay caused by dashed expectations?

Let us look at the myths, myths that once had a basis in reality, but now may only have a basis in our rose-colored memories. What are they? First, there is the myth that we perpetuate when we interview young, impressionable, newly minted second-year law students. We go to the very best schools, seek to recruit the very best law students, to become the very best summer associates. We tell them how wonderful Caldwell & Moore is, that our firm is collegial, easygoing, friendly, values pro bono service, gives young associates meaningful client contact and both intensive hands-on training and compassionate mentoring, how Caldwell & Moore provides outstanding career opportunities, challenging work assignments, ever-increasing responsibility culminating in the holy grail: Caldwell & Moore partnership, with its magnificent income and great prestige, a package that should convince you, young man or woman, now that you have completed one year of law school, to join Caldwell & Moore for a twelve-week summer frolic for which you will be paid the amazing sum of $2,500 or more per week!

Second is the myth we perpetuate once the young law graduates sign on. Put in your 2,000 or 2,200 or, egad, 2,400 billable hours, give up your nights, your weekends, your four-week vacations, your family, make yourself available at all times for our "Big Deals" and our "Big Suits," check your Blackberry at least once every ten minutes, keep your cell phone on at all times, install a fax machine by your bathtub, reach out for ever-increasing responsibility—go from reading thousands of documents to supervising others doing the same thing. The implicit promise is: If you do these things, then at the end of eight, nine, or ten years we will accept you into the exalted group of Caldwell & Moore partners who by virtue of our wonderful leverage can earn splendid profits on the backs of the four, five, or six overpaid associates per Caldwell & Moore partner.

Third is the myth we perpetuate when these lawyers become partners, joining the inner sanctum, learning the secret handshake, gaining entrance to the holy of holies. Partnership means guaranteed financial security for life; you'll be able to put the rat-race behind you, we tell them, while earning prestige and tenure in the great professional partnership that is Caldwell & Moore, privy to the financial information about the firm and what each of its partners make, and with time to join the opera board and engage in bar activities.

Before we skewer these myths, let me make two critical points. First, there was never a time when the myths were entirely true. Most firms came close, but the myths crowded out a more harsh reality even in the good old days. Second, the myths have always reflected, and even today are likely to reflect, the reality at some firms more than others, though the divergence of reality from the myths has accelerated over time; and the process continues, with each passing year reflecting a greater departure than the last, until the perpetuation of the myths gets harder and harder to justify.

## The Reality Fairly Presented

The truth is when we interview law students we shouldn't mention partnership at all. The chances of any given law school recruit, sitting across from an exalted hiring partner in a cramped interview room in West Philadelphia or in Greenwich Village or in Morningside Heights, actually becoming a partner at Caldwell & Moore are so remote and so impossible to predict that discussions of career paths that include partnership should not even be mentioned. Rather we should tell these young lawyers-to-be the truth: that if you come with Caldwell & Moore we will pay you a lot of money but to justify that hiring decision and salary, given the fact you will stay with Caldwell & Moore such a short time, we expect you to work outrageous hours undertaking often mind-numbing work at a high-pressure pace—for as short as our marriage shall last. And while we're being honest, we ought to admit that the summer associate position—for which they are being recruited immediately—is one of the greatest examples of fraud in the inducement since the Wizard was presiding in Oz. For behind the glorious curtain of 9 to 5 work hours, Broadway shows, white-water rafting trips and weekends at fancy resorts is the true state of real associatedom—billable hour quotas, opportunities to dine at nine (at the firm), and other disappointments too numerous to mention.

Even once these young lawyers join the firm, references to partnership should only be in the context of how unlikely it is to occur. Indeed the modern American law firm's economics are premised on the fundamental proposition that many will start the marathon and that very few, if any, will be left running at the partnership finish line.

## Partner as Euphemism

It may be the low odds are now so obvious they need not be candidly addressed. The real issue that can no longer go unmentioned, however, is that the holy grail of partnership in fact is way too glorified, too romanticized, too exalted by the perpetuation of the myths. As a result the truth goes largely unstated. This is because the profession is undoubtedly collectively embarrassed by the fact that the career path to partnership today provides neither a path nor anything that resembles real partnership.

This is true in at least four respects. First, while partnership may bring better financial rewards than those earned by associates, any sense that partnership brings a chance to pause, a chance to reflect, a chance to diminish one's time commitment to firm business is totally wrong. If anything, the entry into partnership increases the pressure on the "lucky" few, not only to keep up the feverish pace, but to become business gatherers, client collectors, fee generators, to keep the economic engine that is Caldwell & Moore improving its revenues per lawyer and profits per partner each and every month.

Second, fewer and fewer of those now called partners really occupy that status. What started as a trickle of a few perhaps less-worthies, assigned to a way station called dollar partner or non-equity partner, has now become a tidal wave as the designation dollar partner or non-equity partner—true oxymorons if there ever were two—provided a splendid solution to a multitude of sins. It postponed difficult decisions about those on the cusp. It retained those whose special skills were deemed essential, who would otherwise be thrown overboard under the law firm's old "up or out" policy, but who were not viewed as being true partnership material. It improved Caldwell & Moore's statistics as to the dismal percentage of incoming associates who were made partner. And, most important, it permitted the firm to show so much better profits per partner ("PPP") for purposes of reporting a firm's PPP to *The American Lawyer*. This was accomplished by the firm's excluding dollar partner income from partner profits and likewise excluding dollar partners from the number by which partner profits were divided, thereby permitting PPP to soar compared with how that calculation might come out if dollar partners were included on both sides of the calculation.

Third, elevation to partnership no longer comes with any sense of tenure. While the outplacement process might not be as speedy as it would be with lawyers who are mere associates, law firms are now free, with little, if any, guilt, to ease out partners who are viewed as less than productive, productive being defined by criteria that were far different from the standards that were applied when these folks were admitted to the partnership, admission that at the time was assumed to carry with it real tenure, not some pale approximation thereof.

Fourth, the model of the law firm of the future that emerges from what now seems an inevitable path is one that will include as partners only those whose books of business exceed a very significant number, say a million, two million, or three, depending on the firm and the city. Everyone else, no matter what name they are given, will be mere employees, even to the point of being kept in the dark about what their "partner" colleagues make. The only real partners at these firms will be the few home-grown lawyers whose originations reach these levels—years after they have pledged as dollar partners for a significant period of time—and, of course, those worthies who are brought into the firm as laterals, lawyers with portable books of business who bring tears to one's eyes as they explain how they are "underappreciated" at their old firms or who are allegedly looking for a bigger "platform."

It is really the latter—the so-called lateral partner—where the action is to be found. Just as at one time it was unthinkable that a law firm partner would ever be eased out, it was equally unthinkable that a successful partner would leave his original firm (they were virtually all "his" back then) and move cross-town to a rival peer firm. Unthinkable, and yet today law firms operate in a free agency world where a combination of the rules of professional conduct—that prohibit virtually any restrictions on lawyer mobility—and the transparency that *The American Lawyer* brought to law firm profitability—anybody can "look up" what each major firm's "reported" profits per partner are—have resulted in lawyers with books of business looking longingly at other firms as places where they finally can be truly recognized for their "excellence" as lawyers, the standard euphemism for maximizing their take-home pay.

The casualties from this process are real. Loyalty is an early victim. So is the concept of firm, all for one and one for all. And if the real rewards go to those with the biggest books of business, what happens to other firm responsibilities such as hiring, training, running a summer program, pro bono services, bar association work, and a myriad of other areas of endeavor? They still might get done, but they will be done by individuals who will be truly under-rewarded and underappreciated for their efforts, in large part because those important skills do not generate offers to move laterally for huge increases in compensation. No firm is worried, in today's world, about having the partner who runs the firm's summer program recruited away.

The lateral partner market has also launched a corollary change in the way the law firm hierarchy is structured. At one time lawyers were generally rank ordered largely on the excellence of their work and the amount of client business they generated. But now the more highly valued partners may not be acting as imaginative and wise counselors or client gatherers at all. Rather, the partners at the top of the firm pecking order spend their days reeling in new books of business by working with legal recruiters to bring in lateral partners and then taking credit for and being compensated not for their own work, or their own clients, but for the work of these other lawyers. This derivative credit, if you will, has very much changed the way partners feel about themselves, diminishing the concept of partnership in subtle but nonetheless very real ways.

Is there a cure for this, one of the saddest developments in the profession, one whose effects at every level are so profound? It's unlikely, in my view, unless it comes from outside of those who are in charge today, because the current vectors suggest that the issues I have identified will only get worse and that current management regimes that attempt to stem the tide are being toppled on a regular basis.

So where do we look? I think of law students and clients as possible hopes for salvation. As to the former, for far too long the prestige has attached to those who are hired at the most lucrative firms. Too many competitive law students, already conditioned by the college entry sweepstakes and its law school counterpart, fall into the next trap, which is to measure their success and prestige in the first job competition by being able to announce, "I'm going to Caldwell & Moore," the firm everyone knows ranks third in profits per partner. But if the very best law students made it clear they were choosing firms that made more partners rather than fewer, that had lower defections and a lower quotient of lateral hires, that had a ratio between highest to lowest in partnership compensation of four to one or less, that rewarded financially the lawyers who engaged in activities other than business generation, then maybe, just maybe, firms would feel the heat.

Similarly, nothing concentrates the mind of the modern American law firm partner like the views of the general counsel of Fortune 500 companies. Simply review how firms have fallen all over themselves trying to demonstrate to the general counsel of SBC or GM that the firms have heard these GCs' message regarding diversity or pro bono. Could it be that these same GCs could affect the practices of law firms seeking assurances that the so-called partners assigned to their matters in fact have that status in some meaningful way?

But, alas, in the end the truth is that it is going to require lawyers of good will and intestinal fortitude within the firms to stop worshipping at the altar of profits per partner and revenues per lawyer, to declare that values other than the raw financial measures count and that these partners are willing to make a "sacrifice" in financial terms (yes, earning only on average $500,000 instead of $550,000 or $600,000) to achieve other non-monetary goals. Do lawyers have the courage to do this? The law firm of Jenner & Block seems to be doing just that. It recently announced it would be consciously getting itself out of any attempt to match the profits per partner of some of its peer firms in Chicago in order to assure the continuation of its commitment to pro bono and other endeavors. Will others follow this courageous lead? When they realize that the continuation of the law as a profession requires just such action perhaps it will occur, with a gentle nudge from law students, general counsel, and the distant memory of why these lawyers went to law school in the first place.

# PART IV

# The Work

# CHAPTER 8

# A New Path to Excellence: Balanced Hours 101

**By Cynthia Thomas Calvert and Natalie M. Hiott-Levine***

The competition for top legal recruits has never been tougher. Client demands for service, responsiveness, and diversity have never been louder. The quest to distinguish your firm above others has never been harder. Yet, at the same time, management of legal talent has never been more difficult for law firms as attorneys clamor for lives outside the office and the treadmill of attorney attrition refuses to slow.

It is time, therefore, for law firms to take a different path to excellence: satisfying clients and managing legal talent through the use of balanced hours.

---

**The authors wish to thank Project for Attorney Retention Co-Director Joan Williams for her contributions to this chapter.*

## What Are "Balanced Hours"?

Balanced hours are reduced hours schedules for attorneys that are designed to meet the business needs of a law firm while maintaining the attorneys' ability to work and develop professionally without stigma.[1] Balanced hours programs involve active management of workloads in proportion to reduced hours, emphasize client service, and promote the values of the firm. Thus, a balanced hours program not only can give employees more time to meet their obligations outside of work, but also can create a climate within the firm that allows balanced hours attorneys to be productive and profitable.

A balanced hours program allows any attorney—male or female, parent or non-parent, associate or partner—to work an individually tailored, reduced schedule. Unlike traditional part-time programs that typically treat alternative schedules as accommodations for mothers of young children, balanced hours programs are business initiatives that align firms' long-term objectives and attorneys' needs for balance between work and personal obligations. The success of balanced hours programs is rooted in an infrastructure that provides for the active management of the balanced hours attorney's workload, and the elimination of the stigma often associated with part-time schedules that frequently derails careers of those who work less than full time.

## Why Do Law Firms Need Balanced Hours Programs? The Benefits

Contrary to conventional wisdom, an effective balanced hours program can increase a law firm's profitability.[2] Law firms can expect to reap a wide range of benefits, including:

- easier recruiting and improved retention of highly talented attorneys;
- diverse legal teams that will better serve and satisfy existing clients;
- more stable client relationships due to reduced turnover;
- improved ability to attract new clients;
- significant cost savings as a result of lower attrition;
- better risk management; and
- improved morale, productivity, and loyalty throughout the firm.

These benefits are real. Compelling examples of success include accounting firms Ernst & Young and Deloitte & Touche USA LLP, both of which have implemented programs to retain and advance women through, among other things, well-designed flexible work arrangements. Deloitte reports that "[s]ince its launch in 1993, WIN [Deloitte's Women's Initiative] has helped us create a more inclusive environment, win the war for talent and build the intellectual capital required to serve our clients, to develop our people and to grow our business."[3] Its statistics evidence its success. In 1991, only 4 of 50 partner candidates at Deloitte were women,[4] but in 2005, 32% of all promotions to partner, principal, and director were women—116 women in total.[5]

Moreover, Deloitte has estimated that it saved *over $41 million in 2003 alone* by retaining professionals through flexible work arrangements.[6] After a dozen years of experience with a formal flexible work program,[7] Deloitte found that the attrition rate of women declined in 2005, and the firm virtually closed the gender turnover gap.[8] In fact, Deloitte now retains slightly more women than men.[9]

Ernst has had a similar experience. In 1996, the firm had only one female director and alarming turnover among its female employees. It started an initiative aimed at retaining women that included a significant flexible work program. The representation of women at the partner, principal, and director levels more than doubled from 7% to 15% by 2003.[10] In 2002, women represented 25% of the partner promotion class, up from 12% in 1996.[11] Significantly, it dramatically reduced its attrition and estimates that it has saved *$12 million annually* in decreased costs.[12] Studies by Ernst have shown that the increased flexibility increased its employees' commitment to the firm, increased the employees' performance and revenue generation, and ultimately improved the firm's financial results.[13]

Extensive additional evidence of benefits can be found in corporate America. Marriott, GlaxoSmithKline, AstraZeneca, JP Morgan Chase, and dozens of others report greater employee loyalty, productivity, customer satisfaction, and profitability from the implementation of flexible work programs.[14]

Law firms are also beginning to see success from their work/life balance programs and women's initiatives, which generally began more recently than the accounting firms' programs. Examples include Dickstein, Shapiro, Morin and Oshinsky LLP, Vinson & Elkins LLP, Pillsbury Winthrop Shaw Pittman LLP, and Kirkpatrick & Lockhart Nicholson Graham LLP. They report easier recruiting, greater retention and advancement of women, receipt of awards and positive publicity, more loyal clients, more productive and loyal attorneys, and reduced expenses. A brief discussion of how such benefits can flow from balanced hours programs follows.

**Recruiting and Retaining Highly Talented Attorneys.** Law firms are in the business of selling talent, and the competition to recruit and retain talent is only intensifying. Over the past decade, law school enrollments have remained level while law firm hiring has doubled,[15] and nearly half of that limited pool of potential recruits are women.[16] Three statistics are important to better recruiting of women: first, nearly 45% of women law school graduates cited "work/life balance" as the number one reason for choosing their current employer;[17] second, nearly 90% of women become mothers during their working years;[18] and third, 93% of mothers work fewer than 50 hours per week.[19] These statistics mean that law firms that require 2,200 billable hours—which translates into workweeks that regularly exceed 60 hours—will potentially eliminate more than three-quarters of women from their labor pool unless they can provide viable reduced hours programs. As the former managing partner of Arnold & Porter, James Sandman, has said, "No well-run business would do anything to limit its attractiveness to half of the talent pool (but that's exactly what law firms do)."[20]

The desire for balanced lives and balanced hours programs in the legal profession, however, is not and should not be viewed as a woman's issue or a "mommy" issue. In fact, recent studies demonstrate that the desire for work-life balance is one of the leading causes of law firm attrition for all associates—including male associates and non-parents.[21] Non-parents report wanting to work less time to be able to teach, travel, do volunteer work, train for sporting competitions, and the like, and some older attorneys have expressed a desire for phased retirement or simply a slower pace of life.[22] Attorneys also need time to care for elderly parents, and sick spouses or partners.[23]

The fact is that a significant proportion of both male and female attorneys cite long work hours as a major reason for leaving law firms and state they would be more than willing to exchange a lower salary for fewer hours:

- Approximately 71% of male and female attorneys who graduated from the top five law schools report experiencing work/life conflict.[24]
- 34% of male law school graduates reported work/life balance as one of their top three reasons for selecting their current employer.[25]
- Gen-Y men are more likely than baby boomer men to insist on work/life balance. Seventy percent of men in their 20s and 30s said that they would be willing to take lower salaries in exchange for more family time.[26]
- Typically, men who leave law firms or other employers for work/family reasons do not admit that is why they are leaving.[27] Thus, law firms that do not have balanced hours programs or offer only ineffective part-time programs could be driving male associates away without ever knowing why that occurred.

Accordingly, to attract and retain the best attorneys in an increasingly competitive market, legal employers must offer more than a sophisticated practice and high salaries—they must provide the work environment and flexibility that the talent pool is increasingly expecting and demanding. Graduating law students and attorneys moving laterally between firms have an increasing amount of information available to them about the quality of life at firms.[28] They want to work for firms with good quality reduced-hours programs, either because they want to work part-time now or in the future, or because they just want to be at a firm that has a people-first attitude. Firms that can provide balanced hours will have a larger applicant pool from which to draw, and lower recruiting costs.

**More Stable Client Relationships Due to Reduced Turnover.** Clients are frustrated when, over and over again, attorneys in whom they have invested and with whom developed relationships leave a firm, and they are forced to expend time and energy bringing new attorneys up to speed. For many, high attrition means a loss of institutional knowledge and well as the loss of all the effort they spent to familiarize the attorney with their business. In fact, despite contrary assumptions, clients do support part-time programs in law firms as a way to stem attrition.[29] Linda Madrid,

General Counsel of Carr America, provides one client's perspective on law firm attrition:

> "It is frustrating when outside counsel don't provide consistent lawyers . . . [N]othing [is] worse than investing in and relying on someone, and then having that person pulled out. Or, even worse, the firm isn't treating them well enough to keep them. We have tried to look at how our outside counsel treat their young lawyers . . . including demands in terms of billing. These are all issues that we think ultimately have an impact on the services we receive."[30]

Firms that address these client concerns by taking concrete action to stem attrition demonstrate their willingness to do what it takes to provide good client service. A 2003 study by PAR found that virtually all corporate counsel expressed willingness to work with part-time attorneys. In fact, the oft-cited excuse touted by law firms that their clients could not be well-served or timely served by part-time attorneys appears to be ill-founded as many corporate counsel have found that part-time attorneys working on their matters were not only accessible, but perhaps even more available to them than full-time attorneys. As one corporate counsel pointed out, "My outside counsel is not available to me all the time anyway because of travel, depositions, and commitments to other clients, and he works full-time. I don't notice a difference if someone works part-time."[31] In fact, one general counsel has observed that balance makes better attorneys:

> There is no question in my mind that outside attorneys who have balance in their lives bring a more well-rounded perspective and provide higher quality service to their clients. . . . not to mention there tends to be higher retention and better continuity of service, which factors prominently into law firm selection decisions.

Lauri Shanahan, Executive Vice President, Chief Compliance Officer and General Counsel of Gap, Inc.[32]

**Diverse Legal Teams That Will Better Serve Existing Clients and Aid Business Development.** Increasingly, clients are demanding that their outside counsel be diverse, in terms of both race and gender. Clients want diverse perspectives when seeking legal advice, as well as the opportunity to forge relationships with outside attorneys who are as diverse as they are themselves. Some large corporations like Wal-Mart have already begun the process of terminating their relationship with firms "'strictly because of their inability to grasp our diversity expectations.'"[33] Other companies, such as Shell Oil Company and Sara Lee, ask firms competing for its business to report the number of female and minority employees at their firms, and some, like Dupont, ask for regular reports of diversity from their outside firms.[34]

Firms' Gen X and Y attorneys tend to be more diverse, and thus retaining them is essential for firms that want to meet client demands. Related to this, clients are beginning to scrutinize law firms' attrition rates and quality of life issues that inevitably affect the diversity of the legal teams serving them.

**The Ability to Attract New Clients.** In addition to new business generated by the ability to meet diversity demands, firms can open up new avenues of business through good balanced hours programs in at least three ways. First, attorneys are a key source of new business for most firms. When an attorney leaves a firm and goes in-house to try to find a better balance, is he or she going to give business to the firm that they feel treated them shabbily? Even if they go to another firm, they are not going to want to refer business to a firm where they were not happy.

Second, clients want to hire firms that share their values. Many companies now emphasize work/life balance as good for business, as well as being the right thing to do. Law firms that have good balanced hours programs show these companies that they have made similar judgments with respect to personnel management and efficient operation.

Third, good balanced hours programs raise the profile of firms within their communities. Firms that offer meaningful alternative work schedules win awards, gain favorable mentions in the press, and generate positive buzz about their culture.

**Significant Cost Savings Associated with Lower Attrition.** Increased retention of trained and talented attorneys likewise saves firms money by decreasing the high costs associated with unwanted attrition or "regretted losses." In fact, by conservative estimates, it costs a firm at least $200,000 to replace a second-year associate.[35] (Other estimates range from $280,000–$500,000.)[36] These costs include, but are not limited to, the value of time spent by partners and associates interviewing new hires; various recruiting expenses, including entertaining, airfare, and moving expenses; hiring bonuses; headhunter fees; lost training costs for the departed attorney; costs of training the new hire; various administrative costs including business cards and nameplates; the value of lost productivity; lost business that the departing attorney takes with him or her; and the value of time written off by the new attorney as he or she gets up to speed on matters. Hence, even by the most conservative estimates, *every time five associates walk out the door, a firm loses at least a million dollars.*

**Better Risk Management.** Legal employers have already been sued more than a dozen times for issues related to motherhood or part-time work,[37] with liability reaching $1.5 million.[38] Employers generally are having to rethink their attendance, promotions, and alternative work schedule policies as more employees are bringing lawsuits for family responsibilities discrimination.[39] Examples of situations that can give rise to liability include personnel practices that deny part-time work to mothers for childcare but allow male employees to regularly take time off for golf or to train for athletic events, failure to consider mothers of young children for high-profile assignments based on the untested assumption that they would not want to work the longer hours necessary for the assignment, and actively discouraging males from taking paternity leave or reducing their hours while not similarly discouraging females. It is crucial for law firms to note that the stigma commonly associated with part-time work often tracks the fact patterns of family responsibility discrimination cases, particularly those based on gender stereotypes. Law firms that have non-stigmatized balanced hours programs that allow part-time attorneys to advance professionally can better protect themselves against such lawsuits. The process of creating and implementing a balanced hours program, moreover, is a perfect opportunity for reviewing law firm policies and practices to ensure that they are free of family responsibilities discrimination.

**Overall Improved Morale, Productivity, and Loyalty Throughout the Firm.** High attrition causes discontent. Attorneys remaining at the firm wonder if they are on a sinking ship, and feel burdened as they pick up the work of those who leave. High attrition also undermines collegiality and mentoring because attorneys are more reluctant to form bonds with colleagues if they expect the colleagues will soon leave the firm. Improving retention through a balanced hours program adds to the attorneys' sense of well-being because, in addition to fostering relationships with colleagues, it demonstrates to the attorneys that their firm has a supportive culture. The attorneys feel less stress, which in turn increases their productivity[40] and enhances their relationships with clients.[41] Productivity is further increased by the reduction in attrition-related distractions such as rumors, farewell parties, and introduction of new attorneys. Furthermore, attorneys who use balanced hours typically demonstrate greater loyalty and commitment to their firms because they feel supported by their firms.

## Why Traditional Part-Time Programs Do Not Deliver These Benefits

Although most mid- to large-sized law firms in the United States offer some kind of part-time program,[42] most firms are not realizing any benefits from their programs. Two primary problems—schedule creep and stigma[43]—prevent those existing programs from satisfying the demand for work-life balance and, therefore, from stemming the tide of unwanted attrition.[44] The reason is not that "part-time just doesn't work"—as is so often stated as a foregone conclusion. The real reason that most existing part-time programs do not work is that they lack the proper foundation and infrastructure to be effectively implemented. When a part-time program is adopted without the corresponding commitment of requisite resources—adequate planning, support, training, and supervision—problems almost certainly will arise. In fact, *many current part-time programs actually exacerbate attrition rates* (of both part-time and full-time attorneys) because these programs—plagued by schedule creep and marred by stigma—are ineffective in large part because they fail to provide viable career paths.

What many attorneys want is not a "part-time" schedule—accompanied by the negative perceptions of partial commitment—but rather the opportunity to have "balanced lives," that is, the opportunity to work "balanced hours" in combination with suitable career development.[45] Balanced hours programs differ in a number of ways from traditional part-time programs, but there are five significant differences. *First*, balanced hours programs are driven by firms' business needs and are adopted to prevent unwanted attrition of a firm's legal talent via the cooperative creation of business plans allowing for a reduced schedule and providing a strategy to meet client needs. *Second,* balanced hours programs value quality work and quality relationships with clients, and clearly separate the concept of an attorney's worth from the number of billable hours he or she works. *Third,* as explained in detail below, balanced hour programs are not stigmatized; rather, a conscious effort is made to ensure that a balanced hours attorney's assignments, client contact, status within the firm, relationships with colleagues and superiors, professional development, and career advancement are protected and not negatively impacted by his or her arrangement. *Fourth,* balanced hour programs treat attorneys proportionally in terms of salary, benefits, hours, workload, and professional advancement toward partnership or within partnership tiers. *Finally,* balanced hour programs treat attorneys fairly by allowing all attorneys the opportunity to establish flexible schedules that meet their personal needs while ensuring that client needs are met and then honor those arrangements by preventing schedule creep and eliminating stigma.[46]

**In Balanced Hours Programs, "Schedule Creep" Is Minimized and Controlled.** "Schedule creep"—the gradual increase of part-time attorneys' hours toward full-time levels while their pay remains at part-time levels—is one of the most frequently recited complaints raised not only by part-time attorneys, but also by full-time attorneys who would prefer to work reduced hours but instead quit discouraged by their firms' unworkable part-time programs.[47] Although one might expect that part-time attorneys might occasionally exceed their contracted weekly or monthly billable hours, schedule creep that occurs regularly is problematic.

Chronic schedule creep is commonly a byproduct of unspoken expectations and mixed messages about what it means to be committed to the firm that subtly (or not so subtly) pressures part-time attorneys to work more and more hours to prove their continued value and worth. For example, supervising attorneys often communicate that their expectations (and the firm's) are inconsistent with part-time schedules when they demonstrate their lack of respect for those arrangements by scheduling non-emergency meetings or conference calls for times when part-timers are out of the office, or when they instruct part-time attorneys to keep their schedules a secret from their clients, inevitably creating situations where clients schedule meetings at inconvenient times.

Moreover, even if firms provide financial compensation for the additional hours worked, chronic schedule creep will nevertheless lead to higher attrition because financial remuneration fails to address the fundamental reasons that part-time attorneys sought reduced hours in the first place. Despite the current trend of raising salaries in an effort to attract and retain associates,[48] high attrition will continue so long as law firms fail to address attorneys' needs for balance. Accordingly, law firms must address the underlying reasons that cause schedule creep and implement mechanisms to manage it if the retention goals of their part-time program are to be realized.

**In Balanced Hours Programs, "Stigma" Is Eliminated to Allow for Continued Professional Development and Advancement.** Part-time work is so stigmatized at many law firms that attorneys who wish to reduce their hours leave their firms rather than jeopardize their legal careers.[49] Stigma takes many forms including:

- Elimination of advancement through a formal or *de facto* policy of not promoting part-time associates to partnership;
- Loss of status demonstrated by a change in treatment by colleagues and supervisors who no longer seek out part-time attorneys to work on matters or to develop new business;
- Erosion of mentoring and social relationships attributable to less time for socializing and negative perceptions of part-time attorneys;
- Transfers to more "suitable" practice areas;
- Financial penalties, including "the haircut,"[50] loss of benefits, and loss of bonuses;
- Diminished quality of assignments and loss of professional development;[51] and
- Diminished opportunities for professional development through non-billable activities, including continuing legal education, bar association leadership, community involvement, and *pro bono* work.

Dissatisfaction with a firm's part-time program can affect all of a firm's attorneys, not just those working reduced hours. This more widespread dissatisfaction often remains hidden as full-time attorneys who want shorter hours choose simply to leave their firms rather than subject themselves to the stigma that would accompany their utilization of an existing part-time program.[52]

## Measuring Your Part-Time Program: The PAR Usability Test

Although law firm management may sincerely believe that schedule creep and stigma do not exist at their firms, the Project for Attorney Retention has discovered that associates' views about the causes of attrition and the effectiveness of part-time programs often are radically different from management's views.[53] This communication gap exists because attorneys cannot openly discuss these issues (or believe that they cannot) without themselves being perceived negatively or otherwise branded. If the rank-and-file attorneys will not or cannot honestly speak up, firms need to find a way to hear what the attorneys won't tell them. Taking the PAR Usability Test is one way to determine if a firm's existing part-time program is "up to par."

The PAR Usability Test focuses on six objective factors that impact and ultimately determine whether a law firm's part-time program is successful:

1. Usage rate broken down by sex;
2. Median number of hours worked and duration of the balanced hours schedule;
3. Schedule creep;
4. Comparison of the assignments of balanced hours attorneys before, and after, they reduced their hours;
5. Comparative promotion rates of attorneys on standard and balanced hours schedules; and
6. Comparative attrition rates of attorneys on standard and balanced hours schedules.[54]

**1. Usage Rate Broken Down by Sex.** Given the increasing demand for work-life balance and reduced hours schedules, low or limited usage rates of existing part-time programs indicate that a firm may have an ineffective and stigmatized program. According to 2004 statistics from the Bureau of Labor, approximately 20% of business and professional workers work part-time; therefore, for most law firms, a usage rate below 6% evidences serious problems. In fact, a firm should aim for a usage rate around 10%.[55] Moreover, gender-specific usage rates are also indicative of whether a program is stigmatized or truly allows for continued career advancement and development.

**2. Median Number of Hours Worked and Duration of the Balanced Hours Schedule.** This criterion examines the average number of hours part-time attorneys work in a given period of time and how long the average balance hours arrangement lasts. With regard to the first, to be successful, part-time schedules cannot exceed what would be considered a full-time schedule in most other professions. For example, a median part-time schedule should not be a 48-hour week (or 80% of a 60-hour week) because working 48 hours is unlikely to provide the work-life balance that balanced hours attorneys are seeking.

Regarding the second component, successful reduced hours programs will be utilized for longer periods of time—*i.e.*, years—by an individual attorney precisely because they are meeting the attorney's needs for balance. Implicit pressures or explicit policies that demand a return to full-time work after a short period of time—*e.g.*, one year after a return from maternity leave—evidence a stigmatized program where balanced hours attorneys cannot expect to succeed or develop and, therefore, undermine the effectiveness of the part-time program.

**3. Schedule Creep.** If attorneys on reduced schedules are consistently working more hours than they negotiated, schedule creep is undermining the effectiveness and usability of the policy. As explained above, chronic schedule creep dooms a part-time program to fail; however, as professionals, part-time attorneys must maintain the flexibility needed to handle true emergencies when they arise and then to be allowed—indeed encouraged—to take "comp time" after the crisis has passed. Supervisors must anticipate and adequately prepare for workflow issues to ensure that schedule creep is truly unavoidable. Looking at hours budgeted and worked over a period of months will demonstrate whether excess hours reflect a passing crisis or chronic schedule creep.

**4. Comparison of the Assignments of Balanced Hours Attorneys Before, and After, They Reduced Their Hours.** To continue developing professionally, part-time attorneys must continue to get quality work assignments. This requires an active commitment on the part of assignment partners and other supervising attorneys so that reduced hours attorneys are not assuming a disproportionate amount of rote, routine, or junior level assignments. One way to ensure that part-time attorneys continue to develop professionally is to seek them out to perform meaningful assignments as part of a team working on high-profile matters for high-profile clients.

**5. Comparative Promotion Rates of Attorneys on Standard and Balanced Hours Schedules.** Despite the fact that nearly half of the graduating law school classes in recent decades were women, only 17% of law firm partners are women.[56] Unfortunately, the current state of part-time programs (or lack of successful balanced hours programs) supports and perpetuates this unfortunate result because, in most firms, working a reduced hours schedule can and does end the road to partnership. Even in firms that do not formally remove part-time attorneys from the partnership track, the large disparities in the promotion rates of standard and balanced hours attorneys may be indicative that part-time status is career-ending at their firm. Being aware of such disparities is critical. Effective balanced hours programs do not just theorize that part-time associates are eligible for partnership; they provide the infrastructure and requisite support so that balanced hours attorneys can be and are promoted to partnership. A persistent imbalance in favor of elevating full-time attorneys to partnership may very well evidence that a firm has a *de facto* removal policy and that part-time attorneys are thus being penalized and stigmatized.

**6. Comparative Attrition Rates of Attorneys on Standard and Balanced Hours Schedules.** As stated above, a program plagued by stigma and schedule creep may actually exacerbate attrition, while usable and effective part-time program can sharply reduce attrition. In a 2001 study, the Massachusetts Women's Bar Association[57] found that in 1997 and 1998, men and women working standard schedules left law firms at the rates of 9% and 12%, respectively; but women working reduced hours had an attrition rate of nearly 23%.[58] The Massachusetts WBA concluded that due to the problems permeating many part-time programs, attrition rates among part-time attorneys were even higher than among other attorneys. Given the intense demand for reduced hours, if the attrition rate for a firm's part-time attorneys significantly outpaces that of the full-time attorneys, the firm's part-time program is flawed.

## The Development of an Effective Balanced Hours Program

**Assess the Firm's Needs and Build a Broad Base of Support.** To build a successful program, a law firm must first lay a solid foundation, doing the "spadework" critical to any new business initiative: articulating the need for a new program, creating a coalition to draft and implement the program, engaging in strategic planning, and building support for the initiative at all levels of the firm.[59] Simply writing a policy without these critical steps is to guarantee failure.

To succeed, the balanced hours program will require the unqualified support of top management and the key players; thus, those spearheading the effort must begin developing the business case from the preliminary data gathered and then begin the process of broadening support. First, the key players must be identified and brought on board. The key players are the individuals who wield the most power in the firm—managing partners, executive committee members, department heads, significant rainmakers, firm visionaries, and other respected and influential partners, associates, or counsel—without whose support the program will fail. Each key player must be personally educated about the business case for the program, that is, how a balanced hours program will remedy existing problems and benefit both the firm and individual attorneys. These personal communications are critical because all key players must understand the reasons for the change.

**Create a Successful Policy.** Once the firm's needs are known and input has been gathered from attorneys at various levels within the firm, a small group of attorneys can begin drafting a balanced hours policy. At a minimum, the policy should cover the following:

- *Eligibility.* The policy should state which attorneys are eligible to work balanced hours. It benefits a firm most to allow all attorneys, regardless of gender or parental status, who make an acceptable proposal to reduce their hours.
- *Process for requesting balanced hours.* A statement of what an attorney needs to include in a balanced hours proposal, identification of decision makers, and a process for resolving disagreements should be included.

- *Schedule.* Each attorney who wishes to work balanced hours should be able to propose an individually tailored schedule designed to meet his or her needs and the needs of the firm. The policy should not limit schedules to rigid reduced hours per day or days per week, but should allow flexibility for fewer hours or months per year. The schedule should also include time for nonbillable as well as billable work.
- *Compensation.* The policy should provide for proportional pay. The days of paying part-time associates a percentage of a full-time salary that is less than the percentage of full-time hours they work (e.g., 70% pay for 80% work) are gone.
- *Benefits.* Most firms provide at least proportional benefits to attorneys who have reduced their hours, while some pay full benefits. The policy should spell out the benefits available (keeping in mind for health benefits that the definition of eligibility in most insurance contracts is based on the number of hours worked, and that the number of hours worked includes all hours, not just billable hours).
- *Advancement.* The policy should spell out what effect, if any, balanced hours will have on consideration for promotions and partnership. For attorneys who have worked full-time at their firm for six or more years, a schedule change may have no effect, for example, while attorneys who are just starting their careers may have their partnership track extended. Note that it is essential that balanced hours attorneys remain eligible for partnership. Removal from the partnership track exacerbates stigma[60] and will doom the balanced hours program to failure.
- *Work Expectations.* It is important for a balanced hours attorney to understand the firm's expectations for not only billable work, but also for administrative work and business development. The policy should also include expectations about complying with other firm expectations, such as responsiveness to clients and mentoring.

### A Policy Is Not Enough: Implementation Essentials

Moving from written policy to everyday practice requires thoughtful implementation. Key aspects of implementation include leadership from the top; training for all attorneys, particularly those who will supervise balanced hours attorneys; appointing a Balanced Hours Coordinator; and holding partners accountable for the success of the initiative.

**Leadership from the Top.** Firm managing partners and key players in the law firm not only have to be committed to the balanced hours program but also have to communicate their commitment regularly. A common failing of traditional part-time programs has been the communication from the top of a *lack* of support—pointed silence, dismissive comments, and even outright statements that one cannot get ahead unless one works extraordinarily long hours. Deliberate and direct communication of support for balanced hours can avoid this failing. Formal communication in meetings and memoranda, informal communication in everyday interactions, and indirect communication such as celebrating the achievements of a balanced hours attorney all play a part.

**Training.** Training is often dismissed as unnecessary, but attorneys cannot be expected to understand how to make balanced hours work on their own. It is far quicker and cheaper to spoon-feed them what they need to know than to let them figure it out by trial and error. Here is a list of some of the topics the training should cover:

- The business case for a balanced hours program, with particular reference to the unique demographics, financial situation, and business goals of the firm;
- The terms of the program, such as eligibility, compensation, and advancement;
- Management and distribution of workloads;
- Meeting client service needs;
- Common misperceptions and stereotypes of attorneys who reduce their hours;
- Ways supervising attorneys can support balanced hours attorneys;
- Each person's accountability for the success of the program; and
- Evaluation of success of the program.

Training can be done in large or small groups, and one-on-one coaching can be a helpful adjunct to the process.

**Adjust Workload.** Of course, adjusting the workload is also key to making sure a balanced hours policy will take hold.

Reducing hours while not reducing workload will sabotage any balanced hours policy, no matter how carefully planned. Excess work might go to lawyers who are underutilized, or you might look at anticipated work needs and hire another full-time or part-time lawyer. Another option is to redesign the work so a balanced hours lawyer can work "smarter," making the most of his or her time through the use of technology or getting support from paralegals who can provide support work.

**Balanced Hours Coordinator.** A Balanced Hours Coordinator is a partner or administrator with a direct report to the head of the firm who is appointed by the firm to oversee the successful implementation and administration of its balanced hours program. Firms need a Balanced Hours Coordinator because even the most expertly drafted, well-intentioned balanced hours policy cannot implement itself. A mere paper policy is essentially worthless or, worse yet, it can be damaging—damaging to the careers of the attorneys who opt to take advantage of it without appropriate guidance and institutional support, and damaging to management's credibility as it creates false expectations and erodes associates' morale. Firms can ensure that their balanced hours programs will succeed by appointing a Balanced Hours Coordinator to keep the program on track, to troubleshoot problems as they arise, and to guide balanced hours attorneys and their supervisors.

**Accountability.** Accounting firms such as Ernst & Young and Deloitte Touche count people-management skills—or the lack of them—as a factor when setting partnership compensation because of the high costs associated with a failure to "keep the keepers." Several law firms have begun to follow suit. Some have made retention and development of valued attorneys a criterion in partner evaluations and compensation; some expressly consider support of reduced hours programs. Tying compensation to results is both a powerful message about the firm's commitment and a powerful incentive to work for the success of the program.

## Reinforce the Program

Implementation takes time and continuous reinforcement. Any initiative, no matter how well conceived and launched, will wither if not tended regularly. A balanced hour program will "stick" and begin to return benefits to a firm when it is reinforced by regular communication from firm leaders about the importance of the program, recognition of successful balanced hour arrangements, and prompt attention to issues or attitudes that undermine the program. A key way to reinforce the program is to celebrate its successes. If a firm gains a new client or retains an existing one because of the balanced hours program, everyone in the firm should share in the good news. When the firm saves money on reduced attrition, attracts a superstar lawyer, or wins an award because of the balanced hours program, that should be trumpeted as well. Success breeds success.

## Conclusion

The established way of doing business isn't going to produce the same results anymore. Hiring associates, grinding them up, and spitting them out is increasingly less profitable for firms in both the short and long runs. New times demand new ways to manage legal talent—and balanced hours programs will provide a new direction for managing human capital and a new path for excellence.

## Endnotes

1. *See generally* Joan C. Williams and Cynthia Thomas Calvert, Solving the Part-Time Puzzle: The Law Firm's Guide to Balanced Hours (NALP 2004) (hereinafter "Solving the Part-Time Puzzle") Joan Williams and Cynthia Thomas Calvert, *Balanced Hours: Effective Part-Time Policies for Washington Law Firms, Final Report* (2nd ed., Aug. 2001) (hereinafter "PAR Balanced Hours Report"), available at http://www.pardc.org/Publications/BalancedHours.shtml.

2. *See* Solving the Part-Time Puzzle at 41–48; Linda Bray Chanow, *The Business Case for Reduced Hours,* available at http://www.pardc.org/Publications/business_case.shtml; Karyn Feiden and Linda Marks, Negotiating Time: New Scheduling Options in the Legal Profession (New Ways to Work, 1986), at 10–12.

3. *See* Deloitte & Touche USA LLP, Initiative for the Retention and Advancement of Women, *2005 Annual Report* (hereinafter "Deloitte 2005 WIN Report") at 5 & 8, available at http://www.deloitte.com/dtt/cda/doc/content/2005_WIN_Annual_Report.pdf; quoted material from summary available at http://www.deloitte.com/dtt/article/0,1002,sid=2261&cid=115199,00.html.

4. *See* timeline of Deloitte's Women's Initiative, available at http://www.deloitte.com/dtt/section_node/0,1042,sid%253D105211,00.html.

5. Deloitte 2005 WIN Report *supra,* note 3, at 5, 8.

6. *See* Corporate Voices for Working Families, "Business Impacts of Flexibility: An Imperative for Expansion" (Nov. 2005), available online at http://www.cvworkingfamilies.org/downloads/Business%20Impacts%20of%20Flexibility.pdf, at 10.

7. Deloitte introduced formal flexible work arrangements and paid parental leave in 1994. *See* WIN timeline, *supra,* note 4.

8. *See* summary of Deloitte 2005 WIN Report, supra, note 3.

9. Deloitte 2005 WIN Report, supra, note 3, at 8.

10. Catalyst, "Ernst & Young LLP: Promoting Change: Developing and Promoting Women" (2003), available online at www.catalystwomen.org/award/files/winners/E&Y%20FINAL%205%20pager.pdf, at 5.

11. *Id.*

12. Williams, Joan, and Cynthia Thomas Calvert, Project for Attorney Retention, *Better on Balance? The Corporate Counsel Work/Life Report* (Dec. 2003), available at http://www.pardc.org/Publications/BetterOnBalance.shtml, at 12.

13. Corporate Voices, *supra,* note 6, at 20.

14. *Id. See also* Charlotte Huff, "With Flextime, Less Can Be More," *Workforce Management,* May 2005, at 65–70, Deborah Epstein Henry, "The Case for Flex-Time and Part-Time Lawyering," 23 PENN. LAW. 42 (2001).

15. Akiko Mikumo, Esq., Remarks at the New York City Bar Committee on Women in Profession, Symposium on Best Practices for the Hiring, Training, Retention and Advancement of Women Attorneys (Feb. 7, 2006) referring to New York City Bar, Committee on Women in the Profession, *Report on Best Practices for the Hiring, Training, Retention and Advancement of Women Attorneys,* Feb. 7, 2006, at 4, *available at* http://www.nycbar.org/pdf/report/BestPractices4WomenAttorneys.pdf. *See also* Ashby Jones, *The Matching Game: Why Firms Follow Firms on Salaries,* Wall St. J. Online (Mar. 22, 2006) http://online.wsj.com/article/SB114295824295604172.html (by subscription only).

16. American Bar Association, J.D. and LL.B Degrees Awarded 1981–2004, available at http://www.abanet.org/legaled/statistics/charts/jdandllbdegrees.pdf (showing 46–49% of law school graduating classes since 2000 have been female).

17. Catalyst, *Women in Law: Making the Case* (Catalyst, 2001), at 19.

18. Williams, Joan C., UNBENDING GENDER: WHY FAMILY AND WORK CONFLICT AND WHAT TO DO ABOUT IT. (Oxford University Press 2000), at 2.

19. *Id.*

20. Emily Barker, "Engendering Change," *American Lawyer* (June 2003), at 2.

21. The NALP Foundation for Law Career Research & Education, *Keeping the Keepers II: Mobility & Management of Associates* (2003) at 98;

*Beyond the Bidding Wars: A Survey of Associate Attrition, Departure Destinations & Workplace Incentives,* The NALP Foundation for Law Career Research & Education (2000) at 17.

22. Solving the Part-Time Puzzle, *supra,* note 1, at 12–13.

23. The Women's Bureau of the U.S. Department of Labor reports that almost one in four American households provide care to an elderly relative or friend, which impacts work schedules. *Work and Elder Care: Facts for Caregivers and Their Employers,* U.S. Department of Labor (1998).

24. Catalyst, *Women in Law: Making the Case* (Catalyst, 2001) at 18.

25. Catalyst, *supra,* note 26, at 19.

26. Survey by Harris Interactive and the Radcliffe Public Policy Center, reported in Kirstin Downey Grimsley, "Family a Priority for Young Workers; Survey Finds Change in Men's Thinking," *The Washington Post* (May 3, 2000), at E1.

27. Keith Cunningham, "Father Time," 53 Stanford Law Review 967.

28. *See, e.g.,* PAR's "The Scoop," www.pardc.org/TheScoop/ (information from attorneys about what it is like to work alternative schedules in particular law firms); Vault.com message boards, http://vault.com/community/mb/mb_main.jsp?forumtype=1&ch_id=242; American Lawyer Associate Surveys, www.amlaw.com (2005 survey available at http://www.law.com/jsp/tal/PubArticleTAL.jsp?id=1096473917144).

29. Solving the Part-Time Puzzle, *supra,* note 1, at 131–134; Project for Attorney Retention (PAR), Corporate Counsel Project, *Better on Balance? The Corporate Counsel Work/Life Report* (Final Report, Dec. 2003) available at http://www.pardc.org/Publications/BetterOnBalance.pdf (hereinafter "PAR Corporate Counsel Report"). The Corporate Counsel Project studied both work/life balance in corporate law departments and ways in which corporate counsel, as clients, can assist law firms in implementing balanced hours programs. Interviews with general counsels and their subordinates have included frequent and frank complaints about turnover at law firms.

30. PAR Corporate Counsel Report, *supra,* note 30, at 52.

31. Solving the Part-Time Puzzle, supra, note 1, at 133.

32. E-mail sent to PAR (March 2006), on file at the Project for Attorney Retention.

33. Meredith Hobbs, *Wal-Mart Demands Diversity in Law Firms,* Fulton County Daily Report (July 6, 2005), available at http://www.law.com/jsp/article.jsp?id=1120579809481 (quoting Wal-Mart's general counsel Thomas Mars).

34. *See PAR Balanced Hours Report, supra,* note 2, at 1. As of April 2006, nearly 100 Chief Legal Officers have signed *A Call to Action: Diversity in the Legal Profession* (List of current signatories to *A Call to Action—Diversity in the Legal Profession,* is available at http://www

.mcca.com/CTA/signatories-print.shtml.), pledging to choose their outside counsel based in significant part on the law firm's commitment to increasing and fostering diversity. (Roderick A. ("Rick") Palmore, CLO of Sara Lee Corporation, *A Call to Action—Diversity in the Legal Profession,* available at http://www.clocalltoaction.com.) *A Call to Action,* which was authored by Sara Lee's General Counsel, Rick Palmore, and endorsed by the Association of Corporate Counsel, (The Association of Corporate Counsel ("ACC") endorsed *A Call to Action* at its meeting on October 24, 2004. *See* http://www.acca.com/public/accapolicy/diversity .pdf.) provides as follows:

> We intend to look for opportunities for firms we regularly use which positively distinguish themselves in this area. We further intend to end or limit our relationships with firms whose performance consistently evidences a lack of meaningful interest in being diverse.

(*A Call to Action, supra,* note 35, available at http://www.clocalltoaction.com.)

35. Wendy Davis, "Associate Flight Leads to New Look at Pyramid," *New York Law Journal* (June 22, 2000); *see* note 5, *supra,* and Chanow, *The Business Case for Reduced Hours, supra* note 1.

36. Lisa Gold, "How to Improve Associate Retention: Old Reward System No Longer Effective," *Legal Intelligencer* (Apr. 19, 1999) at 7.

37. *See Gallina v. Mintz, Levin, Cohn, Ferris, Glovsky & Popeo,* 123 Fed. Appx. 558 (4th Cir. 2005); *Sigmon v. Parker Chapin Flattau & Klimpl,* 901 F. Supp. 667 (S.D.N.Y. 1995). *See also* Brenda Sapino Jeffreys, "Former Associate Sues Godwin Gruber Alleging Discrimination," *Texas Lawyer,* Nov. 3, 2005; John Council, "Motherhood at the Firm," *Texas Lawyer,* April 1, 2004; Diane E. Lewis, "Lawsuit sets precedent against misperception of working moms," *Boston Globe,* June 18, 2000, at F2.

38. Lewis, *supra,* n. 37 (jury awarded $1.5 million to prosecutor in San Diego who was demoted after she had her third child because she needed a flexible schedule).

39. "Family responsibilities discrimination" is discrimination based on an employee's obligations to care for a family member. It arises when employers or supervisors assume that an employee will not be able to do certain jobs because of caregiving responsibilities or make it difficult for employees to combine their work and family obligations. FRD cases typically include claims of gender and/or pregnancy discrimination, Family and Medical Leave Act harassment or interference, or wrongful discharge. *See* WORKLIFE LAW'S GUIDE TO FAMILY RESPONSIBILITIES DISCRIMINATION (Center for WorkLife Law, 2006); Joan Williams and Nancy Segal, "Beyond the Maternal Wall: Relief for Family Caregivers Who Are Discriminated Against on the Job," 27 HARVARD WOMEN'S L.J. 77 (Spring 2003).

40. Numerous studies find stress and productivity to be inversely linked. *See* National Institute for Occupational Health and Safety Job

Stress Research Program, available at http://www.cdc.gov/niosh/stresshp.html, for citations.

41. *See* Solving the Part-Time Puzzle, *supra,* note 1, at 19 (quoting William J. Flannery of the WJF Institute: "If your internal system of how you treat your employees is fundamentally flawed, then the employees' external relationships will reflect that.")

42. NALP's analysis of its 2003–2004 Directory of Legal Employers indicates that 96% of the 625 law firms listed allowed part-time schedules, either as an affirmative policy or on a case-by-case basis. *See* NALP Press Release, *Part-Time Attorney Schedules Still Widely Available, but Remain Rarely Used by Partners, Associates* (NALP, November 7, 2003), available at http://www.nalp.org/press/details.php?id=11.

43. Deborah L. Rhode, for the ABA Commission on Women and the Profession, *Lawyers and Balanced Lives* (2001); Catalyst, Women in Law: Making the Case (Catalyst 2001); Keith Cunningham, "Father Time: Flexible Work Arrangements and the Law Firm's Failure of the Family," Stanford Law Review vol. 53:967–1008 (April 2001); Women's Bar Association of Massachusetts, *More Than Part Time: The Effect of Reduced-Hours Arrangements on the Retention, Recruitment, and Success of Women Attorneys in Law Firms* (2000) (available at http://womenlaw.stanford.edu/mass.rpt.html) (hereinafter *"More Than Part-Time"*); Boston Bar Association Task Force on Work-Life Balance, *Facing the Grail: Confronting the Cost of Work-Family Imbalance* (June 1999).

44. NALP reported that the percentage of attorneys working on a part-time basis was only 4.1% in 2003 (up slightly from 3.7% in 2002). *See* NALP Press Release, *Part-Time Attorney Schedules Still Widely Available, but Remain Rarely Used by Partners, Associates* (NALP, November 7, 2003), available at http://www.nalp.org/press/details.php?id=11. Associates took greater advantage of part-time schedules than did partners, with 5.4% of associates working part-time, compared with 2.6% of partners. *Id.*

45. *See* 1; ABA Commission on Women in the Profession, *Lawyers and Balanced Lives: A Guide to Drafting and Implementing Workplace Policies for Lawyers* (1990); Deborah L. Rhode, for the ABA Commission on Women and the Profession, *Lawyers and Balanced Lives* (2001).

46. Solving the Part-Time Puzzle, *supra,* note 1, at 37–38.

47. PAR Balanced Hours Report, *supra,* note 1, at 15; Lauren Stiller Rikleen, Ending the Gauntlet: Removing Barriers to Women's Success in the Law (Thomson/Legalworks, 2006), at 136–138.

48. *See* Jones, *supra,* note 15.

49. PAR Balanced Hours Report, *supra,* note 1, at 14–15; Cunningham, *supra,* note 27; Holly English, Gender on Trial: Sexual Stereotypes and Work/Life Balance in the Legal Workplace (ALM Publishing 2003) at 201–215.

50. The "haircut"—paying part-time attorneys a lower percentage of full-time pay than the percentage of full-time hours they were required to work (e.g., 75% of a full-time salary for 80% of the full-time hours)—is still common in some cities despite its potential for creating legal claims under the Equal Pay Act and Title VII. For example, in *Lovell v. BBNT Solutions,* 295 F. Supp. 2d 611 (E.D. Va. 2003), a federal district court held that paying a woman chemist who worked a 75% schedule a lower effective pay rate than a full-time male chemist who performed substantially the same work violated the EPA; part-time status alone cannot justify a lower rate of pay.

51. In part, the diminished quality of assignments may be due to supervising attorneys' well-meaning but misguided attempt to accommodate the reduced schedule. The quality of assignments an attorney receives is directly related to the attorney's professional development and readiness for advancement, so diminished assignments exacerbate the advancement difficulties part-timers face.

52. *See* Women's Bar Association of Massachusetts, *More Than Part Time, supra,* note 41.

53. PAR's Balanced Hours Report, supra, note 1, at 13.

54. Joan Williams, *PAR Usability Test,* reprinted by permission in SOLVING THE PART-TIME PUZZLE, *supra,* note 1, at 31.

55. *See* "Up To Par" (February 17, 2005), available at http://www.pardc.org/UpToPAR.

56. NALP Press Release, *Women and Minorities Continue to Make Small Gains at Large Law Firms* (Nov. 17, 2005), available at http://www.nalp.org/press/details.php?id=57.

57. *More Than Part Time, supra,* note 41.

58. *Id.* at App. B, chart.

59. *See* SOLVING THE PART-TIME PUZZLE, *supra* note 1 at 51–60; e.g., John P. Kotter, LEADING CHANGE (Harvard Business School Press, 1996).

60. *See* PAR's Balanced Hours Report, *supra,* note 1 at 25–26; Rikleen, *supra,* note 49 at 358.

# CHAPTER 9

# Solving the Legal World's Problems: A Sole Practitioner's Perspective

**By Roland Baggott**

I love my job. I'll say it again: I love my job. I love the satisfaction of getting results for my clients. I love the intellectual challenge posed by the law. I love the hard work. I love being a lawyer. Being a lawyer is a significant part of who I am. I aspire to be the best at what I do every day.

I am a sole practitioner. This essay is mostly about me. The reason it is about me is simple: my opinions about the practice of law, its problems and possible solutions to those problems have been formed based upon my experiences. Without knowing and understanding my background and my experiences, it will be difficult to understand how my opinions have been formed. Understanding me will make it easier to understand and accept the opinions I espouse about my profession, my colleagues, and that which should be changed about the practice of law.

Here we go:

## Family History

I grew up in Dayton, Ohio. My family is a family of lawyers. Our family firm was founded in 1850 by my great grandfather's uncle, James H. Baggott. During his career, he was the Montgomery County Prosecutor and a Probate Judge and had a successful private practice. At the time he started practicing, he was one of 37 lawyers in Dayton. My great-grandfather, Roland W. Baggott, was a lawyer and then became a Probate Judge, Juvenile Court Judge, and Domestic Relations Judge. My grandfather, Horace W. Baggott, and his brother, James C. Baggott, both were attorneys. My grandfather also was a member of the Ohio Senate. My uncle, Horace W. Baggott, Jr., was an attorney. My father, Thomas M. Baggott, is an attorney. His career has taken him from private practice to a Probate Magistrate and back to private practice. I am the fifth consecutive generation in my family to practice law. There are few firms that still exist in Ohio that can claim the longevity that ours does. Even fewer, if any, can make a claim to such familial history and ties.

Needless to say, I could not get away from being an attorney. It is in my blood. Although I did not know it at the time, I grew up on cross-examination. Every night at the dinner table, my father, a litigator, cross-examined me and my younger sister about the day's events. Similarly, he cross-examined us about our homework, our friends, and our coaches. Family gatherings were no different, except that the cross-examination was conducted by multiple attorneys.

These conversations were, in many ways, formative. I learned how to listen to the question being asked and then how to answer it, usually directly so as to avoid having the question rephrased and posed again. I also learned that I was likely to be caught in any lie I told. My family lawyers knew how to dig to find the truth.

My family, to this day, holds a prominent spot in the history of the bar in Dayton, Ohio. Whenever I return to the city, I am reminded of it through my interaction with judges, other attorneys, and family friends. I frequently am asked whether I will be "as good of a lawyer" as my grandfather and father. My reply of course is: "No. I am going to be better." Joking aside, the prominence that my family holds within the legal community is based upon a respect that my father and forefathers earned. That respect was earned through diligence, hard work, ethical representation, honesty, integrity, and professionalism. Gentlemen at the bar, we all have been, are, and will continue to be. Excellence is our standard. It is one that we bear daily. It is one that cannot be compromised, for to do so is to compromise our integrity. Without integrity, we cannot represent our clients effectively.

This history is where my legal career began. I carry it with me daily.

## My Early Years

I won my first case when I was in elementary school. My fifth grade class took a field trip to the historic Montgomery County Courthouse. As part of the field trip's educational program, the court reenacts the murder trial of Francis Dick. My great-grandfather's uncle, James H. Baggott, was the prosecutor. The Mr. Dick had beaten his victim to death with a shovel.

My mother and father were present on this field trip. I wanted to play the judge in the reenactment. However, when the court personnel learned who I was—the descendent of the prosecutor—I was asked to play his part. I did so and won. When the verdict was read, someone said to me: "You've won your first case." As the story is recounted to me, I replied: "And it won't be my last."

While growing up, I was forced to observe the dedication that the practice of law requires. My mother stayed at home and raised my sister and me. My father worked. Saturday was, and still is, a work day. Evenings, similarly, also required work. My father often would return to the office after eating dinner with us. His dedication to the profession and his practice forced him to miss numerous Little League baseball games, soccer games, swim meets (which I can easily understand because they are incredibly boring), gymnastics practice, and even some of my hockey games. His choice was not his own. Rather it was made for him after he became a lawyer. His dedication to work was both necessary and expected. His brother and father, with whom he practiced, did the same. To me, because I knew nothing different, I had no other expectation. I now know that his dedication came with sacrifices.

While in high school, I learned the value of hard work. My first job was as a paper boy. I delivered the local twice-weekly paper. It was a small route in my neighborhood. I could service it on my own from my bicycle. I had to pay for my papers and collect the amounts due from my customers. This job was the first where I learned that adults can be dishonest: some of my customers tried not to pay or would dispute the amount due. I was not discouraged, however. I found one effective collection technique: either the customer paid or I would quit delivering the paper. I also reported delinquencies to the paper.

Eventually, I sold that route and moved to delivering the daily evening paper. I also started cutting grass, pulling weeds, and trimming bushes, and I became a caddie. I quit delivering papers, however, when the paper route duties started to conflict with playing hockey. It was very difficult to find regular subs when I was traveling for games on the weekends or had practice immediately following school. Also, it did not pay as well as the other jobs. Thus, it had to go.

As a caddie, I rose through the ranks to become the top caddie at my club. I learned that a caddie is a service provider. The better the service I provided, the higher the base pay I earned and the greater the tips. Eventually, I had a regularly scheduled loop, an attorney named Hugh Wall. I would learn his tee time, arrive early for my loop, caddie, and then go home. This was a privilege that I earned through quality service. Frankly, it was not that hard to get it right. The key was simply staying a step ahead of my player, watching where his ball landed and anticipating what his next club selection would be.

Cutting grass and lawn care was my first entrepreneurial job. My business grew because I took the time and care to ensure that spots were not missed, and I knew how to trim without destroying flower beds. This job required diligence and discipline. Overgrown grass was not acceptable to my neighbors or other customers. If I got rained out, I had to find the time to make it up. My business grew to the point that I eventually employed three other people full time. That summer, which was between my freshman and sophomore years of college, was the last summer I cut grass. To this day, my father claims that I made more money than he did that summer. That job taught me the joy of running my own business, the value of hard work, and that diligence pays off.

Another formative experience during high school was playing hockey. My high school did not have a team. Thus, I played for a different high school. My sophomore year we were terrible, winning only 8 games out of a 52-game season, three of which came at the end of the year at a tournament that we won. My junior year, we were better, putting together a winning season. My senior year, we won 38 games and we were a powerhouse. We practiced four days per week. We played games on Friday, Saturday, and Sunday. Thus, hockey required a lot of dedication. It was hard work and a lot of fun.

Hockey was a good training ground for my future career as an attorney. Among other things, I learned how to fight, but to fight fair. Our coach was particular about our team's appearance. We were required to wear a coat and tie to every game. It may seem strange, but when you walk in unified in look (and looking good, as only a teenager in the 1980s could), you foster camaraderie. I also learned about teamwork, leadership, and perseverance. One of my favorite memories was when I was a senior. Going into the third period, our team was losing by a score of 5 to 1. Most people would have been broken at that point because scoring five goals in one period against a team that was kicking your ass and shutting them out is highly unlikely. That's exactly what we did: we came back and won. Perseverance, and a little luck, carried the day.

## College

From high school, I went to Vanderbilt University. As a freshman, I thought I wanted to attend Medical School after I graduated. Thus, I enrolled in many pre-medical classes, including advanced Calculus and Chemistry. I continued these studies through my sophomore year. However, I did not enjoy the program. Although I enjoyed the Chemistry courses I took, I realized that I did not want to complete a pre-medical program. Consequently, during the second semester of that year, I declared English as my major. I have a flashbulb memory of the moment I made the decision. It was as though a weight had been lifted off of my shoulders. When I called my parents to notify them of my plan to declare English, my father bluntly asked: "What the hell are you going to do with that?" I replied:

"Whatever I want," and proceeded to argue my position about the benefits of having the ability to read critically and write cogently. Little did I know, on that very day I had taken the first substantial step to becoming an a lawyer.

I had a number of amazing experiences studying English, not the least of which was that it gave me the opportunity to attain the benefit of realizing the value of a true liberal arts education. By the time I was graduated from Vanderbilt, I was able to see the interwoven web that links all subjects. For example, my astronomy course helped me in my Chaucer course because I knew who Ptolemy was; my Spanish courses helped me in my course on *Ulysses* by James Joyce—a book on which as a senior, I wrote an honors thesis—because I better understood the Latin roots of many of the obscure words; and my history courses helped me in my Southern Literature courses. Fortune's fair wheel was good to me from this standpoint.

I had one undergraduate professor who significantly encouraged me to attend law school: Margaret Doody. Professor Doody, during her Eighteenth Century Novel class, taught us *Oroonoko; or The Royal Slave* by Aprha Bhen. I do not remember the specific assignment, but I wrote a paper about a portion of the book where the narrator and Oroonoko traveled down river to an Indian tribe camp. Oroonoko, until this point in the book had been a protector of the narrator. However, when he and she exited the canoe and were greeted by threatening Indians, he hid behind a bush. She then walked confidently into the Indian settlement and he followed. I argued that the narrator's recounting of this incident was revisionist history: that it was she who hid behind the bush and it was Oroonoko who walked into the settlement. Professor Doody did not buy it. However, she recognized the interest I had in the argument and how I supported it. She stated directly that I should think about going to law school and she proceeded to encourage me to go to law school from then on.

## Law School

So, with the support of my parents, I applied to law school. When I was accepted at The Ohio State University College of Law, I was very excited. Not only is it the best law school in the State of Ohio, but it gave me an opportunity to join the ranks of my forefathers. I was the fourth consecutive generation in my family to attend Ohio State for Law School, starting with my great-grandfather, then my grandfather, then my uncle, and then me. Both my mother and father had attended Ohio State as undergraduates, as had many of my other relatives on both sides of my family. Law school tied me to all of them in one more way.

Make no mistake about law school: it sucked. Anyone who tells you differently is a liar. Law school is the place where new lawyers are "minted." The process is three years of abuse, cutthroat competition, and hard, high-stakes work. It would seem as though this type of competitive experience would benefit a young lawyer—teaching tenacity and critical thinking, and causing the student to question that which he does not know. Stated directly, this cutthroat atmosphere is not beneficial. Instead, it merely fosters the development of and promotes singular achievement at all costs. Students will go so far as to create and distribute outlines for classes that either omit pertinent information or, worse, actively misrepresent the rule of law, its legal standards, and the burden of proof for the rule. This type of competition is commended by the legal academic community. It is my belief that many schools' administrators pride themselves on how much they can abuse their students, believing that they are doing the right thing. What they do not understand is that this atmosphere is not collegial and it does not foster professionalism. It does not accommodate the idea that students should help each other or that by working with an adversary, the student will benefit. This competition has become acceptable because she who earns the highest grades will be all but guaranteed that high-paying job at the prestigious large law firm. Unfortunately for our profession, that which is learned is not easily unlearned. Too often that view of competition follows the young lawyer into practice, taking on the form of deceit, obstructiveness, obfuscation, bending rules because of "gray lines," hiding facts, misrepresentations, refusal to turn over probative evidence, and active destruction of evidence.

Law school is not limited to academic study. There are extracurricular activities that every student is told should be on his or her resume: moot court and law review. Both of these are very competitive and both are time consuming. I did both, and excelled at them. I was given an award for best brief in moot court by Ohio Supreme Court Justice Paul Pfeiffer, who was the primary author of the decision that we re-briefed and argued. When presenting the award, he commended me for my investigation, research, and presentation. He even went so far as to say that had he known some of the facts that I had uncovered, he probably would have decided the case differently. I did not "grade onto" law review. Rather, I wrote my way on through a writing competition. I was one of four students selected that way. On law review, I co-authored a student note that was published and which later was a finalist for a national award for best student note. I also was an editor for our symposium issue.

Today, I have little doubt that my participation in moot court and law review activities was beneficial to me. I learned the fine art of legal citation; honed my grammar, punctuation, and capitalization skills; and learned the craft of brief drafting, including the benefit of cogency. These skills were further honed during a judicial externship that I had with Hon. Walter H. Rice, then the Chief Judge for the United States District Court for the Southern District of Ohio. Judge Rice supplemented my education. He taught me the importance of correct legal citation and, to my amazement, showed me how many lawyers have no problem either omitting portions of a citation (e.g., the pinpoint cite) or not citing the case correctly at all, making the case difficult to locate. He specifically had me work on cases where lawyers would omit portions of passages that they were quoting or, worse, would actively misrepresent the holding of a particular case. He taught me that the sheer volume of matters that judges hear forces them to read an unbelievable volume of poorly drafted, incoherent pleadings. He taught me that written materials must be clear, cogent, and direct in order to be effective.

Approximately seven months after I was graduated from law school, I had the distinct honor of drafting a brief and arguing it in front of Judge Rice. I won. I won because my client's position was right. Judge Rice drafted a lengthy decision that was published in the Federal Reporter. That the decision was published is not remarkable. Rather, that the judge quoted liberally from my brief was.

I will admit that during law school, I had a number of positive experiences. I had more than a few great professors. The standouts were excited to teach every day. They excelled in their pedagogical skills. I took my notes on a laptop computer. One professor, whose teaching seemed at first to be disorganized, I quickly realized had a perfect outline of everything that he was going to say that day. It was nothing less than amazing. His motto was: "The law is a seamless web." He helped teach me how my Torts class overlapped with my Business Associations class; and how the Legislation course overlapped with my Contracts course. Very simply, he showed me that the law, like liberal arts, is not made up of distinct compartments but rather is interwoven. He was a fabulous teacher.

Another professor who was a great influence on me was my contracts professor. She also was the Associate Dean of Students. In many ways, she became my mentor. I now consider her a friend, hold her in high esteem, and am proud of her accomplishments. She cared about the student quality of life. She understood the students' desire to make their own school better. She fought for it. Our law school, while I was there, was in the Stone Age technologically. New computers were being produced with Windows 95. The school's computer systems, and the network we were expected to use, were still DOS based. To put the school's technological obsolescence into perspective, since the use of DOS was pervasive, Microsoft had developed Windows, had upgraded Windows twice, and then had released Windows 95. Only those law schools that were unwilling to expend the capital on technology, or which struggled financially, were still employing DOS systems. Ohio State fell into the former category. To me, particularly after the school completed a major renovation and expansion, this computer system was unacceptable, particularly because none of the programs, documents, and electronic mail that I produced with my laptop computer were compatible with the school's systems. I fought the administration and lobbied for new computers. This professor supported me. She made it possible for me to attend a committee meeting, which was presided over by the Dean, to present my case. When asked where the money would come from, I argued that the school had many avenues for raising money, including raising tuition, taking more out of state students (which would improve geographic diversity at the same time) or pumping palms and kissing babies. Most of the committee members were astounded that I would actually tell the Dean he needed to go out and raise the money, let alone that I thought it was his duty. At the end of my presentation, this professor merely smiled—that telling smile of satisfaction. The next academic year, the school replaced all of the computers. Thus, I won. Without her support, I probably would not have been the opportunity to fight for my law school colleagues. During this process, she taught me that you have to take advantage of the opportunities that are put in front of you; and then you must perform. She also taught me that battles that seemingly are a joust with a windmill may in fact have significance for others.

Finally, another professor who had an impact on me taught me criminal law during my first semester of my first year. He had little enthusiasm for the subject and made it clear that he had been forced to teach it. One day, late in the semester, however, he stopped class to discuss his career. He did this because he felt like there was too much pressure put on the students to earn high grades so that the spring interviewing season might land them a summer job. He said that before becoming a professor, he had worked for a large, prestigious law firm in New Orleans. There, he enjoyed everything that law students are taught is the goal of law school: the high-paying job, partnership at a prestigious law firm, the fancy sports car, the big house in the nice neighborhood, and the trophy wife. He went on to say, however, that he worked his ass off. He never had time to spend his money, never drove his sports car, never spent any time in his house, and rarely saw his trophy wife, let alone his children. Although he had everything that he had been taught that he should want, and thus, he should have been happy, he was miserable.

He then speculated that most of us in that class that day would be miserable in that situation too. He thought, instead, that most of us would be happy if we could, as lawyers, help people. He surmised that earning an "A," instead of a "B" (or a dreaded "C"), in his criminal law class was unlikely to have any affect on our future happiness as lawyers. Almost condescendingly, he said most of us were not cut out for large law firm life. He was right. Only a few of my friends and colleagues who went to work at large law firms still work at large law firms eight years later. The primary reason they left was that, despite getting paid a lot of money, they were unhappy.

## Work History

After graduating from law school, I took and passed the Louisiana Bar Examination. I was living in New Orleans. While studying for the bar and waiting for my bar results, I did not have a job. Many employers were suspicious that because I had not attended law school in Louisiana and had not studied Louisiana Civil Law, I would not pass the bar. They candidly wondered whether my "common law" education would give me the knowledge base that would allow me to pass the Louisiana bar.

Fortunately for me, a friend of my family, David Deutsch, helped support me while I was waiting for my bar results. Mr. Deutsch is a sole practitioner in Dayton. He hired me as a contract attorney to work on the Pig Case. This case involved a high school girl who was involved in the Greene County, Ohio, 4H Club. She showed pigs. One of her pigs, Big Fat, won Grand Reserve Champion (second place) at the Greene County Fair. Pursuant to the rules of the 4H Club, because of the award to her pig, it was to be slaughtered. Six weeks later, she showed a different pig at another county fair. This pig looked very much like Big Fat. The 4H commissioner, because of the similarity between the two pigs, disqualified her. She and her family were labeled cheaters. Her disqualification at that county fair also disqualified her from participation at the Ohio State Fair. By not being able to participate in the Ohio State Fair, she was ineligible for college 4H scholarships.

She had not cheated. She sued the commissioner and the State of Ohio. During the development of the case, the expert testimony revealed that it was physically impossible for the pig that caused her to be disqualified to be the same pig as Big Fat. Quite simply, pigs grow at an approximate rate of two pounds per day and the second pig weighed six pounds less than Big Fat did six weeks previously!

The State defended with the doctrine of qualified immunity and won at the trial level on summary judgment. My job was to draft the appellate brief. I spent weeks working on this project. We lost the first appeal. We then appealed to the Ohio Supreme Court, using almost the exact same brief that we filed with the Court of Appeal. We won. In the process, we developed an exception to the state doctrine of qualified immunity.

Unfortunately for our client, the win was hollow. The win merely gave her the opportunity to have a trial. That win came too late. By this time, our client and her family had become outcasts in their rural community and she had almost completed her college studies. The State, by refusing to take responsibility for its own wrongdoing, had delayed justice so long that its harm was irreparable.

From this experience, I learned a number of lessons. The first was that justice does not always come timely. Second, I learned that there are many people who have no intention of accepting responsibility for their own actions. Simply, if they do something wrong, they think that they can avoid being held accountable and will take every necessary step to avoid accountability. Their lawyers, too often, will fight merely for the purpose of delay, knowing that time has a way of working to their wrongdoer client's benefit. Too often, those lawyers are right. Finally, and equally important, however, I learned that working for a just cause has merit. Justice delayed may not be effective, but it nonetheless is justice.

I think about this case regularly when conducting litigation on behalf of my clients. I try to follow the lessons that I learned from it when advising my clients as to our strategy and as to the expected outcome. I also use this experience as a guidepost for determining when settlement may be in my clients' best interests. I honestly can say that many attorneys fail their clients because they have not developed the perspective, or simply lack the integrity, that will allow them to stand up to their clients and tell them when they have done something wrong and should make amends for it.

## My First Firm Job

I have not always been a sole practitioner. My first job after graduating from law school was just outside of New Orleans in Metairie, Louisiana. I worked for a mid-sized firm, primarily defending products liability cases that arose from asbestos and silica sand exposure. I was an asbestos lawyer.

This firm gave me my first real introduction to what is expected of young lawyers. My billable minimum was 200 hours per month, 2400 per year. I had to meet this requirement despite holidays, vacation, or sickness. Thus, if I wanted to take the two weeks of allowed vacation, I had to bill on average 48 hours per week. My starting salary was $50,000 per year.

I was fortunate that this firm gave its young associates significant responsibility early. Shortly after being hired, I spent many days taking depositions. I also spent many days drafting motions. When those motions were to be heard, I was the lawyer in court arguing them. On "Rule Day," when others had motions to be heard, if it was my turn, I was directed to argue motions (often minor discovery motions) that were drafted by others in cases in which I was not actively participating.

Fortunately for me (because of my billable requirements), there was plenty of work to do. I always made my numbers, often exceeding them by 20 to 30 hours per month. I spent days on end attending depositions all over Louisiana and Mississippi. I saw a lot of backwater towns. I listened to the same questions over and over and honed my skills for identifying when my clients had an advantage. I learned that an aggressive motion practice can be very successful. Over a period of six months, I had over 30 cases against my clients dismissed. Many dismissals came after deposition testimony of a plaintiff who could not state a cause of action against my clients. Often, the plaintiff's counsel would be willing to dismiss a case without prejudice, merely to avoid a motion for summary judgment. I thought I was doing a great job.

It was after I had so many cases dismissed, that my bosses pulled me aside and said: "You don't get it, do you?" I was then told that I was doing too good of a job. They explained that defense firms make money by defending lawsuits, not by getting lawsuits dismissed. Thus, I was to find a way to continue working my cases until the point when the client, an insurance adjuster, felt that the case should either be settled or did not understand why we were still defendants in the case. This conversation was my first introduction to the business side of practicing insurance defense.

I understood my bosses' position, but did not like what they were telling me. I did not think it was ethical when we could get the case dismissed to continue to represent the client merely so that we could charge the client more money. They rationalized their practice by stating that there were additional probative facts that should be developed in the event that a case could not be dismissed on summary judgment. How this rationalization applied in cases where the plaintiff's attorney was willing to dismiss our clients, I did not know. Further, they informed me that our client, the insurance adjuster, had a reserve in place that anticipated a certain amount of fees and expected to pay most of those fees. Finally, they explained that the hourly rate that we were being paid by the insurance company was artificially low because of the carrier's knowledge of this practice in general—meaning that this practice was not limited to them, but was pervasive throughout the insurance defense bar (which I now believe is true). Essentially, their attitude was that if everybody else is doing it, the client expects it, and the hourly rate reflects it, is there really anything wrong?

They made it clear during this conversation (and others) that if I did not follow their directions, I would lose my job. Thus, they put me in the position of having to choose between engaging in what I considered an unethical, arguably fraudulent, practice and being unemployed. Ultimately, the decision as to whether to leave was made for me: my section's biggest client went bankrupt. My billable hours fell from 220 per month to 80. The firm partners generously gave me 30 days to use my office to find another job. During that time, at least I could say I was employed. My primary boss and the other attorney in our section left the firm.

## Job No. 2

My next job was with a smaller firm in downtown New Orleans. It was a split off of a large firm. I had the same billable minimum, the same long hours, and the same pay. The work was far worse, however. Very simply, this job sucked. I was miserable while I was there.

When hired, I was told that I would be defending products liability cases, as I had with the previous firm. That proved to be untrue. Instead, I ended up doing low-dollar insurance defense, mostly auto defense and a little bit of worker's compensation defense. I had 170+ open files. I was nothing more than a glorified insurance adjuster. My billable rate, as set by the insurance company, was $85 per hour. I saw one bad back after another. There was no intellectual challenge to these cases.

Generally, I was not permitted by the client to work up my cases. Because the client would not pay for it, my bosses would not allow the firm's paralegals to organize the files. Rarely did I get to depose a plaintiff or a treating physician. The only time I tried a case was when Allstate was a co-defendant (they try everything).

Despite the real limitations on my ability to defend the cases I was handling, my bosses expected high productivity. They wanted and expected me to make money for them. To assist me, they gave me (and the other associates) a seminar on how to "capture our time." The essence of this seminar was that the client should be billed for every second that you spend thinking, talking, or doing anything associated with the case. Thus, if you were in the shower thinking about a case, that time should be billed. If you dreamt about a case, that time should be billed. During this seminar, they also informed me how to artificially inflate my bills without expending much more time by taking advantage of the billable minimum of .1 hours. For example a two-minute phone call with opposing counsel would be billed as .1. Then a short letter would be drafted to the client and, even though it took only two minutes to dictate, billed as .2. Then, a short memo to the file on what to do next would be dictated and billed as .1. Total time spent on the matter might be eight minutes, but the client was billed a total of .4 for the work. At the end of this seminar, one attorney proclaimed with pride that if he had actually lived all of the hours he had billed, he probably would be five years older than he is. All I could think was that we associates were just directed to commit fraud. I silently refused to do it.

While at this job, I started to develop clients. One matter that I developed was a commercial transaction where I was to represent the buyer of a bakery chain that had 52 stores. My bosses made me refer it to another firm. It generated over $40,000 in fees for the firm to whom my clients were referred. I was told that the firm did not want to take on that type of business. I now know that the reality was that my bosses did not want me to have my own clients. When you have your own clients, you have power. To this day, none of the associates have made partner. Further, all but one of the associates with whom I worked have left the firm. It is clear that my bosses never intended to share their firm's success. Rather, I was there for one reason only: to make money for them. They did not care about me or my professional development. I would quit the practice of law before I went back to doing that type of legal work or that type of atmosphere. It's simply not worth it.

### Going In House

My next job was an in-house position with a medium-sized franchisor. I was their General Counsel. At the time I was hired, I was one of the youngest General Counsels in the country. This job was a pretty good gig. It, however, was not the cushy 9:00 AM to 5:00 PM job that almost every attorney envies. Rather, it was 7:30 AM to 8:00 PM, with lunch catered daily. As with my previous jobs, I worked my ass off. During the process, I learned the law and the trade that now is the focus of my practice: franchising. I have a lot of reasons to be thankful that the company gave me the opportunity. My boutique practice exists because of my experience at the company.

This job also taught me how bigger businesses are run. There are endless, mind-numbing, wasteful meetings where every numbnut in the room gives his two cents, even if the discussion has no bearing on his department. I learned that meetings are not productive unless there is a set agenda; and then only the person who presides over the meeting follows the agenda. I try to remember my frustration with these meetings when preparing for a meeting with a client. I do not want to waste the client's time.

I also learned that there is no such thing as ethics in business. Businesspeople are not licensed professionals. There is no person, regulatory body, or governmental entity that requires businesspeople to be "ethical." Businesspeople's actions are either legal or illegal. If they are illegal, rarely are there criminal penalties, even for fraud. Usually, the only recourse for a victim of a company's illegal actions is through the civil justice system. Businesses owners, executives, and employees know this fact. They do and will exploit it to their advantage, weighing the risk of civil liability against the gain. Often they will insure these risks so that they can avoid paying the actual civil penalties. Many businesses will not pay for services rendered or goods that were delivered, and then will try to get the vendor to negotiate for a lesser price. This practice is pervasive. The only penalty is that they might be sued for the unpaid portion of the bill. Of course, the vendor who was stiffed has to pay a lawyer to get the money. Faced with that fact, the vendor is likely to negotiate first.

When you add a licensed professional to this mix on an inhouse basis, one who is knowledgeable about the law, you create a tension. The lawyer has a higher standard of conduct for which she is accountable. The licensing body and the highest court of the state will take away her ability to practice law if she actively advises her clients on how to break the law, allows her services to be used so that her client—the company—can break the law, or simply appears to be a complicit adviser by standing by idly. I know a former in-house lawyer who lost his license and went to jail for his active participation in his company's illegal conduct. The President and founder of his company, however, did not go to jail and is still out there doing business. The lawyer lost his ability to practice his chosen profession. The businessman is free and still sells his widgets.

Every company that has an in-house lawyer has this tension. Mine did too. Just before I went in-house, a friend of mine who had been an in-house attorney with Amoco for over 27 years gave me his sage advice: "Your answer never is 'no.' Rather, it is 'we can do what you want, but this is how we have to do it.'" The in-house lawyer is not an internal police officer who tells the executives and employees how they must conduct their business. Rather, the in-house lawyer's job is to ensure that the objectives of the company are accomplished in a manner that is permissible under the bounds of the law and to advise of risk associated with deviating from those bounds.

The real dilemma for in-house lawyers comes when her company decides not to follow her advice. For example, the company has engaged in a course of action that is illegal but has not notified the attorney until the process is almost completed. She advises that the company needs to backtrack, take some remedial action, and then move forward along a compliant path. The company executives, recognizing that there may be substantial cost associated with the course recommended by the lawyer, refuse. Further, the company executives want her to substantially assist in the completion of the project. It is at this point that she is confronted with the ethical rules, specifically Rule 1.16, which requires that the lawyer withdraw if the client demands that the lawyer engage in conduct that is illegal, violates the Rules of Professional Conduct, or violates other law. She cannot participate in the project and must withdraw. Withdrawal, however, means losing your job.

When I was faced with this dilemma, I sought the opinion of outside counsel on the company's matter. The opinion of outside counsel about the matter was the same as mine. The day outside counsel delivered this opinion was my last day as General Counsel.

## Solo Practice Beckons

Of course, being unemployed and having no clients, I took the most logical next step: I started my own firm. Initially, I worked out of my house. I slowly built up my number of clients. I did not receive any payment for the work that I did during the first four months. Fortunately, my wife was in a residency at the time. We struggled to make ends meet. Just before I was about to give up on my solo practice because of the mounting financial pressure, I was paid approximately $5,000 for fees that I had earned while helping a friend settle his deceased mother's estate. My wife and I breathed a sigh of relief.

Over the next four years, I built my practice to where it is today. Many of my contemporaries have made more money (some, such as the ones working for big firms in major metropolitan markets like Chicago, substantially more) than I during that time. I, however, have enjoyed my practice more. When I work until midnight, it is for me, not an uncaring boss who won't look at my work for at least three weeks. When I get paid, the money is mine. I have the ability to control my expenses and overhead, rather than simply being given an allocation over which I have no control. I do not worry about someone taking my clients away from me simply because a senior partner has lost some of his—something that happened to a friend of mine *after* he made partner at a big firm. My clients are mine. I get to choose who I represent and who I do not represent.

I have been fortunate to be able to build my practice so that I do not have to practice what some attorneys call "door law"—i.e., whatever walks in the door. My practice is almost exclusively commercial in nature, focusing on franchising, business transactions, commercial litigation, and health care, in which field, I represent physicians exclusively. I choose not to represent insurance companies, health care companies, and hospitals. I choose not to represent individuals in family law matters, not to defend criminal matters, not to close real estate transactions, not to prepare wills and trusts, not to represent debtors in bankruptcy (rarely doing anything more in the bankruptcy arena than filing a proof of claim for a creditor) and not to represent victims of medical malpractice. On rare, select occasions I will represent a victim of injury, a victim of employment discrimination, or a whistleblower (e.g., *qui tam*). When I accept these types of representations, however, it is only after substantial investigation. I have to believe the client's story, that the client has been wronged, that the client is entitled to recovery, and the defendant must be able to pay.

I work hard—as hard as, if not harder than, I did when I was employed by someone else. Frankly, one of the keys to my success is that I work harder than most of my opponents. I put in long hours, regularly working late into the evening and on weekends. I am dedicated to my job and my clients. I refuse to compromise on quality. I have high expectations for myself and those around me.

My dedication to my firm and my clients does not come without sacrifices. A friend of mine, who may be one of the best trial lawyers I know, David Greer, says that "the law is a jealous mistress." By this he means that once you have become an attorney, the law will require your time and will take you away from your other obligations, including your family, as would a jealous lover. For me, the primary sacrifice is time spent with my wife. When I come home late in the evening, we have little time to spend together before we go to bed. When I work on the weekends, we do not run errands together, do not play tennis together, do not do yard work together, do not go hiking, biking, etc. Because my office landlord allows me to bring my dog to the office (I have a fabulous landlord), I spend more time with my dog than I do with my wife. Unless I am traveling, my dog goes to work with me every day. My wife, a professional herself, recognizes the dedication that I have to my work and respects it. That does not mean she always accepts it.

The balance between family, home, and work can be difficult to strike. However, because I am a sole practitioner and answer only to my clients, not some managing partner who claims my numbers are good enough, I have the luxury of flexibility. If I need to be at the house to meet a worker (I recently acted as the general contractor for our kitchen renovation), I simply schedule it. If I want to take a vacation, again, I simply schedule it. If I need to go to the dentist, I do. If I want to close my office for any reason, I can, and do. This flexibility is one of the reasons that I have a high level of job satisfaction. The only downside to this flexibility is that when I am not working, I do not get paid.

Another reason that I have high job satisfaction is that I have responsibility. I am the only attorney that performs the clients' work. I manage, direct, and control their litigation. I make strategic calls. I am the one who must provide the advice. I am the one they trust. An eighth-year senior associate at a large law firm, who has another two years to go until she is promoted to non-equity partner (assuming she makes it), may have some of these responsibilities, but always will have someone else who makes the final decisions for her. She also will always have someone else to whom she is beholden, simply because of her lower status. She is unlikely to have substantial client contact, primarily because of the fear, particularly if she is good, that she will develop too strong of a relationship with the client. She is unlikely to be fully supported in client development. For any client she does develop, her senior partner is likely to be given the origination credit, not her. Her job satisfaction, guaranteed, is less than mine.

Business is booming. My success has been my own. I get results for my clients. With those results, my reputation in the community has grown. I regularly get referrals from attorneys in the community who know what I do and who respect me. I also regularly get referrals from large law firms when they have a conflict. After the representation is over, I send their clients back to them. They keep sending me this business for a few reasons: (1) I get results for their clients; (2) they trust my judgment; and (3) because business for big law firms is so very competitive, they can have confidence that the risk posed by having the client develop a relationship with another lawyer is minimized. Let's face it, if the big firms were to refer that business to each other, they, with reason, would be concerned that their client relationship might be put at risk.

Another key to my success is my ability to create financial relationships with my clients that are aligned with their interests. I have the flexibility to enter into flat fee, mixed flat fee and hourly, straight hourly, retained, contingent, partially contingent, and/or deferred fee arrangements. I do not have to get approval from anyone to enter into these arrangements. I can simply create an arrangement that best fits the client's need and still compensates me well. I know of no senior associate who has this flexibility—another barrier to that attorney's ability to develop clients.

Client development is the key to the success of any attorney. If you have clients, you have stability, both professionally and financially. You also have power. You have responsibility. If you have a client base that generates substantial, sustainable revenue, no matter where you work, you will become a partner. If the firm decides not to make you a partner, then you can, and should, take your business elsewhere. Understanding this reality is the key to an attorney's success and, in my opinion, personal satisfaction.

Without a doubt, the hardest part about being a sole practitioner is staffing. Support staff is the single largest expense that I have. It is not the expense that is difficult to manage, however. Rather, it is the employee's expectations and attitude. I found that there are a lot of people who believe that simply because their body is warm, they deserve to be paid a lot of money. Newly minted paralegals with no experience during interviews have stated that they expect to be paid $45,000 per year—which in my market is the salary of a seasoned paralegal who has a billing requirement. I have had employees who cannot show up on time or who miss work and think that I should accommodate them. I even had an employee who thought she should be able to practice real estate brokerage from my office (she was a licensed realtor) while on my clock. It baffles me. I have yet to find a solution to this problem. From what I understand, this problem is not limited to my firm or me.

As mentioned above, I work as hard as I ever have. Unfortunately, not all of the work that I do is legal work. I spend a significant amount of time on administrative matters. The most time consuming are managing finances and billing. Fortunately, for me, almost all of my clients pay their bills on time. Thus, I do not have to spend much time managing accounts receivable. However, I do have to ensure that my bills are accurate, both with the description of the work and the amount of time spent, and then have to send them. This sounds easier than it really is. I spend at least one day, usually more, finalizing and sending my bills to my clients. Daily throughout the month, my time is entered on the bills. Thus, the day or more that I spend on my bills is time that is not generating new revenue. I also have to make sure that I have sufficient revenue coming in to meet all of my financial obligations, including staff salaries, tax payments, rent, insurance, student loan payments and other personal obligations. Managing cash flow can be difficult, particularly when there is an unexpected event that dramatically affects my practice, such as a hurricane. Hurricane Katrina blew approximately $10,000 to $15,000 per month in revenue out of my practice. Only now, nine months later, is that portion of my practice starting to come back.

Despite the drawbacks to being a sole practitioner, specifically staffing and managing administrative time, I know that I would not be happier in a different setting. I also know that I would not have higher job satisfaction if someone else were handling my staffing, managing my firm, and doing my billing. Simply, I would be trading one set of problems for another, specifically office politics.

### The Profession: Problems and Solutions

So, having learned about me and some of my experiences and having heard my career path, I finally come to the heart of the topic of this article: What's wrong with our profession and what solutions exist?

The problems with our profession are multifaceted and have many layers. Thus, solutions to the problems that we face must be implemented in more than one place and in more than one way. Like the law itself, the problems with our profession are not distinctly compartmentalized, but rather are interwoven.

Let's start with the law schools. The law schools are where we are first introduced to what it means to be a lawyer. Skills and habits that are developed during law school carry through and follow us for the remainder of our careers. The current law school atmosphere needs to change. Law schools need to start treating their students better and must change their atmosphere from cutthroat competitiveness, where winning at all costs is praised, to one of collegiality. The schools must start encouraging their students to work cooperatively, rather than pitting them against each other. When my father attended law school, the practice was that only one-third of entering students graduated. It was the: "Look to your left. Look to your right. At the end of your three years here, only one of you will remain." This practice is no longer a hallmark of legal education. However, the competitiveness that was fostered by that system remains. It needs to go.

In order to effect such a change, the law school administrators and professors will have to shift their attitudes. They also may have to change their teaching methods, including creating group projects and administering examinations more frequently than once a semester.

The law schools also need to stop failing their students. Law schools fail their students on many levels, including by not providing them with sufficient scholarship funding and by taking too many students. The university cash cow that is the law school needs to be slaughtered. Law schools enroll too many students, provide too little financial assistance in the form of scholarships, and take no responsibility for the end result: graduates who are overburdened with educational debt who have to enter a marketplace that cannot support the volume of newly minted lawyers. For example, in the State of Louisiana, there are four law schools, one of which is not accredited by the ABA, that combined produce approximately 1000 graduates per year. Although some of those graduates leave Louisiana after graduation, the overwhelming majority stay within the borders of the state. Simply, there are not a sufficient number of jobs being created annually to support the raw number of students. There are even fewer jobs being created that will allow the graduate to service her educational debt fully and live modestly.

The law schools, and the universities associated with them, have accepted no responsibility for the glut of new lawyers they have created. Rather, they have merely reveled in the increased revenues and expanding alumni base. It has to stop. They need to decrease enrollment and increase scholarship funding. That means that the administrators, particularly the deans, need to go out and raise money. Then, after raising money, they need to keep it in the law school's endowment, rather than letting it slip into the hands of the larger university.

Next, moving to young lawyer expectations, the law schools need to provide their students with a more realistic expectation of the legal marketplace. Most lawyers will not work for a large law firm. Even fewer will stay at a large law firm. Placement of students into large law firm jobs is the brass ring by which law schools measure their success. Those students who are not in the top 10% of their graduating class, or who want a public service job (e.g., prosecutor or public defender), are neither cherished nor supported by their law schools. The reason is simple. These graduates do not make enough money to donate back to the school. Regardless, the law school needs to prepare its students for the reality of the marketplace: that good, high-paying jobs are not the norm. Rather, they are the exception. Teaching students that they should expect to fall within an exception to the rule when seeking employment after graduation is wrong. However, unless and until the educational debt structure of legal education changes, they have no choice but to encourage, and hope, that their students will get that big firm, high-paying job.

Students, similarly, need to better investigate what it means and what it takes to be a lawyer. It is my opinion that the students who are best prepared to deal with the reality of the commitment required by the practice of law are those who grow up around lawyers. While growing up, I saw the dedication required of my father. I had little expectation that anything different would be my fate. Thus, my eyes were more open than those of my colleagues who did not have the benefit of having a parent who is an attorney. My experience with my law clerks has confirmed my opinion. Those clerks that have attorney parents better understand the commitment that our profession requires and, frankly, handle it better. This is not to say that my colleagues who did not have an attorney parent are less qualified to enter the workforce after graduation from law school. However, their expectations about the reality of the practice of law are often mismanaged. That reality comes crashing down on them when either they find themselves working endless hours at the large law firm or they find that they struggle to first find employment and then make a living. Simply, the graduates need to learn that a law degree is not guarantee of a good, well paying job. Rather, not unlike a franchised business opportunity, it is nothing more than a tool that, if used properly and combined with a lot of hard work, should help them achieve a higher standard of living. The expectations of students need to change to meet the reality of the legal marketplace.

The next problem that I see in this profession that needs to be corrected is the attitudes of lawyers regarding billing. The institutional fraud that has been caused by the overreaching control of insurance companies needs to end. Similarly, the insurance companies, who are well aware of the practices of the attorneys they hire, instead of condoning the practice and then merely negotiating downward the hourly rates of their lawyers, need to take action against their attorneys. Unfortunately, for this to happen, the insurance industry would have to want to change—something that is guaranteed not to happen. The attorneys that they hire, many of whom are no better than the unlicensed non-professional who is directing their actions, thus, will have to change from within.

Personal integrity and honesty are things that I am convinced cannot be taught to an adult. Either the adult has it, or he does not. Change, thus, will only come through strong leadership. That leadership must require honesty in billing practices. That leadership must also stand up to the unlicensed client, the insurance company, to restore professional independence. Additionally, it would be helpful if more attorneys would take the self regulatory facet of our profession more seriously and report their colleagues to the Disciplinary Counsel (or other regulator charged with enforcing our ethical rules) when they know that they themselves or others have breached our rules.

The insurance defense bar is not the only place where leadership needs to effect a change. The plaintiff's bar also needs change. Too many attorneys will take a matter for which they have done no pre-litigation investigation and then prosecute it regardless of its merits. These attorneys often do their clients a disservice by not providing meaningful representation. Rather, their client is nothing more than a paycheck. Ironically, these attorneys often are paid by the same people who pay their opposing counsel: the insurance company. They rationalize their conduct because they have seen so many legitimate claims be denied by insurance companies that they see no reason not to abuse the insurance company. It's wrong. The leaders within the plaintiff's bar should work proactively to stop these types of matters from being filed.

Next, too many lawyers treat their jobs like they are a business person at a corporation. They take on the personalities of their clients. They accept their clients' mindset and then forget that there is no such thing as ethics in business. They let their clients direct their activities. In the process, they lose their professional independence and compromise their ability to provide honest, impartial advice. They become nothing more than their client's whore. These lawyers need to stop fighting their clients' battles merely because their clients want to fight and are willing to pay to fight. Too few lawyers have the guts to stand up to their clients because they fear that the client, upon hearing their independent opinion rather than merely being the client's parrot, will take its business elsewhere. These lawyers need to understand that their professional judgment, independence, and skill are that which the client needs and are that which the client is really buying, regardless of the client's wants.

Lawyers, when providing advice, should identify to the client when the client has engaged in wrongdoing. Then they work to resolve any dispute associated with the wrongdoing. They need to be independent, however. They also need to recognize that their opponent is (or should be) independent. Taking back independence will require accepting the risk of losing business. Moreover, the rationalization of, "If I don't do it, someone else will" needs to disappear.

Lawyers need to stop abusing each other. Throughout the process of building my practice to the point where it is today, I have encountered many attorneys. The majority of these lawyers have been honorable and professional. However, I have also encountered my fair share of obstructionist scumbags, shysters, and outright liars. These lawyers almost universally have one thing in common: they have no qualms about misrepresenting facts, omitting material facts, misrepresenting the law, changing material terms in transactional documents without notifying you of the change, and actively encouraging their clients to lie. Without fail, these lawyers abuse the legal process and have no respect for the law, our judicial system, rules of procedure, their opposing counsel, or their clients.

These lawyers exist in all types of practices, from the sole practitioner who represents malingering worker's compensation claimants to the senior partner at the "white-shoe" law firm. Unfortunately, their presence in our profession is more than simply tolerated. Law partners often will take no action, so long as the attorney continues to show financial productivity and is not sanctioned too often. Additionally, the people with the authority to discipline these attorneys for their abuses, particularly judges, rarely exercise their authority.

For example, I sued a woman and her husband as community debtor for the debt she incurred during her divorce from him, but before the divorce was decreed. His lawyer filed an answer and then immediately filed a Motion for Sanctions. The Motion for Sanctions was without merit, was abusive, and was designed for one purpose only: to intimidate me personally. The Motion for Sanctions was denied and eventually we took a judgment against the husband. The judge in the case, however, despite her knowledge that the lawyer's actions were meritless, abusive, and intended for an improper purpose, did not even admonish the attorney for his conduct. By failing to address the abuse in any way, she tacitly condoned his actions. Had she taken action, she might have been able to prevent future abuses by this attorney. Instead, she encouraged them.

When committing these types of abuses, which include litigation abuses and transactional abuses, many lawyers will hide behind the aegis of "zealous advocacy." The idea of that which constitutes zealous advocacy has become perverted. This perversion has led to more and more egregious abuses by lawyers who, due either to their ineptitude, sloth, or outright dishonesty (or a combination thereof), believe that it is acceptable to gain an advantage by any method available. Amazingly, this type of conduct was probably first learned in law school, where it was rewarded. Then, it was further rewarded when it may have produced the results wanted by a client. Then it became acceptable because neither law partners, colleagues, judges, or the disciplinary board would take action. If the conduct is acceptable because it is nothing more than zealous advocacy, then it does not need to change, right? Wrong.

How do we effect the change that will stop these abuses? First, the attorney who engages in the abuses needs to stop being rewarded for the abuses. Stopping the reward can come from judges, disciplinary counsel, colleagues, and even the client. Realistically, it should come from all of them. However, there is little likelihood that the client will take action, particularly if the lawyer is getting results. Second, there should be a penalty, one that is effective as a deterrent. The penalty should be imposed swiftly. Finally, there should be education. The education has to come from leadership, not merely from a 50-minute "ethics and professionalism" seminar designed to fulfill CLE requirements. This education should be ongoing, if not constant and on a peer to peer level. It will require that the leadership take the abuses seriously, rather than promote them. This change will be difficult, particularly when, as with my second job out of law school, billing fraud is encouraged.

The next problem that needs to be fixed is that law firms need to quit abusing their associates. The abuse of associates can be observed both from the standpoint of the volume of work required and the standpoint of the respect for the associate. Abuse of associates makes them miserable. Because the abuse is so pervasive, they learn that treating people badly is acceptable and treat everyone accordingly. The associate who has so much debt that she has no choice but to find the big firm job, if she manages her finances correctly, can escape the abuse in a few years. Hence we see attrition at years 3–4. The partners consider the attrition an act of disloyalty. However, they need to understand that their associates, and even their partners, are not an annuity from which they are entitled perpetual payment. If they continue to treat their associates like an annuity, they will be doomed to repeat the cycle and perpetuate the development of unethical, rude, unprofessional, miserable lawyers. Because there is a sufficient supply of young associates, particularly ones who must withstand the abuse because they need to service their educational debt, there is little incentive for the law firm culture to change. If the law schools, however, decrease the supply of young lawyers who are overburdened with debt, then the only reason the associate will have to withstand the abuse is the promise of financial reward. That reward, however, will come to any attorney who works hard, represents her clients honestly, and gets results for her clients, regardless of whether she is at a big firm or in solo practice.

I truly love the practice of law, its challenges, and the joy it can bring. I cannot imagine being happier doing something else for a living. The problems with the profession that I have identified and discussed here should be addressed. Changing any one of them is unlikely to have much effect. All of them will need to be changed. However, it has to start somewhere. Let it start with us individually.

# PART V

# Associates and Mentoring

# CHAPTER 10

# Mentoring: Alive and Well?

**By Louise A. LaMothe**

Mentoring is the time-honored method of transmitting and thereby preserving the best values of our profession. It has always been the way in which values have trickled down from the senior to the junior members of the organization. While my particular focus is the difficulties women and minorities face, *all* lawyers need one or more mentors. Yet finding them seems to be ever more challenging, as lawyers switch firms and practice modalities at a pace unknown even a generation ago. Mentoring opportunities have particularly been lacking historically for women and minorities, which in turn has contributed to their lack of advancement in and dissatisfaction with the legal profession.

In 1992, when I first wrote on this subject, it was from the vantage point of being the first woman partner in what was then considered—by Los Angeles standards—a large law firm. While around me I saw ever increasing numbers of women law school graduates, they seemed to be only ineffectively absorbed into the profession. True, there were growing numbers of women judges and law professors, but there were almost no women at the top—partners in large law firms, general counsel of significant-sized corporations. Moreover, there were very few minority students in law school and an almost complete absence of minorities in law firm and corporate ranks. For women and minorities, there seemed to be both a glass ceiling and a revolving door.

Now, 14 years later, I was asked to revisit this subject. How has the landscape changed? During the entire intervening period, women have been gushing out of law schools, graduating in numbers about equal to men. So, does the door for women still revolve at the same pace now? And are minorities any better off? How about women lawyers of color, who have been doubly discriminated against?

I do see cause for hope in the legal profession on this subject. We have many more women judges and law professors, excellent role models for women starting out. We have seen a recognition in many places that mentoring for all lawyers is a need and programs have been put in place in many firms to formalize it. We have also frequently been reminded that the lack of diversity of all types is a crisis in our profession, and goals and timetables have been established to address it. Given all the progress that has been made, the reader might ask—why are we still talking about this?

Old ways die hard, and not unless they must. We need to continue to monitor the situation because the glass ceiling is still a barrier. While it has lifted somewhat for women, it is still firmly planted in the profession and especially affects the advancement of minorities, particularly women of color. Women and minorities consistently report that they still must prove their capability over and over again, despite many years of legal experience. When we achieve success, it is still attributed to luck, rather than competence and hard work. Minorities continue to face even greater problems than women in our profession. Some recent statistics tell the story: a National Association of Law Placement survey shows that only 4% of law firm partners and 15% of associates are people of color. That simply is not significant progress toward diversity, by any measure.

Moreover, in the intervening 14 years, there has been a continuation of the trends in the legal profession that I noted then—the ballooning size of firms, the inexorable increase in required billable hours. We have seen relentless consolidation of law firms as globalization continues apace. There is a concomitant decline in the personal commitments that used to be the glue in law firms—more partners leave for greener pastures and fewer clients are secure. It appears that there are diminished personal investments in all firm personnel. To combat these trends, many large firms have mentoring programs, consciously formed in response to observations that associate retention rates, particularly for women and minorities, were far below what they should be. How effective are those? And what is the prognosis for mentoring for the thousands of lawyers who are not in those large firms?

My own situation has changed dramatically since my first writing on this subject. First, I am no longer in the midst of a law firm litigation practice. Indeed, I no longer practice law at all. A half dozen years ago I segued out of litigation practice to work full time as an arbitrator and mediator. Second, having moved outside of the Los Angeles metropolitan area to a smaller community, I have become aware of the diverse practice situations women encounter and the similar and different issues they face here.

This chapter asks whether firms are doing a better job of mentoring women and minorities now than they have in the past. I want to know whether women and minority lawyers now know the questions to ask. Firms need to assure that all attorneys learn better how to connect with those who can help them chart a successful and satisfying professional course. We need to enlist the support of clients to help make mentoring and diversity a reality. We need to export creative solutions to other practice environments, including smaller firms, where mentoring is still hit or miss. To assist those attorneys who want to learn more about mentoring programs and those firms that want to adopt mentoring and diversity plans, a list of resources appears at the end of this chapter.

## Signs of Danger in the Legal Landscape

Many law firms have been slow to adopt modern business methods, and now, it seems, they've gotten mostly the bad ones. There is an increased emphasis on the "bottom line" issues, such as billable hours, without the professional personal commitment that used to glue a firm together for decades. Firms are failing to recognize that turnover of attorneys is enormously expensive.

This is shortsighted management and there is much room for improvement.

It used to be claimed that the dearth of women partners was a "pipeline issue." Women should just bide their time until a significant enough percentage were employed as associates and partnership rates would also climb. But for many years now, close to 50% of law school graduates have been women, and a significant percentage of them have been seeking work in private firms. Yet many firms' retention rates for women are stubbornly low—on average, women comprise only about 17% of large-law-firm partners, and by definition many firms can't boast a percentage even close to that. Firms need to ask themselves: what de-motivates women, what causes them to be shunted aside to "of counsel" positions or leave law firms after just a few years?

The answer is many faceted. Looking at basic area of work allocation, one managing partner observed that without complaining the women lawyers stayed too long in dead end areas of the firm's practice. Male lawyers, meanwhile, took the first case or two they were assigned and then found a way promptly to move on to other areas. Why does this happen? Do the women misread what it takes to be considered a "team player," or is a different standard applied to them? What are the likely effects of this laissez faire staffing?

When women and minorities arrive at a firm, they may find themselves without an established firm structure on which to rely. Meanwhile, they report that the mostly male lawyers identified as being in the "in crowd" get better assignments. Those assignments enable them to hone their skills and in turn enhance their visibility within the firm and with clients. Such practices become a self-fulfilling prophecy; the lawyers outside that group feel that they do not belong. After feelings of alienation continue unrecognized and unaddressed for some time, lawyers up and leave.

Going to a smaller firm may not be the answer. While some smaller firms may be a much better fit for women seeking a balance of work and family life, many smaller firms do not offer other benefits taken for granted at larger employers. For example, I discovered that reasonably sized firms of 15 or 20 lawyers in the smaller legal community where I now live still lack paid time off for maternity leave, a basic for women lawyers.

Weak management practices may also hinder mentoring at smaller firms despite their advantageous size. Since there is no perceived need to institutionalize mentoring programs, it is left to chance if a junior associate connects with a mentor in the firm. Moreover, if the legal practice is not experiencing growth, the firm's practice stagnates. When this occurs, there is no room for new blood and no investment in the development of junior lawyers. A revolving door of associates or contract attorneys is just what these firms want due to the economics of their practices. No one can become a partner until an older partner retires or dies. This is not a recipe for professional growth and career satisfaction for the junior attorney.

Big firm or small, for good or ill, the values of the more senior partners are passed down. When older partners eventually retire and younger ones take their places, the existing firm system is perpetuated. Given these realities, it seems to me necessary to speak of mentoring from two different perspectives—the individual attorney and the firm or other employer. For that reason, I address the subject from both viewpoints—the lawyer and law firm.

## It's Your Career

From the viewpoint of the junior lawyer, the most important point continues to be that mentoring is a long-term proposition. The junior lawyer needs to take personal responsibility for her/his own development and career. Landing a job is only the beginning.

I earlier suggested that women interviewing at law firms needed to ask questions to help them choose firms where they would be more likely to receive mentoring. This continues to be the case.

One obvious question is the number of women partners. If there are no women partners, this is an obvious red flag. Find out why and dig for more information. If there is only one woman, also find out why. Find out from her why she thinks there are not more. Her answers will tell you a lot, not only about the firm, but also about her, particularly whether she is likely to be interested in mentoring other women. A woman partner who says that the reason there are not more women in the firm is because they were not "good enough" or "committed enough" is someone to be avoided. Cross that firm off your list.

Minority lawyers should treat similar statistics and responses in the same way.

In evaluating the firm, you need to be honest with yourself about how much of your career you want to spend there. Is this a job you are taking to pay off your student loans, or do you want to stay at this firm for the foreseeable future? Though some mentoring relationships survive the end of employment, in order for mentoring really to pay off, a long-term commitment helps. Firm partners, too, don't want to invest their time in mentoring someone whom they believe will soon leave. That reluctance explains much of the past refusal of white male partners to mentor junior women or minority lawyers. They could not envision those associates remaining at the firm because they looked different from themselves.

Once you join a firm, continue to be proactive and entrepreneurial. Evaluate the projects you are given based on what you are learning, not just on meeting your immediate work assignments. Women and minorities need to speak up and ask for what they want. Ask for projects that expose you to many partners in the firm and to many different types of issues. Look for possible mentors throughout the firm.

For example, a number of years ago an opportunity came to me as a firm partner to work for the Christopher Commission, formed to conduct a top-to-bottom review of the Los Angeles Police Department and its use of force policy in the wake of the Rodney King beating. I did not need to ask for the help that I obviously needed on this project. Junior lawyers from all areas of my firm's practice volunteered to help. This period of intensely working together formed bonds among us that never would have been forged otherwise and that, in some cases, still exist many years later.

When I speak of mentoring, I am not just speaking here of someone correcting your work for style or content, or critiquing your oral argument. That training is only a start. A mentor is someone who takes an interest in your advancement more broadly, and outside of the workplace as well as within it.

Try these questions to determine whether you really are being mentored in your firm. Is there anyone who really has an investment in your success there? Speaking more concretely, who will take you along to a deposition and write off your time? Who will share their professional contacts with you? Who will introduce you to their clients and praise your importance to the firm in front of them? Who will set aside time for you? Who will promptly return your phone calls or emails? Who will care about your non-firm life, your family, your interests outside the office?

Judged by this standard unfortunately, most law firm relationships are shallow and unsatisfying. You need to demand better for yourself and your career.

## Whom Should You Choose as a Mentor?

If you are in a firm and don't have a mentor, there are ways to find one. The greatest likelihood is that it will be a man. A special report in California's statewide legal newspaper in late 2005 profiled 75 top women litigators. Not surprisingly, the vast majority paid tribute to the male lawyers with whom they had worked. It is still true that most women will be mentored by men since there are still so many more of them in the senior ranks of the profession. And it is not necessarily a bad thing. Besides, if only women mentor women and only minorities mentor minorities, it may actually take longer to inculcate diversity in our profession. Be open to establishing relationships with more senior lawyers and seek opportunities. If golf is not your thing, or you are not invited to play, either suggest a round or look for a charitable or community project on which you and a more senior lawyer can work together.

The project need not be as all encompassing as the Christopher Commission was for me and my team. It can involve working together on a child advocacy project, or advising a political campaign, or counseling an environmental group. Offer to help if it's a subject in which you are genuinely interested.

Be alert to whether those who claim to be your supporters really are. Just because someone declares himself your mentor does not make it so. For example, the male partner who professed to be my "strongest supporter in the firm" never invited me to lunch or any other social activity in the almost two decades I spent there. I submit that that was not a mentoring relationship at all.

Likewise, don't assume that all women are interested in the professional advancement of other women. Some women litigators who are now at the top of the profession had no chance to have woman mentors. That makes some of them want to mentor other women and some of them not want to mentor at all.

It is also prudent to have more than one mentor, for several reasons. Multiple mentors may assist in giving you differing perspectives on the firm's culture, your strengths, opportunities for your growth, and information on activities outside the firm that could advance your career. The other, practical reason to avail yourself of many mentors in the firm is that if you don't have more than one, you could be left high and dry if your mentor leaves.

## New Ways to Mentor

As the number of women and minorities in the profession continues to grow, the focus of mentoring has shifted and expanded, adopting many forms. Whether you have sources of support in your firm or not, it is useful to seek mentors outside, too.

Many women's bar associations have now started mentoring programs for their members. In California, for example, California Women Lawyers, www.cwl.org, has launched a statewide mentoring program, matching more senior and more junior attorneys who seek contacts in different legal communities. To aid the newest of lawyers, the New York Women's Bar Association, www.nywba.org, has a unique program of individual mentors for women law students in their last year of law school and first year of practice.

One problem is that many lawyers fear one-on-one mentoring will be too time consuming and therefore hesitate to make the commitment. For this reason, Women Lawyers of Los Angeles, www.wlala.org, has tried a somewhat different tack. While this organization helps to match more senior with more junior women attorneys for individual mentoring, it also has sponsored a successful program of mentoring "circles" modeled on a program also begun by the New York Women's Bar Association.

WLALA circles are composed of two or three more senior women "anchors" who meet monthly for a brown bag lunch or after work refreshments with a group of more junior women. Since the mentoring relationship is more communal, shared among all of the members, if one member can't make a monthly circle, the meeting goes on without her. Over time, these circles develop into remarkable support groups, sharing joys and supporting members during times of challenge, both personal and professional. Another benefit of bar-sponsored programs is that, as one woman expressed it, in a group not connected to the firm she could more openly express her concerns about the firm's management and how that affected her own professional development.

After a few years of practicing as a mediator and arbitrator, I found that I missed the camaraderie of the law firm environment. I decided to reach out to the women attorneys in my community and began a program of mentoring circles for my local women's bar association, many of the members of which practiced in very small firms or alone. I asked a few more senior women to join me as anchors, and we invited more junior women attorneys to sign up. Though our bar association is small, we have grown to three active circles, each of which meets monthly.

Use your contacts with women faculty and women judges also to advance your career. Volunteer to serve on committees and meet as many other lawyers as you can, both within and beyond your practice specialty. These networks may introduce you to others who can help your career or become your clients. Mentors can alert you to an opportunity to make a zig-zag move out of your firm into an in-house counsel position for a few years, after which you can return to private practice at a more senior level.

Minority lawyers are finding ways to network as well. Bar associations devoted to the concerns of minority lawyers are good resources for mentoring opportunities. In California, the Minority Counsel Program, www.cmpc.org, offers statewide support for minority lawyers as well as firms seeking to increase diversity in their ranks.

## Clients Demand Diversity

A welcome source of support for increasing diversity in our profession is coming from firm clients. In the corporate world, the advancement of women has already been driven by client demands. For example, an October 31, 2005, Wall Street Journal article, *50 Top Women to Watch,* reported that while 50.3% of all managers and professionals are women, just 1.4% of Fortune 500 CEOs and 7.9% of Fortune 500 top earners are women. Those women are concentrated in the fields of consumer products, media, financial services, and retail, places in which women customers are well represented. With a large female customer base, companies are paying attention to how many women managers they have.

In our profession, I suspect that we have already seen a similar advancement of women due to client demands. In the field of employment litigation, for example, a lot of women have achieved prominence. When I mediate or arbitrate employment cases, I see many more women attorneys than I see in commercial cases.

There is mounting evidence that large corporate clients, populated by increasingly diverse employees, managers, and in-house counsel, expect a more gender diverse and ethnically diverse population of lawyers. Those clients are gravitating to the firms that offer diverse attorneys. If clients demand a more diverse law firm, the firm will respond

In fact, clients are emerging as an important key to stepping up the pace of mentoring. We are seeing many large clients that make diversity one of the most important criteria in their selection of outside counsel. Many corporations have signed a Call to Action, www.clocalltoaction.com, announcing that they demand diversity from the law firms they hire. Those firms that lack diversity are losing their business.

While many larger law firms have learned this and are now responding, progress is not as tangible in smaller firms and smaller legal communities where this corporate pressure is less likely to exist. Only time will tell if the techniques used by large corporate clients to ensure diversity will trickle down to the typically smaller businesses that hire firms in these markets.

## Firms Must " Walk the Walk"

From the law firm or other employer perspective, mentoring is a management issue. Well-run firms mentor, knowing that it is a vital component of the development of their lawyers and therefore an investment in the firm's future. It's as simple as that.

Either mentoring is a part of a firm's culture, or it is not. It is not enough to talk about it. If it is left to chance it won't work. The firm's leaders must incorporate mentoring and diversity into the firm's culture as priorities. First and foremost, those aspirations must be tangibly promoted. A firm's compensation system is designed to reward the behavior the firm intends to encourage. If the firm truly values mentoring and diversity, it will structure its compensation to reflect those priorities.

Partners could be held accountable for the number and quality of the relationships they have fostered with junior lawyers, what community and social activities outside the office they have established to include participation opportunities for junior lawyers, and how creatively they have expanded the firm's identification and promotion of its upcoming generation of leaders.

Since the values of the firm are passed down from the more senior partners, the highest ranks of the partnership must be held responsible for creating these priorities and implementing agendas for achieving them. This is the biggest single stumbling block for most firms. There is a gap between what firms say their values are and what behavior they actually reward. Firm compensation systems these days are set up largely to reward those with high billable hours and those who generate business for the firm. Other activities are not encouraged since they are not compensated as highly. Entering associates can find this out, if they bother to ask.

If a firm above all rewards business generation—or the mentality of "eat what you kill"—it is not likely to encourage mentoring or place a high priority on increasing its diversity. Firm partners have a tendency to hoard business rather than hand it off to more junior attorneys and share it as a team.

Rather than just talking about being "team players," the firm should reward teamwork instead of individual accomplishment at compensation time. That reorientation may be especially appealing to women attorneys, who may not like to be seen as "self promoters."

If clients are successfully institutionalized, difficult as that may be to accomplish, then teamwork is rewarded, and junior lawyers work in an atmosphere in which they can grow and develop. Of course, it is difficult to institutionalize work when partners and whole practice groups leave the firm, but this is the challenge firms must face and overcome if they are to be successful.

From the firm's viewpoint there are several prongs to a successful program of retention and advancement of associates and increased partner satisfaction. Sexual harassment policies must be in place and enforced. Work assignments cannot be left to chance. In the assignment of projects, low-grade case assignments need to be rotated. Moreover, powerful partners cannot be allowed to override the system once it is set up.

All firm lawyers need to believe that the firm has an investment in their success. Tangible evidence of this is the firm's promotion of work/life balance through programs such as day care, sabbaticals, and part-time work. To assist attorneys in developing their skills, the firm can offer executive coaching, leadership training, and marketing assistance.

Mentoring should not be assumed to be the "job" of the women or minority lawyers alone. Many more senior women, for example, believe that they have no time for this added responsibility, especially if they are the only or one of only a few senior women. They may be barely holding things together for themselves, in their careers and in their family lives. Mentors throughout the firm need to be developed and encouraged. Numerous resources are available, some of which are listed at the end of this chapter. One, the Project for Attorney Retention, www.pardc.org, is devoted to innovative ideas for balancing work and family commitments.

Law firm mangers should look to who sits on their key committees—the management committee, the partner compensation committee, the executive committee, the associate evaluation committee, for example. Is there more than token representation from women and minorities?

Progress in achieving diversity goals through the hiring and retention of minority lawyers must be measurable. For example, the Association of the Bar of the City of New York, www.nycbar.org/diversity, and the San Francisco Bar Association, www.sfbar.org/diversity, have established diversity goals for women and minorities. The firm can sign up to meet those goals. If the local legal community lacks an organized program to measure progress toward diversity, the firm can enlist the support of other firms and establish one.

To demonstrate its support for diversity, the firm should also require participation in women and minority bar associations and pay for membership in those organizations. It should sponsor local diversity bar events.

If it happens that a woman or minority lawyer does gravitate away to join a minority-owned firm, as many do since they feel more comfortable in that environment, there are many reasons why the firm should not lose touch with the departing lawyer. The firm can refer business to the lawyer after she leaves or can partner on cases with the minority-owned firm to the benefit of both firms.

No law firm should allow itself to be in the dark as to why associates or partners leave. It has long been assumed that women leave law firm practice for "personal reasons." This is not necessarily true. For example, many women decide to leave because they do not see how within the existing structure they can manage both work and family life once they have children. In many cases, their departure could have been averted by better support from their firm, including the ability to telecommute or job share.

Even if the woman does leave for personal reasons, the firm should not believe that it is thereby absolved. The firm's managers should be asking, what happened to the woman lawyer who said she wanted to take a few years off? Did the firm bother to track her when she left? Did firm partners stay in touch with her? Did the firm offer her a re-entry ramp if she were interested in it?

The best way to find out why lawyers leave law firm practice is to ask. The answers to these questions may shine the spotlight on deficiencies in the firm's approach to mentoring. While exit interviews are common in the business world, they are surprisingly rare in law firms. Exit interviews are a way to see if firm policies and structures need attention and if there are issues with some partners or practice groups that need to be addressed. One word of caution here, however; the firm must be prepared to act on what it learns from the lawyers who depart. If the firm is not prepared to act on the appropriate information it receives, it could merely be creating a discoverable document in later litigation if complaints have been consistent.

All of the suggestions here, and many available in the sources listed at the end of this chapter, mean that firms have many resources to achieve better retention of women and minorities. Success requires the commitment of firm management and holding individual partners accountable for the results. This is the only way to ensure that the firm leadership "walks the walk" rather than just "talking the talk" on mentoring and diversity.

## Conclusion

Over the entire length of my professional career, for some thirty-five years, I have mentored others. It has been one of the greatest satisfactions of my life and one that any lawyer can achieve. This satisfying relationship of colleagues over decades gives life to our profession. Mentoring relationships are truly circles. As the relationship matures, you can no longer tell who is mentoring whom. Many of those whom I have mentored in the past I find now open doors for me.

The legal profession has made satisfying progress toward a goal in which women and minorities will have the support of their firms and professional colleagues to develop into the best lawyers they can be, but we are not there yet. We must not only announce our aspirations, but be willing to measure our progress in achieving them.

## Mentoring and Diversity Resources

The list that follows gathers resources for law firms seeking to enhance mentoring:

Snyder and Greene, eds., *The Woman Advocate* (ABA Section of Litigation 1996)

ABA, Commission on Women in the Profession, www.abanet.org/women, produces many publications of interest on the advancement of women:

*The Burdens of Both, The Privileges of Neither*
*Walking the Talk: Creating a Law Firm Culture Where Women Succeed*
*Empowerment and Leadership: Tried and True Methods for Women Lawyers*
*Balanced Lives: Changing the Culture of Legal Practice*
*Fair Measure: Toward Effective Attorney Evaluations*

Publications of Catalyst, www.catalystwomen.org; Note in particular a 2006 report on the results of its 2005 survey of women serving on for profit boards of directors

Nossel and Westfall, *Presumed Equal: What America's Top Women Lawyers Really Think About their Firms* (second edition forthcoming) (the first edition was published by Career Press 1998)

Rikleen, *Ending the Gauntlet: Removing Barriers to Women's Success in the Law* (Thomson Legalworks 2006)

Numerous publications by Ida Abbott, including *The Lawyer's Guide to Mentoring* (NALP 2000), and other publications. www.idaabbott.com

NALP, www.nalp.org, has developed many excellent surveys and publications. Of particular interest is its *Diversity Best Practices Guide* (2006), available for download free from its website.

Association of the Bar of the City of New York, www.Nycbar.org/diversity, *Diversity Signatory Law Firm Benchmarking Report* (2005)

Bar Association of San Francisco, www.sfbar.org, particularly its Glass Ceiling initiative

California Minority Counsel Program, www.cmpc.org, works statewide to promote diversity in law firms. Either It is patterned on the ABA Minority Demonstration Project of the ABA Commission on Racial and Ethnic Diversity in the Legal Profession, www.abanet.org/minorities. Also part of the Commission is the Multicultural Women Attorneys Network, www.abanet.org/minorities/mwan

For the list of corporations promoting diversity, see Call to Action, www.clocalltoaction.com

Corporate Counsel Women of Color, www.ccwomenofcolor.org

National Native American Bar Association (NABA), www.nativeamericanbar.org

The Project for Attorney Retention, an initiative of the Center for Work-Life Law at the UC Hastings College of Law, www.pardc.org

# CHAPTER 11

# There's No Turning Back: Five Practical Ways to Motivate the New Breed of Associates

By Coke Morgan Stewart

## Introduction

Many associates lack motivation. Proof lies in the countless books, articles, and seminars written to help older attorneys work with Generations X and Y. Partners know this is true and yet they scream: "Lack motivation? How can an associate who is paid $150,000 a year (or more) lack motivation!" Easily.

At most law firms, the unwritten contract between the generations has been broken. In the old days, if associates were loyal, competent, and professional, they were invited into the partnership ranks, at which time the apprenticeship ended and they became responsible for making a name for themselves in the community, solidifying their expertise, managing cases, and bringing in business. Over the past ten to fifteen years, this system eroded. More firms have taken to what many call the "New York" model, where partners provide high salaries and short-term job security, rather than realistic opportunities for partnership. Under this model, despite exorbitant associate salaries, partners generally benefit from higher revenue and profits—although many bemoan the loss of collegiality.

A byproduct of the New York model is that associates who face uncertain prospects for partnership are more likely to be "in it for the money." Motivation is down, salaries are up. Many partners long for the good old days when associates were partners' dedicated servants.

Since we can't turn back the clock, partners and associates must learn to cope with—even thrive under—the new model. Associates can design a career that does not implode when they are denied partnership. Partners can learn to motivate associates by being great managers, rather than by relying on the traditional dedication that resulted from more realistic opportunities for partnership.

As Peter Pantaleo, managing partner for the New York office of DLA Piper Rudnick, puts it: "Professionals are free agents and I need to decide how to get them to play on my team." Here are a few ways partners can get associates to play ball.

## Motivate by Tying Compensation to Performance

**Salaries.** Partners are very sensitive—to the issue of associate compensation. They think that associates are generally overpaid and that the enormous salary increases of 1999 and 2000 have hurt law firms. Although firms will never be able to reduce salaries, they can take the same money and allocate it in a better way.

Salaries are a huge motivator for students looking to join law firms. Even a few thousand dollars can impact the decision of which offer to accept. Unable to distinguish among law firms, students use salaries to find the most prestigious firm—in the same way they used U.S. News & World Report rankings to identify the most prestigious law schools. Firms understand this and monitor starting salaries very closely.[1] What firms often do not understand is that once law students become your associates, their attitudes about salaries change.

This change in attitude can be attributed to the combination of lockstep compensation and high job security. Under the lockstep system, associate salaries are fixed regardless of how hard they work or how well they perform. Thus, salaries provide no incentive for associates to work harder or perform better. At the same time, associates know they have an extraordinarily low probability of being fired. This creates a highly frustrating situation for partners who have trouble grasping why associates who are paid $135,000 or more have a casual attitude about their work.

Firms reinforce this problem with the lockstep promotion system. Under this system, associates who meet minimum performance standards are virtually guaranteed a promotion and a significant raise. Worse, the exact amount of the raise is predetermined by when they graduated from law school. How many other businesses pay their young executives according to how many years they have been out of school?

Why do most firms cling to such a system? Because it's easy to implement. Partners do not have to make subjective judgments about each associate's performance. A committee does not have to agree about appropriate salary adjustments for individual associates. And partners do not have to give serious feedback to the associates whom they rely upon to do their work.

It's not all the partners' fault. Associates are not clamoring for change either. They like the certainty of the lockstep system and they like not having to compete against fellow associates.

Unfortunately, while this system may be popular, it's ineffective.

Firms can create a compensation system that is relatively easy to implement, that provides a degree of certainty for associates, and that encourages substantive feedback and healthy competition. In order to create such a compensation system, firms have to change the system of guarantees. After their first year at the firm, associates should be grouped by quality of work rather than the number of years they have been out of law school. To create these groups, firms can use the three categories already informally used to describe associates: junior associates, mid-level associates, and senior associates.

Within the junior associate ranks there would be opportunities for promotions depending on whether partners judge their work as fair, good, or exceptional. After a few years, associates who are performing well would be promoted to mid-level associate. The same pattern would take place among the mid-level associates and the senior associates until the senior associates are promoted to partner. How long an associate remains at each level and how long it takes to become partner depends upon how the associate is progressing. Top-notch associates would be considered for partnership within six or seven years. The majority of associates would be considered for partnership within eight to twelve years.

There are numerous benefits to this system:

- first and foremost, associates will be motivated to perform better because there would be real benefits to generating exceptional work
- associates will truly care about meeting partners' expectations because those partners will be determining their salary
- associates will be able to progress at their own pace
- firms will have a way to identify and reward star performers
- firms will identify and assist laggards earlier in their careers
- associates will know where they stand well before they are considered for partner
- firms will no longer have associates coming up for partner en masse
- firms will move away from evaluating associates primarily on billable hours

One predicament with this model is that firms have to decide what to do with associates who have trouble moving to the next level. Should a firm retain an associate who reviews documents well, but does not write well? There are pros and cons to retaining or dismissing such an associate, but at least under this system the firm would not be paying a fifth-year to perform second-year work. Additionally, the associate would not be sailing along with his class, unaware that his performance is considered weak.

A criticism that I have heard about this model from both partners and associates is that it injects too much subjectivity and politics into associate salary decisions. My response is that this is the reality of professional life—a lesson associates often do not learn until they are considered for partnership. The sooner associates learn to cope with this subjective, political reality the better.

In order to create excitement rather than animosity over implementation of such a system, firms will have to keep their current pay scale as the range for each group and even provide a little more upside. Associates will therefore not perceive that the firm is reducing salaries and may be excited about the opportunity to earn even more.

Dickstein, Shapiro, Morin & Oshinsky implemented a similar system in 2001. Far from hiding its compensation system, Dickstein touts it to prospective associates. (*See* www.dicksteinshapiro.com/careers/attorneys/compensation.) Have associates responded well? Since implementing this change, Dickstein has received consistently high rankings in associate satisfaction. In 2005, the firm was ranked *first* among AmLaw 100 firms in the annual associate survey.

**Bonuses.** If you're not ready to overhaul your compensation system, you might try overhauling your bonus system. Most firms give bonuses almost entirely based on billable hours. Rewarding billable hours makes sense. If an associate bills more hours, she brings in more revenue to the firm, so why not reward high billers? The problem is not in rewarding billable hours, the problem is that most firms use billable hours as the primary or exclusive method to determine bonuses. This encourages associates to value billing hours over all the other aspects of practice that are important to a firm's success. Additionally, it creates a troublesome situation in which mediocre associates may make more money than star associates just because they spent 200 more hours reviewing documents. Associates see this situation all the time and infer that the firms care more about billable hours than quality of work. The truth is firms want high billable hours and top-notch work. The bonus system should more accurately track partners' expectations.

One way to do this is to use hours as a starting point in determining bonuses and increase (or decrease) the bonuses *significantly* according to associates' performance. Performance can take into account many factors such as research, writing, oral advocacy, work ethic, expertise, efficiency, and business development.

In order to minimize drastic variations in bonuses, firms should agree in advance on which factors will be considered and how they will be weighed. Then explain the system to associates so they understand what the firm's expectations are.

## Motivate by Making Nights and Weekends More Bearable

Have you ever noticed that most paralegals and secretaries don't mind working occasional nights and weekends? Some even like to. Are they more committed to their jobs than associates? Of course not—they receive overtime when they work nights and weekends. What would happen if associates received overtime? I can assure you, many would be lining up for more work.

There are numerous reasons, legal and otherwise, why associates should not receive overtime, but there's no reason why law firms should not make working nights and weekends a little more bearable. One way many law firms make working nights and weekends more bearable is by generously reimbursing associates for meals. Associates who have to work late into the evening can soften the blow by ordering a gourmet meal from an upscale restaurant.

Firms can do something even better. Rather than reimbursing associates for their actual dining expenses, give associates a *generous* stipend for meals when they work nights and weekends. Associates would receive a fixed amount per meal and could spend some or all of it on food, save it, or use it when they actually have time to enjoy a nice meal. If they do choose to use the money when they're working late, rather than buying the most expensive meal the firm is willing to pay for, they might think about minimizing their meal expenses and maximizing what goes into their wallets. Associates need these opportunities so that they can learn to think like business owners.

Make the stipend generous enough that it would cover most associates' actual meal expenses, but not so generous that associates would want to work nights and weekends simply to receive it—although don't be surprised if some associates do want to work more nights and weekends after you implement this system.

Another idea is to help associates set up a functional home office. Subsidize the purchase of a laptop, an all-in-one (printer, fax, copier, and scanner), and some basic office furniture. With a functional home office, associates will be able to spend more time at home. Associates who are married would see their spouses more often. Associates with children could have dinner with their families and work after their children go to bed. Associates wouldn't have to go to the office on Saturdays just to print cases, read email attachments, or send a fax. Working nights and weekends will become more bearable and associates may very well bill more hours. An added benefit: when your office is closed due to inclement weather or some other catastrophe, your associates can keep billing.

It's better to subsidize the home office than to buy the equipment outright. With a subsidy, associates can be responsible for choosing what equipment they want and for maintaining it. They would decide whether to spend more for more features. As with the meal stipend, firms would be encouraging associates to think like partners. Instead of buying the most expensive laptop the firm will pay for, the associates will think: "How can I get the most features for the least amount of money?"

After a few years, when the equipment is of little value to the firm, the associates would own it outright. They'll think it's a good deal and it will save the firm the trouble of recycling or redistributing the used equipment.

Subsidizing a home office is not a huge investment; $1,500 would do the trick. You're spending $135,000 or more on their salaries; spend a tiny fraction of that on their home office. You'd probably recoup the expense within a few months.

## Motivate Through Developing Good Relationships

If you want associates to care about you, your clients, and your assignments, you have to care about them, or at least make them think you do. The stronger the personal connection, the more likely the associate will be to help you in a pinch. Treat associates well and reap the rewards.

A partner walks into an associate's office a few days before Thanksgiving. The partner is desperate. He needs someone to help prepare for expert witness depositions. The associate is not assigned to this case, and her plate is full with other work. She has plans to travel out of town for the weekend. She helps him anyway—willingly. Why? He's an important partner and she can't say no? No. It's because this partner is a friend. Helping out is not about fulfilling an obligation; it's about helping a friend in need.

A partner calls an associate. He needs immediate research and help late into the evening. The associate is not assigned to the case and has a meeting that could provide an easy out. The associate agrees to help. Why? It's the associate's duty to help a partner in an emergency situation? No. It's because the associate has worked with this partner in the past and he has treated him well.

Associates will put forth all sorts of excuses (legitimate and otherwise) to get out of work they don't want to do and to avoid people with whom they don't want to work. Partners have very little recourse when this happens.

Some partners will think this is backwards. Partners say, "Jump!" Associates should ask, "How high?" Unfortunately, motivating this way only works for the most powerful partners and it doesn't work very well for them. It generates bitterness that leads to less cooperation, not more.

Even if you dislike working with certain associates because you think their work is marginal, it still pays to treat them with respect because you never know when they might be able to help you in a pinch. You might have no choice but to call on the services of a weak performer. In fact, it's often the associates who produce "so-so work" who have the time to help in an emergency.

Jim Hibey, a litigation partner with whom I worked for many years, had a gift for developing friendships with his associates (as well as with his partners, clients, and even opposing counsel). One way he accomplished this was to make time for small talk. He never began a meeting or conversation with business. He was funny, sincere, and a little irreverent. He ate lunch with associates. He also regularly entertained associates in his home. As a result, most of the associates he worked with knew his wife and his children and he knew their spouses and their children. Although Hibey did not develop friendships with associates simply to motivate them, that's the effect his goodwill had. Hibey could call on a dozen or more associates to drop what they were doing to help him in a pinch.

Hibey recently became chair of the partnership committee at his firm. What's the first thing he did? He made sure someone from the committee personally met with each associate who was up for partner. Never underestimate the power of relationships—even relationships with the most junior associates can inure to a senior partner's benefit.

## Motivate by Rewarding Great Work with Better Work, Not More Work

I recently asked a partner how he rewards associates for great work. He said, "I give them more work." I then asked how he punishes associates who do mediocre work: "I give them less work." More work is a reward if associates have time to manage it. If they don't, it's a punishment that can have the unintended consequence of driving your best associates away.

Case in point: a great associate left a prestigious law firm after a few years even though he liked the firm, his work, and his peers. He left because he was overworked. For the first year or so when he was new, his schedule was fine, but after partners found out he did great work, they buried him in it. All the partners in his group wanted him to do their work and because many associates in his group had left, there was no one to help. No one at the firm monitored the situation and the associate wasn't the type to complain. The associate eventually left and went "in-house." Now that he's been away from a law firm for over a year, part of him wishes he were back, but he wants a career where he'll be rewarded, not punished, for great work.

When partners think about how to manage their best associates, they need to think strategically. Like any valuable asset, associates need to be treated well so they will stay in good condition. How would you treat a fine automobile? Would you drive it into the ground or maintain it so it would last for years?

Consider the story of two partners. They own the same three cars: a Porsche, a Toyota, and a new model made by a new manufacturer. The Porsche is a high-performance car and a classic that can perform well forever. The Toyota is a great, reliable car that they know will perform well for at least 10 years. The new model has no performance record.

Partner 1 only wants to drive the Porsche. It's the best car and he wants the best all the time. Every time he needs to go somewhere, whether it's the garden center or a drive on the open road, he takes the Porsche. Only when the Porsche is unavailable does he drive the Toyota. He tries to avoid the new model at all costs. After a few years, the Porsche is wearing out. It's full of dings, has high mileage, and needs serious maintenance. On the other hand, the Toyota is doing very well. It has a decent amount of miles, but it's in great shape. The new model isn't doing so well. Because the partner seldom drives it, it won't start. The lines are clogged. The belts are rotten. If the partner wants the same performance and coverage from his cars, he's going to have to replace the Porsche and find another new model.

Partner 2 also loves his Porsche, but he knows that if he wants to keep it a long time he's going to have to keep the mileage in check, store it in the garage, and make sure it receives regular maintenance. So Partner 2 uses his Porsche for his most important trips and for long drives on the open road where it can really perform. He uses his reliable Toyota for less important trips and errands. He uses the new model for errands closer to home so he can find out how it performs.

Most partners are like Partner 1. They want the best performance all the time, so they ask their best associates to handle almost every assignment they have. They don't allow these associates to delegate any significant part of the assignments because they want the best. If they wanted less than the best, they would have asked another associate for help.

Partners who operate this way often lose their best associates because the associates burn out and start looking for other jobs. Unfortunately for these partners and their firms, there are plenty of other firms, companies, and government agencies looking for used Porsches. After several Porsches leave the firm, partners are left with too many late-model Toyotas—associates who partners want to retain but may not want to promote to partner. Partners are forced to go out and find new Porsches and new, new models. However, unlike Porsches and new model cars, associates, especially exceptional associates, are hard to find and a lot more expensive to replace.

If partners want their star associates to stick around longer, they have to be strategic. This means giving them the most challenging, interesting, and sophisticated assignments they have time to handle. They can't give their best associates every assignment they have or even every important assignment they have. In order to keep these best associates from burning out, partners have to give the work that the best associates do not have time for to other associates who may not produce the best work, but who are adequate for the job. Partners will also have to give some work to associates who are unknown quantities. In fact, partners should give work to these new models because some of them may turn out to be Porsches.

Firms can implement this strategy by monitoring their best associates' hours. In the same way that firms monitor the hours of low billing associates to help bring them up to pace, firms should monitor the hours of their best associates to make sure they're not burning out. Most people agree that a 2,400 pace is not sustainable long term, so if your best associates bill more than 200 hours a month two months in a row, visit them to see if they need help. If they consistently bill more than 200 hours, speak to their supervising partners. Often the supervising partners do not even know the associates are working at such a high pace. If you think 200 hours per month is too low, choose another benchmark, but do begin to monitor your associates' hours.

One response to this suggestion is that associates need to take responsibility for their own schedule. As one partner commented in a recent article about billable hours: "The quality of your life is *your* responsibility! It is not my responsibility to give you a quality of life."

The problem with this response is that the best associates, the ones who are considered the most dependable, are the least likely to complain about their hours. So if you put this responsibility on associates, firms will end up with the same problem they have now: star associates leaving because they are burned out.

If firms take this approach, their best associates will thrive and their adequate associates and new associates will want to become best associates. They will see that the reward for great work is better work, not more work. Firms that implement this approach will end up with more Porsches and fewer late-model Toyotas.

## Motivate by Helping Associates Find a Sense of Purpose

Every year *Fortune* magazine issues its list of "The Best Places to Work." Read about those successful companies and you will learn that they have one thing in common: their employees have a sense of purpose. Most law firms aren't trying to become best places to work. They're trying to become profitable places to work. Unfortunately, what many law firms overlook is that motivated employees make their employers exceptionally profitable.

The publicly traded companies on *Fortune's* "best" list (accounting for about half of the list) outperform other public companies in 1, 3, 5, and 10 year returns by a huge margin—*double* the S&P. Additionally, the companies on *Fortune's* list stay in business *four times longer* than the average company. We're not talking about mom-and-pop companies. *Fortune* only includes companies with more than 1,000 employees.

So help your associates find a sense of purpose and you'll be improving your own bottom line. I'm not suggesting that partners become guidance counselors. Associates must find meaning for themselves, but partners can play an important part in the process by following the suggestions below.

**Articulate the Vision of the Firm.** Firms need to articulate their vision. It's not nonsense. Look at a list of the largest firms in the United States. Take away profits. Take away geography. How do you distinguish one firm from another? How do you distinguish your law firm? To have a sense of purpose, associates need to understand why they are working for one firm over another.

I asked a senior partner what distinguished his firm from others in its treatment of associates. He said the firm offered associates challenging work early in their careers. Unfortunately, every firm makes a similar claim. Choose something specific. For example, almost all firms have associates committees with associate representation, but these committees typically spend their time on the usual associate gripes. At Latham & Watkins, the associates committee makes recommendations for partnership—and, according to Washington, D.C., managing partner Rick Bernthal, those recommendations have been accepted without alteration for 20 years. "We're telling associates they will have a deep say in how the firm is run. Other firms say that, too. But as far as I know, we're literally the only law firm in the world that entrusts a committee—half of whose members are themselves associates—with the ultimate decision: who makes partner in the firm, and who does not."

Many law firms try to articulate their vision through their website. Often the message sounds generic. Here are two exceptions:

> We value winning. In litigation there are winners and losers, and we do not sleep well when we lose. When clients hire trial lawyers, they do not want someone to "handle" their cases; they want someone to win them. They want someone who hates losing at least as much as they love winning. . . . .

You may like or dislike this philosophy, but it undoubtedly helps the firm communicate with its associates. Here's another reason to care. The firm in question—Quinn Emanuel—began with four lawyers in 1986. It now 50 times that size. With per partner profits well above $1 million (a record $1.9 million in 2004), Quinn's one of the most profitable law firms in the country. One reason Quinn has been able to grow so quickly and so profitably is its ability to articulate how it is unique.

How about this statement from the recruiting page of another firm's website:

> [We have] a long tradition of sophisticated legal practice in an informal, friendly atmosphere. The high morale and unusual degree of personal satisfaction experienced by our lawyers arises from our client-centered approach to lawyering that teaches personal responsibility for clients. We expect our lawyers to "own" their clients' problems and do their late night worrying. Enthusiasm and a spirit of camaraderie pervade the firm. Our firm values family and desires that all our lawyers maintain an appropriate work-life balance.

While many firms are turning away associates who seek work-life balance, Miles & Stockbridge embraces it as a distinguishing feature. The firm is bent on combining challenging professional opportunities with high job satisfaction. John Frisch, chairman of the firm, states: "All else being equal, we'll sacrifice dollars to keep our firm culture." That's a powerful statement. But the firm hasn't had to sacrifice dollars because it has very low attrition and per partner profits that have been increasing substantially for years. Miles & Stockbridge also has the recognition to back up its claim of great culture. The firm has been ranked among the top ten in associate satisfaction year after year. It's no surprise then that Miles & Stockbridge is able to articulate a vision for associates that not only distinguishes the firm, but also sounds genuine.

**Articulate the Vision of the Practice Group.** Another great way to help your associates find a sense of purpose is to promote the vision of your practice group. Call it a mission statement. Call it a strategic plan, but put it in writing and share it with associates. Most associates enter large law firms with no idea of what expertise they want to develop. It's another reason that so many associates lack motivation. They still haven't decided what they want to do.

Practice groups that identify their mission will help associates decide whether they want to join the group and will then motivate the associates who do join the group to fulfill that mission. On the other hand, associates who have no idea what their group's goals are can hardly be expected to advance them. I know several associates who spent years developing expertise in government contracts not knowing that their firm was phasing out the practice. I know other associates who developed relationships with clients that the firm would not pursue because of conflicts. The associates had no idea what the mission of the group was.

**Articulate the Vision of the Matter.** Stephen Covey, the outrageously successful author of *The Seven Habits of Highly Effective People*—a book which has sold over 15 million copies—offers a lot of advice, but one of his best tips is to "organize and execute around priorities." How many associates understand the goals of their matters? Most have only a vague sense of what the partner and client are trying to accomplish. If partners *really* want to motivate their associates, they need to articulate the goals of their cases very clearly.

Take the example of Alan Fisch. A few years ago, while Fisch was still in his mid-thirties, he led a small team, comprised mostly of associates, to a $62 million jury verdict against Microsoft—the eighth-largest federal jury verdict of 2003. How did he do it? One way was by searing the goals of the case into the mind of every associate on the team. Fisch had a formula describing how each of the major elements of the liability case fit into his damages theory. He repeated the formula in almost every team meeting he held. There was never any doubt among team members how they were going to develop the case. The results speak for themselves. By continuing to articulate the case mission, he empowered the associates to have a positive impact on the outcome of the case.

**Explain the Purpose of Assignments.** You might wonder whether individual assignments should have mission statements. Yes—but just don't call it one. Ross Guberman, one of the country's most acclaimed legal writing experts, advises law-firm partners to explain how they plan to use written work product before the associate starts writing it. Seems like simple advice, but how many partners follow it? Partners who do, don't receive law review articles when they want a two-page memo. The principle holds true for all assignments. You'll be amazed at the effect it has on the quality of associates' work.

## Conclusion

Some partners who read these suggestions will undoubtedly still be thinking that motivating associates is not their problem. Or as one partner said, "It's not my responsibility to give you a quality of life." Unfortunately, these partners are living in the past, when partners made far less money and far more associates became partners.

A new model has taken hold of law firms and there's no turning back. Partners who adapt and learn to motivate the new breed of associates will be able to take advantage of associate talent and enjoy incredible financial gains and great personal satisfaction. Those who do not? They are likely to remain frustrated.

Remember the advice of DLA managing partner Peter Pantaleo: "Professionals are free agents and I need to decide how to get them to play on my team." Implement these ideas and you'll be able to recruit and motivate the best associates. They may even decide to stay on your team for a few more seasons.

## Endnote

1. In 2006, large firms raised starting salaries again from $125,000 to $135,000 for first-year associates.

# CHAPTER 12

# Developing Young Lawyers

**By Dean Zipser**

## Introduction

I doubt that you can find anyone in the legal profession who would not agree with the need for and importance of developing young lawyers. Despite such a universal sentiment, however, we are not doing the job we must—to the detriment of all involved. And, unfortunately, it appears to be growing more and more difficult each year to reverse the trend. But it is something we must do. Indeed, the success and prosperity of law firms and the reputation and quality of the legal profession itself depend on it. Moreover, I submit that taking the time and effort to develop our young lawyers not only is necessary, but also is enjoyable and rewarding—both personally and professionally.

Developing and retaining our young lawyers must always be a top priority. It needs the same attention and resources as those devoted to other aspects of firm's practice development, such as targeted clients, practice areas, and industries. And maintaining that priority is more critical now than ever before. Mentoring, training, and developing our young lawyers is becoming more difficult every year. Firms are getting larger. Billable hour requirements continue to go up. Clients are more demanding.

There are more pressures on all of us. Among newer lawyers, disillusionment, impatience, and, ultimately, dissatisfaction are on the rise, making retention all the more difficult.

Our newest lawyers represent the future of our firms and our profession, yet who is taking responsibility to help them develop? Law schools do not necessarily train lawyers for actual practice, and leaving junior associates to "sink or swim" on their own does not result in their becoming better—and certainly not happier—lawyers. More than ever, developing young lawyers must be a priority. It is not easy. But it is important—indeed essential—and it can be the most rewarding aspect of one's career.

## The Need for Development

While law schools prepare students to think like a lawyer, they can only go so far in preparing a student to be one. Clinical courses certainly help, and externships and judicial clerkships are invaluable. A summer clerkship at a law firm provides insight to the practice. But none of these is a substitute for the development young lawyers need, and must have. The need for development of new lawyers includes, but goes far beyond, ensuring the adequate training and experience in substantive areas of the law. Developing young lawyers should include every facet of the practice of law—from interacting with colleagues and clients, to conduct outside the office. In addition to learning how to draft a complaint and take a deposition, for example, young lawyers need to be trained in areas such as professionalism and ethics.

The need for training and development both increases and becomes more difficult every year, as firms increase in size, billing rates increase, and the cases get more sophisticated. Hours requirements continue to rise, placing more pressures on all of us to spend our time on client billable matters, to the exclusion, or at least minimalization, of the rest of what it means to be a lawyer. As rising associate salaries and billing rates accompany increasing hours' requirements, there is further strain on developing young lawyers. Partners are under additional pressure to do work themselves, and avoid write-downs. Associates, on the other hand, are under increasing pressure to "bill their hours," which sends a message that development and training are secondary. And things like attending seminars, bar association events, doing *pro bono* work, and getting involved in the community tend to fall by the wayside.

When I was a young associate, I had the privilege of "tagging along" with the partner with whom I was working. I would be able to attend and observe court appearances, depositions, and client meetings, among other things. While that still happens today for others, it does not happen as much, or nearly enough. Too often, associates in large firms find themselves assigned to massive cases where their responsibilities are limited. While being part of a big litigation team is an invaluable learning experience, other facets of a young lawyer's training and development cannot be ignored.

Further, mobility among lawyers has increased over the past 25 years. In addition to movement between firms, we are seeing more and more associates leave the practice of law altogether. Without the necessary mentoring, training, and development, associates are more likely to see their work as just a job, rather than a career, and not feel a part of the noble profession they chose.

Yet, despite the increased pressures, demands, and hours, the development of young lawyers does not have to take a back seat. Lawyers can be trained, firms can prosper, and those involved can have incredibly rewarding experiences in the process.

Developing young lawyers is by no means a one-way street. Development must start with the motivation and drive of the young lawyers. They must want to develop, and the firm or organization or individual senior lawyer must not only facilitate that process, but also support and encourage it.

## Some Suggestions on What to Do, and Ways to Do It

There are a number of things that firms and organizations can and should do to develop young lawyers. While specific programs will necessarily differ among firms, one foundational aspect must be present in each—a supportive and encouraging environment.

As part of the ABA "Raise the Bar" colloquium that kicked off this project, our working group identified the overriding need for an environment that enables all lawyers to reach their full potential by taking charge of their professional development with the support of the firm. In other words, development must become part of the firm's culture—from the most senior partner to the most junior associate. Young lawyers should both be expected to, and supported in their efforts to, develop professionally.

To be successful, the commitment must be real. Merely paying lip service to development will not get it accomplished. On the other hand, once the real commitment is there, the rest will follow easily.

While it can be debated what is the cart and what is the horse, it is clear that all of the planning and programs will not be successful without motivated participants. Although it can be argued that the programs are needed to motivate the young lawyers, and a good mentor will provide the direction and encouragement, the young lawyer remains the single most important participant in this triangle he or she forms with the firm and the firm's lawyers. Fortunately, while many finish law school without a firm grasp of the nature of the practice, nearly all young lawyers are eager and anxious to learn.

Developing young lawyers requires a comprehensive and broad approach. It should include, among other things, practice training—through both formal and informal programs—a constructive feedback and evaluation system, a case load that contributes to the associates' development, and a mentoring program. Just as no two individuals are alike, nor should there be a single developmental program implemented by all firms and individuals. One size does not fit all. What works for some will not work for others. Rather, training and mentoring of new lawyers will depend on the person, firm, and organization. With that in mind, I offer some suggestions to consider.

**Formal Training.** The most obvious, and perhaps common, method to develop young lawyers is through "formal" training. This includes both outside and in-house programs. Both should be an essential part of any development program.

The scope of outside seminars is quite broad, and young lawyers should be encouraged to seek out and attend those relevant to their practice. To that end, bar associations and other professional organizations should be encouraged to regularly develop and present programs of interest to young lawyers. The Orange County Bar Association, for example, holds two "Bridging the Gap" programs each year. These programs are specifically directed toward newly admitted attorneys, and cover a broad range of subject matter, as well as professionalism and ethics.

Although outside training seminars may be a logical and obvious developmental tool, they are underutilized by young lawyers. First, many do not receive the encouragement to attend them. Second, the billable hour requirements act as a governor on attendance. Associates are constantly faced with a choice of spending an extended lunch period attending a seminar or continuing to work on the billable projects they have on their desk. The seminars typically lose out. One easy "fix" would be to give associates some form of "credit" for attending training programs beyond simply recording it as "non-billable time." Whether it's treating the time as equivalent to billable time or requiring a certain minimum of seminar hours, attendance should be encouraged and fostered in a tangible way.

Firms also need to develop and provide a comprehensive formal training program for its associates. While attending outside seminars should be strongly encouraged, attending in-house seminars should be mandatory. Indeed, this is the opportunity for the firm and its partners to teach the associates what they believe is most important to learn.

The training program should run continuously throughout the year and, ideally, track the stages of a matter from beginning to end. For example, a litigation training program should include sessions on pleadings, both complaints and responsive pleadings, legal writing, oral advocacy, written and oral discovery, settlement, and trial. For example, a hypothetical fact situation could be developed and then used as a basis for teaching the various aspects. At larger firms, the associates could be placed and work in teams, perhaps also with an assigned partner to be a guide and resource along the way. Although such a program would perhaps be more time-consuming, it might be much more rewarding and instructive, and would provide a boost to morale in the process.

A successful in-house training program benefits greatly from the participation of both partners and associates. In fact, the most beneficial in-house training seminars occur when in addition to the associates being trained, a number of partners attend. That way, issues presented can be discussed and debated among the partners—as we all know there is no one way to do things, and none of us have learned it all. Again, partner participation—both as presenters and attendees—should, ideally, follow naturally from the firm's emphasis on an environment supporting professional development.

Besides offering a variety of subject matter, in-house training programs should strive to offer a variety of formats. Simply holding one lecture after another, no matter how important, will lose effectiveness. To the extent possible, training programs should be interactive and participatory. We have found it helpful to enlist an associate to help plan the program itself, and then act as one of the presenters.

While all of the partners should be encouraged to participate in the training, the development of the program should be left to a qualified and motivated person or group. More and more, large firms, recognizing the importance of formal training and professional development, are hiring individuals specifically and exclusively for the purpose of developing and implementing training programs and monitoring professional development. Of course, these individuals cannot do it all; they must have the support and participation of the lawyers.

**The Importance of Constructive Feedback and Evaluations.** Timely and constructive feedback is one of the most important factors to developing young lawyers. Like so many other aspects of development, feedback can and should be both formal and informal, structured and unstructured.

Both the firm and the young lawyers benefit when the young lawyers are kept fully apprised of their progress. At a minimum, this requires a formal, structured feedback program. Such a program, however, should by no means be a substitute for case-by-case, or assignment-by-assignment, feedback. Rather, such a program provides an institutional opportunity to ensure feedback on a systematic and uniform basis.

The feedback should be constructive and helpful; the more specific the better. For example, comments like "improve your writing" will not help develop young lawyers. Rather, they should be provided with specific examples of how to make their work product better and what steps are necessary to further their progress within the firm. And the partners providing feedback should be held accountable and be willing to discuss their comments with the associates. The greatest value of a feedback system occurs when the atmosphere of the firm and the process is one of openness. Associates should feel welcome to ask specific questions about their development and advancement within the firm, and should expect and receive honest responses. The feedback also should be timely and periodic, rather than sporadic. This is especially critical for junior associates, who need more regular attention.

Ideally, this structured periodic feedback program will add nothing but confirmation to what the associates and partners already know, that is, with a healthy environment and the willing participation among the partners, associates will not be surprised when they receive their "formal" evaluations. One would hope that they will have been receiving feedback regularly up to that point—from all of the lawyers for whom they have worked—so that the formal evaluation will merely be confirmation, and an opportunity to discuss development in a formal setting. In fact, the evaluation itself should be an opportunity for a dialogue: This should be an opportunity for the associates to voice any questions or concerns about their development.

While a structured evaluation program is essential, there is no substitute for the benefit of on-the-spot, immediate, task-based feedback. Nor should the existence of a formal program be an excuse not to give task-based feedback—particularly to the young lawyers. Each and every task provides an opportunity for feedback and an exchange between partner and associate. Each task is a learning and training experience. This task-based feedback need not be overly lengthy or comprehensive. It is more important that it be timely and constructive. For example, when editing, a partner should make sure to explain to the associate the changes made to the written product at appropriate places in the document. At times, even a single word can make a world of difference in a brief; the associate should understand why in this case that was so.

The feedback to the associate also must be put in context. Was the work product appropriate for the lawyer's level of experience? Merely handing back the written product with edits or discussing the changes made may not tell the whole story. For example, I am a notoriously heavy editor. Thus, I believe it is important to remind associates that the amount of red ink on a document does not necessarily reflect my level of satisfaction with it. Often, I will make heavy edits to a document, yet feel that the associate did a good job drafting it—and certainly produced work product that was appropriate for his or her level of experience. Quality feedback should include the "big picture," so that reality matches perception. Too often, partners feel they have given feedback by noting specific improvements, but failing to put those comments in context; in turn, associates later are surprised by the overall message of their formal review because the feedback they received along the way did not address developmental concerns and how the work product matched up to expectations.

Obviously, there will not be time for a formal "sit-down" for each and every assignment. Nevertheless, it is important that both partner and associate do not have different perceptions of the associate's work on that assignment. If the project needed improvement, the associate should know what and why.

Like the structured evaluation process, the task-based feedback process is a two-way street. Here, the young lawyer also plays a critical role in his or her development. Although it would be nice to expect every partner or supervising lawyer to provide constructive and instantaneous feedback on each and every assignment, that is neither realistic nor practical. That said, however, a young lawyer interested in his or her development should not hesitate to solicit feedback on a regular and ongoing basis, and the environment of the firm or office should encourage it. Using the same example of an edited brief, developing lawyers should not simply ensure that the partners' changes are made in the final document, but they should strive on their own to understand why the revisions have been made. And if they do not understand, they should ask.

**There Is No Substitute for Experience.** All of the formal training in the world, whether through outside seminars, or in-house programs, can only go so far toward developing young lawyers. There is no substitute for the actual experience gained "on the job." We learn more, and faster, by doing, rather than listening.

Yet, here too, the task is much more difficult now than in the past. Current demands on our practice make it more and more difficult to give meaningful responsibility to young lawyers. As cases get larger, partners and other more senior lawyers are forced to take greater responsibility. But we must remain focused on and dedicated to giving younger lawyers the opportunities that will enable them to develop as lawyers.

Despite the ever increasing demands, it can be done. To begin, there is nothing wrong or detrimental to the development of younger lawyers with having them play a lesser role on some larger cases. Being part of a large team, and learning how the different parts come together, are vitally important in their development.

At the same time, that does not mean that a new associate should be consigned to one large case after another, or spend every waking hour in front of the computer or in a warehouse staring at document after document. Even when the young lawyer is the most junior member of a large team, a young lawyer should, whenever possible, also have the opportunity to participate in, or at least observe, various events in the matter and have the opportunity to attend and participate in team meetings and strategy sessions—even if it means that the time will not be billed to the client. In this way, lawyers who may be just reviewing documents can still feel like part of the team. You might also be surprised how much the associate who has been reviewing client documents for several weeks has learned about the case and what that person may have to offer the team.

Firms and individual partners should encourage "shadowing." Young lawyers should have regular opportunities to observe more senior lawyers in court and taking depositions, meeting with the client and with opposing counsel. It can be quite demoralizing for a young lawyer to spend hundreds of hours on a matter only to see the more senior lawyers be the ones to go off to court, or to work feverishly in connection with a trial, yet never be offered the opportunity to even visit the courtroom. Besides the obvious training benefits, bringing young lawyers along builds teamwork and increases loyalty and job satisfaction. While I am not suggesting that young lawyers become a permanent appendage, and I recognize that client and case sensitivities will not permit multiple lawyers in all instances, too often partners or other senior lawyers are overly reluctant to include younger lawyers or, even worse, do not even think to do so.

Here, again, the environment of a firm and the incentives it establishes can help immensely. Partners should be encouraged and rewarded, rather than discouraged, from training and involving young lawyers. Similarly, no one should be penalized when junior lawyers accompany more senior lawyers, even if the time cannot ultimately be billed to the client. Whether the firm utilizes a "training" or "shadowing" non-billable number, or does not mark down a partner who writes off time based on training, both partners and associates should not face resistance for spending time on training through case work.

While young lawyers benefit greatly from being part of a large team, they should also be regularly afforded the opportunity to work on smaller matters. They will be able to take greater responsibility on those individual matters. But that does not mean that the young lawyers should go completely without guidance. Habits and styles are being formed, and it is important for senior lawyers to be there to steer the young lawyers through these particular new experiences. (I sometimes liken it to being the lifeguard standing by offering words of advice and encouragement while a child learns to swim.) Often, supervising young lawyers handling these types of cases takes more of a partner's time than may be called for by the matter itself, but it is an investment worth making. Not doing so is a disservice to the young lawyer and, ultimately, to the firm itself.

One wonderful way to provide young lawyers actual experience is through *pro bono* matters. While a firm's regular case load and clientele may not afford young lawyers sufficient opportunities to handle smaller matters, there is always a pressing need for *pro bono* legal assistance—regardless of practice area or geography. Young lawyers not only can learn their craft, they can "do good" in the process. Too many people do not have meaningful access to our legal system, and their rights are not protected simply because they cannot afford a lawyer.

Here, again, firms can provide an invaluable asset. *Pro bono* work not only should be encouraged, it should "count" the same as billable work. And, just as with billable client work, partners should be there to guide and supervise as needed.

To ensure the proper development of a young lawyer, case assignments and responsibility cannot be a mechanical task. While the nature of the assignments to be delegated naturally is reflective of the specific matters in the office at any particular time, the individual(s) responsible for associate assignments should, to the extent possible, tailor specific case assignments with the development of the individual lawyer in mind. Providing a mix of work that is appropriate for that specific young lawyer is critical for a number of reasons.

Lawyers develop at different rates. Some are able to both accept responsibility and perform well from the outset. Others do well in some areas, but not as well in others. And still others are reticent to take responsibility and may not catch on to the nuances of practice as quickly. Aided by an involved mentor, the assigning lawyers should take care to give assignments that are appropriate to the young lawyers' abilities and responsibilities so that they can develop to the greatest extent possible.

Particularly at the early stages of their career, young lawyers will benefit greatly from being exposed to a number of different supervising lawyers and their respective styles of practice. While working relationships and substantive specialties develop over time (and ever more quickly these days than previously), new lawyers should have the opportunity to work for and receive guidance from as many different lawyers as reasonably possible. As each individual lawyer is unique, he or she will be developing his or her own unique style of practice. The more lawyers and styles they are able to observe and learn from, the greater their development.

Creating a mix of assignments and cases with different lawyers should not, however, be an end in and of itself. Rather, it should be a factor to consider when assigning work so that new lawyers receive a full breadth of experience—particularly during the first few years of practice. Quite often, strong working relationships develop between partners and associates, many times driven by work styles or substantive legal areas. Those relationships should be nurtured.

Through a development program and the individuals responsible for administering it, the mentors, and the partners, each associate should have his or her own "development plan." That plan should be reexamined periodically and adjusted as needed. For example, does the lawyer lack work experience in one area (such as depositions or court experience), or need work in certain practice or substantive areas? Case assignments should reflect and further that development plan—a plan of which the young lawyer should not only be apprised, but also, help to create and achieve. In the end, thoughtful and appropriate matter assignments will play a key role in the young lawyer's development and will improve both morale and retention.

**The Intangibles—The Need for Mentors and Role Models.** The value of mentoring cannot be understated. And the benefits are not limited to young lawyers. Indeed, one of the most wonderful things about mentoring is that, while it is important to begin a mentoring relationship early on, the relationships and the benefits from mentoring continue throughout your career. Here, again, I have been blessed to have a number of different lawyers guide me throughout my career with respect to various aspects of the practice and profession. Although some of my mentors naturally developed through my firm, there are many outside the firm who helped me as well.

No one is too old or experienced not to have a mentor; nor does anyone have an excuse not to be one. Mentors can take different roles and serve different functions depending upon the individuals. For example, for a brand new lawyer, it helps to have a mentor just to learn what it means to be a lawyer, as most new lawyers beginning their career have no idea what to expect from the practice. And then there is so much more than the mere nuts and bolts of the practice. Young lawyers need guidance, mentoring, and training to learn how to conduct themselves responsibly and professionally, how to best serve their clients, and how to learn to get and give the most to the profession.

Although, ideally mentor/mentee relationships should develop naturally, firms and organizations still should have a formal program in place. Each new lawyer in a medium-sized or large firm should have an individual he or she can utilize as a mentor. The "assigned" mentor should be chosen carefully, with input from the professional development group. The aim should be to provide a mentor who will give the new attorney the greatest opportunity to develop and succeed. Certainly, the number-one requirement should be a lawyer who possesses the requisite skills and motivation to do the job. Indeed, having an assigned mentor who does not follow through may be more disenfranchising for a new attorney than not to have anyone at all. The mentors' charge should be bold and broad. Mentors have the responsibility to help the new lawyer succeed within the firm and in the profession.

The roles and responsibilities of both mentor and mentee should be clearly articulated. In addition to clarifying expectations, creating a defined list of responsibilities creates accountability, and should help ensure that the job gets done.

Being a mentor is a job that must be taken seriously. It cannot be "phoned in." Rather, a successful mentoring relationship requires time, and a lot of face time. Mentors should meet regularly with their mentees, taking them out to lunch, and otherwise checking in to see how they are doing.

The mentoring program should be part of the overall development system, and the group or individual in charge of the professional development should monitor the progress of the mentor program and the individual relationships. Like the formal training programs, having such a person in place will help ensure that the mentors are carrying through on their responsibilities, and that the young lawyers are receiving the desired benefits.

Having a mentor program in place is by no means a substitute for the responsibility of every other partner and senior attorney to guide and mentor new lawyers. Indeed, as I have noted elsewhere, this should come naturally—particularly if the firm fosters a constructive and cooperative attitude. Such an environment will enable other mentoring relationships to develop and flourish naturally. Indeed, the greatest value to a formal mentor program probably is in the first several months to one year after the new attorney joins the firm. After that point, they often will develop mentoring relationships independently—a result that should be encouraged to the same extent as the formal mentoring program.

**Outside the Courtroom, the Boardroom, and the Office.** Developing young lawyers involves more than training them in the practice of law. Young lawyers should be assisted in their development as a member of the profession itself. While the firm mentors can and should play a major role here, the responsibility for this part of a young lawyer's development does not rest only with the firm, company, or employer. Rather, professional organizations can and should step forward—as many already have done.

For example, during my recent year as president of the Orange County Bar Association, one of our initiatives was to revitalize our mentoring program. A survey of our membership—some

9,800 members and growing—confirmed my suspicion that lawyers need and want their bar association to step forward to assist in mentoring younger lawyers. Thus, we developed a program within our bar association where more experienced lawyers would each mentor a new member. In contrast to development within a law firm, this program specifically *does not* focus on substantive legal practice. Rather, the program is designed to help younger lawyers develop outside the office—from law office management to community involvement.

Given that most lawyers do not work at large firms and do not have an institutional training program, it is incumbent upon bar associations and other professional organizations to step forward and assist in and contribute to a young lawyer's development. Whether through a mentoring program or simply having resources available, organizations should do all they can to facilitate a young lawyer's development. As the number of lawyers increases year after year, it becomes that much more difficult for lawyers starting out on their own to successfully develop—particularly those who are not part of a large firm or organization.

To the extent that professional organizations and their membership take responsibility for, or even just a role in, the development of young lawyers, they can only help toward furthering the goals of professionalism and ethics among us, and making the practice more collegial. The more lawyers reach out to others, the more acrimony can be replaced by collegiality, resistance by cooperation. As the number of lawyers in a community increases, some lawyers find less reason to be civil to each other, as there is less likelihood that they will run into each other again. That trend can and must be reversed. Zealous representation does not have to equate to discourteous advocacy. Nor does it help achieve a better result. Creating and continuing a hostile, contentious relationship does not advance the cause. What it does do is increase the cost of litigation or transactions for all involved. To the extent that more experienced lawyers reach out to less experienced ones, we can help restore our reputation as a noble profession.

## Concluding Thoughts

All of the programs and ideas to develop young lawyers will not succeed unless they have motivated participants—the young lawyer, the experienced lawyer, and the firm/company. Although the obvious benefits to a firm from developing its young lawyers, the increased loyalty and job satisfaction, and the individual, personal rewards, should be more than enough motivation, sadly, they are not for many lawyers. At the same time, while the importance of developing young lawyers should not need to be encouraged, firms should not have systems in place that effectively "penalize" lawyer development. Creating and fostering an atmosphere and culture that emphasize development will be a gigantic first step. If the ends and objectives are clear, the means to achieving them can be easily tailored. The result will benefit all involved: the young lawyer, the firm, and the profession.

# PART VI

# Serving the Wider World

# CHAPTER 13

# Pro Bono: More Than a Professional Responsibility

**By Joanne Martin and Stephen Daniels**

Pro bono publico—for the public good. Lawyers serve their clients to the best of their ability every day of their professional lives. At the core of the legal profession, however, is something more fundamental—the responsibility to further the critical relationship between law and democracy. This responsibility involves ensuring access to the fundamental rights guaranteed by our laws for all of the nation's citizens. One avenue available to meet this responsibility is participation in the provision of legal services to underserved and underrepresented individuals on a pro bono basis.

The need for pro bono legal services, which has always been substantial, has increased over the past several decades in the wake of declining federal funding for providing legal services to the poor and underserved and increasing restrictions on the use of funds that are available for that purpose. As some aspects of the legal services provider market shrink, lawyers in private practice, corporate settings, and government have—as volunteers—become the major providers of legal services for individuals of limited means. They often do so through a growing array of private, nonprofit entities that have arisen to channel and support pro bono activities. In addition, national, state, and local bar associations, long supporters of pro bono legal services through referral networks and direct funding, are providing information, training, malpractice insurance, and CLE credit to further support the efforts of attorneys who contribute their time on a pro bono basis to individuals and entities in need.

Pro bono work is more than a professional responsibility. For some lawyers, unlike their day-to-day practices, it offers the opportunity to work with individual clients. For others, it provides an avenue for participating in causes of public interest. For still other lawyers, pro bono work provides the opportunity for continuing training and the development of new skills. More importantly, the provision of legal services on a pro bono basis is not just about lawyers and their professional lives. Respect for our system of laws and its legitimacy is built upon a perception that these laws are fundamentally fair, and fairness requires meaningful access to the rights and remedies the law provides. Meaningful access, in turn, requires adequate legal representation. The provision of legal services on a pro bono basis is a means of ensuring that access to the rights and remedies that the law provides regardless of wealth.

## Legal Needs

Legal needs studies conducted by national and state bar associations over the years continue to document the demand for legal services for Americans of limited financial means and demonstrate that the volume of unmet need remains substantial. These studies, and others more specifically tailored to the inquiry, also collect information on the level of pro bono hours contributed by the nation's lawyers. It is clear from these efforts that the need for legal services among persons of limited financial means far outstrips the supply—which is not to say that the contributions of law firms and individual lawyers in terms of their time and financial resources are not substantial.

As federal dollars available to support legal services to the poor and underserved Americans declined over the past decade, the delivery landscape for these services changed considerably in response. Law firms and individual lawyers are providing both substantial direct funding and, equally importantly, legal talent through the significant contribution of pro bono hours, to address the demand for legal services among the underserved components of the American population. Where once federally funded entities dominated the organized aspect of the delivery system, over 1,000 nonprofit organizations now function to address various demands of the market. Law school clinical programs have grown in number as well. Collaborations and partnerships across firms, corporations, law schools, bar associations, and nonprofit provider organizations are enhancing the delivery mechanism for legal services to the poor as well. State and local bar programs and provider organizations offer additional incentives for participation in pro bono work such as training programs, malpractice insurance, and CLE credits. Yet the demand continues to outstrip supply.

In moving toward the future with regard to the delivery of legal services, it is clear that while substantial efforts are being made, more needs to be done. The Legal Services Corporation needs the continuing support of the profession to maintain, and hopefully to increase, the level of its federal appropriation. States should be encouraged to recognize their responsibility for serving their citizenry. Existing legal service efforts require continuing support for programs already in place and assistance in identifying and crafting innovative ways for the legal system to deal with the legal issues that confront Americans of limited means. The importance of the pro bono efforts that address more systemic reform of the system must be recognized as a critical aspect of the delivery mechanism for legal services. Within the legal profession, pro bono service should be formally celebrated not only as a professional obligation, but as a means toward achieving professional development and satisfaction.

## The Demand

Barbara Curran's seminal study, *The Legal Needs of the Public* was published in 1977. It showed a staggering amount of unmet legal need among people of limited means—over 80% of the reported legal need for these individuals was unmet.[1] Since 2000, nine states have conducted similar studies (Oregon, Vermont, New Jersey, Connecticut, Massachusetts, Washington, Tennessee, Illinois, and Montana). The volume of unmet legal need as measured by these efforts suggests that little has changed with regard to the volume of demand. For example, the recent Illinois legal needs study released in early 2005 found that "low income households had legal assistance for only one out of every six legal problems encountered in 2004. . . . [T]he most common response (65.8%) to a legal problem was to attempt to resolve it without legal assistance. . . . Many of these problems were complex matters with potentially serious consequences."[2] To some degree, the types of matters for which legal services would be productive have changed over time—for example, immigration-related matters have increased in number—but generally, the substantive areas remain the same, focused on very basic needs—family matters, housing, consumer issues, and employment concerns.

Matching this demand with the number of legal aid attorneys presents a rather stark picture of one aspect of the gap between supply and demand in this market for legal services for the poor. A recent report issued by the Legal Services Corporation indicated that in 2002 there were 6,581 legal aid attorneys serving the nation's low-income people—(3,845 lawyers in LSC-funded programs and an estimated 2,736 lawyers in programs that do not receive LSC funding).[3] The report puts these figures in a comparative context with the number of lawyers serving personal civil legal needs of the general public, noting that there is one legal aid lawyer per 6,861 low-income people in the country compared to one lawyer providing personal civil legal services for every 525 people in the general public.[4] Deborah Rhode, a distinguished scholar and researcher, offered a similar characterization of the disparity of the availability of legal services:

> The facts speak for themselves. An estimated four-fifths of the legal needs of the poor . . . remain unmet. Only one lawyer is available to serve approximately 9,000 low-income persons, compared with one for every 240 middle- and upper-income Americans. . . . Entire categories of the "unworthy poor" have been denied assistance.[5]

## The Supply

Federal funding for the delivery of legal services to the poor through allocations to the Legal Services Corporation peaked in 1981 at $687,063,000 (in 2005 dollars). The appropriation for the Legal Services Corporation in 2006 was $326,600,600. The *Documenting the Justice Gap* Report issued by the LSC in 2005 noted that for every person who receives service from LSC-funded entities, one applicant was turned away. LSC entities are also prohibited from assisting certain individuals—based on a maximum income threshold (about $16,500 for a two-person household)—and from taking certain types of cases, such as criminal matters, class actions, or particular types of immigration issues.

State funds and IOLTA dollars supplement the funding available to support the provision of legal services to the poor, but even more significantly, over the past decade a substantial number of nonprofit, non-LSC entities have been established to broaden the scope of the legal services delivery system. It is estimated that over 1,000 of these organizations are currently in existence. In Chicago, Illinois, for example, there are over 50 entities in addition to the one LSC-funded organization in the metropolitan area that provide some level of legal assistance to individuals of limited means. These efforts are largely supported—in terms of funding and legal talent—by the practicing bar. In a recent, lengthy and fascinating article, Scott Cummings argues that lawyers' pro bono activities have become "the dominant model of delivering free legal services."[6] He identifies a major shift in the delivery mechanism, which he characterizes as the institutionalization of pro bono, as follows:

> A much more important story was in fact taking shape—one which was transforming the nation's system for delivering free legal services to poor and underserved clients. The defining feature of the 1990s boom [for law firms] was not that private lawyers were prioritizing profit over pro bono services. This had, to some degree, always been the case. Instead, the real story was the radical change taking place in how pro bono services were being dispensed. Whereas pro bono had traditionally been provided informally—

> frequently by solo and small firm practitioners who conferred free services as a matter of individual largesse—by the end of the 1990s pro bono was regimented and organized, distributed through a network of structures designed to facilitate the mass provision of free services by law firm volunteers acting out of professional duty.[7]

The ABA's Model Rules of Professional Conduct provide that "Every lawyer has a professional responsibility to provide legal services to those unable to pay. A lawyer should aspire to render at least (50) hours of pro bono publico legal services per year."[8] A national survey of 1,100 lawyers conducted by the ABA's Standing Committee on Pro Bono and Public Service in 2004 examined the extent of pro bono work being done by lawyers in the United States. The report based on this study noted that two-thirds of the respondents reported providing some level of free pro bono services to people of limited means and/or organizations serving the poor—an average of 39 hours of free pro bono services over a twelve-month period. Only 14% reported that they had not done even one hour of pro bono work during the twelve-month survey period. About 46% of the lawyers surveyed met the ABA's aspirational goal of providing at least 50 hours of free pro bono services. Similar figures are reported in the three states that have mandatory pro bono reporting requirements (Maryland, Florida, and Nevada), as well as in the states that have voluntary reporting procedures such as New York.

Across the various studies that examine the levels of participation in pro bono services and lawyers' satisfaction with their careers, the most frequently cited reasons by lawyers for *not* doing pro bono work revolve around notions of lack of time because of the demands of their current positions and family obligations. Other reasons cited for not participating in the delivery of legal services to persons of limited means or to organizations who serve these individuals include lack of skills or experience in the practice areas needed by pro bono clients (or an absence of opportunities that would best utilize the professional skills that lawyers, such as transactional attorneys, already possess), a lack of information about opportunities, and a lack of malpractice insurance. The ABA's survey captured information on factors that would motivate attorneys to perform pro bono services. First and foremost is the sense of professional responsibility. Other factors include free training, CLE credit, free malpractice insurance coverage related to their pro bono activity, employer encouragement, the opportunity to take on discrete legal tasks rather than an entire representation, and encouragement from a judge.

## Types of Matters

Because LSC-funded entities are limited to working with certain clients based on their income levels and further constrained in terms of the categories of matters that they are permitted to handle, law school clinics and an increasing array of nonprofit provider entities address these gaps. Many of these entities are very narrowly niched as a function of their funding and staffing limitations. Some address the legal needs of individuals living in particular geographical areas, some focus on particular substantive areas such as housing or immigration, others deal with the needs of individuals who are similarly situated such as the elderly or the disabled, and other providers are grounded in ethnic or religion-based communities. Some of these organizations are set up to specifically address the needs of individuals, and others are more cause-oriented and engage in class action–based work, which LSC entities are expressly prohibited from undertaking. There are also conservative legal advocacy organizations such as the Pacific Legal Foundation, Americans United for Life Legal Defense Foundation, and the Center for Individual Rights.[9] While the proliferation of these entities works positively to expand the coverage of legal needs across a broader community of individuals who need them, all of these entities compete in the same market for funding and legal talent.

## The Real Picture

The various survey efforts that gather data on supply and demand briefly noted above offer snapshots of the aspects of the elephant (from the joke about the blind men identifying the object before them) that is the delivery system for legal services to individuals of limited means. These surveys serve several important purposes. The legal need studies, by identifying the volume of demand, provide support for funding requests from provider entities and for encouraging participation of the legal profession. The studies that measure the contribution of pro bono hours identify the areas where services are being provided and measure changes, hopefully increases, in the landscape of pro bono service. These studies also have their weaknesses.

As dire a picture as the legal needs studies may portray, when the array of services that are actually provided is examined, it becomes apparent that the scope of demand might be understated. The needs of individuals who are wrongfully incarcerated, of children, or of immigrants are examples of the aspects of demand that may be undercounted. The immediate and sudden needs of groups of individuals that arise as a result of the events of the moment—the Katrina victims, for example—are also not factored into the "traditional" legal needs calculations. The assessments of services offered in these studies do not really count, for example, the hundreds of hours and thousands of dollars that a firm may invest in the defense of one individual in a wrongful conviction matter. In short, the legal needs studies, while similar in their findings, are not set up to capture the full array of demand and the reports assessing the level of services provided don't match the demand as identified by the legal needs studies with the services actually provided.

However, the essence of the message is that there is a huge volume of demand for the expertise that the members of the profession have to offer their communities and the individuals who live in those communities. The legal profession—through its professional associations, firms, and individual lawyers—makes a substantial contribution in pro bono services and financial contributions to providing legal services to the underserved population. The issue at hand is how to continue increasing the coverage and the level of services that address real everyday need, while recognizing and supporting the contributions of the profession aimed at systemic reform.

## Law Firms

Law firms have become a very significant component of the delivery mechanism for legal services to the poor and underserved. Many American law firms have a long tradition of making substantial commitments to pro bono service—both in direct dollars and contributions of legal talent. The pro bono cultures within firms vary widely, but at least within large firms, many of these cultures are built around the business plans of those firms.

Reasons underlying the commitment of law firms to pro bono include the desire to support the sense of professional responsibility imbued in their legal professionals. Pro bono work also improves firm morale, enhances a firm's reputation in the legal community and with their clients, provides a vehicle for the development of lawyering skills, assists with recruiting and training new associates, and strengthens community connections.

Just as there are different cultures within firms, there are numerous models for structurally organizing pro bono work within law firms. Some employ pro bono partners who spend all of their time organizing and pursuing pro bono opportunities; others have individuals designated as pro bono partners who still produce substantial billable hours, but also coordinate the firm's pro bono efforts. Some firms utilize committees supported by a pro bono coordinator—a super legal assistant—to orchestrate and monitor pro bono efforts. Firms with multiple office locations—including foreign offices—have structures that bring together the efforts of individual offices under regional or national committee umbrellas.

The ABA's statement with regard to best practices in law firms recognizes various structural and procedural models:

> Law firm best practices include most predominately a wide variety of administrative policies designed to encourage and promote pro bono and community service among lawyers, paralegals and staff, and to efficiently and effectively match attorneys with appropriate pro bono projects. Many of the best practices include, for example, providing "full credit" or "billable hour credit" for time spent on pro bono matters for purposes of hour targets and bonuses, creation of pro bono committees and in some cases positions for full time attorneys or staff who coordinate the firm's pro bono program, and written policies governing the firm's pro bono program. A number of firms also have developed systems to recognize pro bono work within the firm, such as through officewide emails, newsletters, annual reports, and awards. Several firms work in partnerships with bar associations and other community organizations, and have developed focused pro bono projects targeted at specific community issues. Also a number of firms have a rotation of externship projects that offer an opportunity for attorneys,

> paralegals and staff to spend significant portions of time working with a particular nonprofit legal services provider. (www.abanet.org/renaissance/bestpractices/lawfirms.htm)

The Pro Bono Institute Challenge offers another incentive for law firms to make a formal commitment to pro bono activities. It calls upon large firms to contribute three to five percent of firm revenues to pro bono efforts. Unfortunately, although many firms have become signatories to the Challenge, a substantial number do not meet its requirements. Another incentive is the commitment of the *American Lawyer* magazine to regularly rank the largest 200 firms, taking into consideration in their evaluation the pro bono contributions of these firms.

One issue that proves to be a hindrance to the efforts of private practitioners to contribute their time to pro bono efforts is that of conflicts of interest. Whether such concerns should be considered a major deterrent is questionable, not because the potential for conflicts does not exist, but rather because the panoply of opportunities for pro bono service is so large that projects can certainly be found that will not run afoul of such concerns. Some pro bono partners and coordinators also report that where the pro bono projects are considered particularly important, they have approached the clients who interests might be affected to discuss the possibilities of granting waivers to remove concerns about conflicts.

Another area of expressed concern among lawyers, particularly transactional lawyers, is that their skill set does not lend itself to addressing the types of needs for which pro bono efforts are sought. The fact is that bar groups and pro bono provider organizers recognize these concerns and offer many opportunities that call upon the special talents of transactional lawyers and, for those that are interested in providing the type of legal services that are so desperately needed by individuals, they offer training programs geared toward those matters. Nonprofit legal service providers are more than willing to work with law firms to identify projects that will provide a good fit between need and available legal expertise.

The ABA's Pro Bono study reports that older lawyers were more likely to report doing some pro bono than younger attorneys. This is not necessarily a startling finding. Within larger firms especially, the demand on young associates' time is extensive and as a result, lack of time is often cited by young lawyers as a reason for not participating in pro bono efforts. As the demand for billable hours rises in response to firm business models, this is perceived as an even greater deterrent than was the case in the past. In a 1,400-billable-hour world it was one thing to ask that pro bono be taken on one's own time, but at 2,000 hours, it is necessary to have firms recognize and make the commitment to give credit for such efforts if they wish to encourage participation, particular among the younger associates. Other concerns about opportunities for pro bono service expressed by young lawyers include the perceived lack of mentors and structured projects.

For new lawyers who are interested in the pro bono cultures of their potential employers, there are readily available resources that provide that information. The online NALP *Directory of Legal Employers* lists the pro bono policies of the vast majority of law firms in this database. Also the Vault *Pro Bono Directory* provides more detail on the pro bono efforts of the nation's larger law firms. The topics covered in this volume include information on recent clients and programs, partner contacts, supervisory structures, and formal policies. Most large firms also make information on their pro bono policies and activities available through their websites and firm newsletters.

One example of a law firm's efforts to enrich its pro bono efforts and to enhance the professional training of its young associates is reflected in the hiring by Mayer, Brown, Rowe & Maw in Chicago of Marc Kadish, a former clinical law professor, as the firm's Pro Bono Partner. Mr. Kadish is quoted in a recent article in the *Wall Street Journal* on vanishing trials as making an offer to federal judges in Chicago that the firm would represent, pro bono, any prisoner with a case set for trial who didn't already have counsel. The purpose behind this offer is to provide the firm's young associates the opportunity to hone their courtroom skills, an opportunity they might not get in the near future given a perceived decline in formal trials.

While large firms have the financial resources and personnel to support organized pro bono service programs, mid-sized and smaller firms are not necessarily in a position to formally support such efforts, nor do they necessarily have the long-standing pro bono traditions that are found in older, more established firms. Once again, the growth of nonprofit provider organizations, bar association programs, and law school clinics provide opportunities for lawyers in all work settings who wish to offer their services on a pro bono basis. It might be noted that many personal injury firms, because they handle cases on a contingency fee basis, deal with clients who may be members of the underserved population as a matter of course. In fact this is one of underlying logics of the contingency fee structure. These efforts should not be discounted in assessing the level of services provided to individuals of limited means simply because there may ultimately be a financial return for the lawyer.

## Corporate Counsel

The survey underlying the ABA's Report on Pro Bono Work of American Lawyers found that the level of pro bono participation among the respondents employed in corporate settings was lower than that among private practitioners and those lawyers working in government settings. Corporate counsel face constraints to pro bono service unique to their practice setting. The dynamics of in-house corporate settings, even within the largest corporate entities, generally do not offer the pro bono culture or support mechanisms found in large law firms. Whereas large law firms may provide billable hour credit for pro bono service, even large corporate entities are not usually set up with the same system of recognition and rewards for these activitives. Some corporate law departments are indeed structured around a billable hour model and have a system in place through which pro bono activities may be undertaken once cleared through the general counsel. However, before credit is given for the pro bono efforts or projects are undertaken that involve collaborative participation by several members of the corporate law department, the case must be made to the corporate management using a business model format. Another impediment to pro bono participation by corporate counsel is the fact that because most corporate legal departments do not have the kind of contacts and long standing pro bono traditions that are present within law firms, identifying pro bono projects deemed appropriate and consistant with the corporate identity may be perceived as difficult.

The ABA's statement of best practices for corporate counsel participation in pro bono efforts provides:

> The best practices in a corporate counsel setting involve partnership or collaboration with law firms, a bar association or pro bono services provider. For in-house counsel, collaboration is effective as it allows that corporate client to build its relationships with outside counsel, foster involvement of legal and non-legal staff in pro bono cases via a bar association who can also provide skills training, and enhance the image of the corporation in the process. In-house counsel will likely also participate in public service projects that give back to the community by assisting children, the elderly, low-income families, domestic violence victims, disabled individuals and others with needs that do not necessarily involve legal advice. The key to the success of these programs is a willing corporation and general counsel, collaborative projects with firms and or bar associations and community recognition of the lawyers as well as the corporations. (http://www.abanet.org/renaissance/bestpractices/corporate.html)

The notion of collaboration with law firms or other entities is a very effective model for a number of reasons. Corporate counsel are in the unique position to encourage the outside firms with which they work to have a strong pro bono policy and to suggest that collaborative efforts in this area will strengthen the professional relationship they have with their outside counsel colleagues. Also, working with entities that can better provide the necessary infrastructure for such projects makes it easier for corporate counsel to participate more effectively.

Another issue that often is cited by inside counsel as a potential hindrance to participating in pro bono activities is the fact that they are transactional lawyers and finding pro bono projects that utilize their unique skills is often perceived as a problem. However, as mentioned earlier, there are numerous nonprofit legal service providers that recognize and value these talents by offering projects specifically geared to utilizing this particular skill set. An example of such an entity is the Lawyers Alliance in New York. Such nonprofit providers and some law school clinics are specifically set up, for example, to extend pro bono or low-cost services to start-up entities, nonprofits, and individuals in the arts who need the type of legal advice and assistance that transactional lawyers have to offer.

The American Corporate Counsel website offers its members a very extensive Corporate Pro Bono Infopack (www.acca.com/infopak/probono.html). This collection of material contains information on making the case for pro bono participation, legal malpractice options, a guide to multi-jurisdictional practice issues, and listings of possible projects. ACCA and the Pro Bono Institute have partnered to establish Corporate Pro Bono, which provides resources for in-house corporate counsel seeking to engage in pro bono activity, including a worldwide database of pro bono volunteer opportunities geared specifically to the skills of these lawyers.

## Government Lawyers

Government lawyers also face rather substantial constraints on their ability to participate in pro bono activities imposed by the organizations for which they work due to natural conflicts of interest and express provisions in their contractual relationship with their employers. While such constraints exist, they are not insurmountable. As recognized in the ABA's best practices statement for government attorneys regarding pro bono, an initial hurdle to participation in pro bono work may be the lack of a formal policy within the governmental entity.[10] Support for rectifying this situation, at least at the federal level, was provided in February of 1996, when President Clinton issued Executive Order 12988, which provides that "all Federal agencies should develop appropriate programs to encourage and facilitate pro bono legal and other volunteer services by government employees to be performed on their own time, including attorneys, as permitted by statute, regulation, and other rule or guideline." In response to the desire of government attorneys to participate in the provision of pro bono services, the provider world is quite willing to accommodate the constraints placed on these attorneys by matching projects to their particular situation.

Outlines and procedures for the development of pro bono policies for government entities, as well as sample policies, can be found on the website of the ABA's Government and Public Sector Lawyers Division (www.abanet.org/govpub/probono.html) along with links to selected pro bono projects. Many state and local bars, recognizing the special requirements of government and public services lawyers, have information on programs and information geared to the unique situation of these lawyers. An example of such a website is www.probono.net/dc.

### Law School Programs

Law schools are in a position to initiate and grow the ideals of professional responsibility among soon-to-be lawyers and to encourage them to serve the underserved, to contribute to their communities through public service, and to use their legal skills to promote social justice. The ABA's accreditation standards were modified in 1996 to provide that every law school "should encourage its students to participate in pro bono activities and provide opportunities for them to do so." In its 1999 report, *Learning to Serve: The Findings and Proposals of the AALS Commission on Pro Bono and Public Service Opportunities,* the AALS Commission on Pro Bono and Public Service Opportunities recommended "that law schools make available to all law students at least once during their law school careers a well-supervised law-related pro bono opportunity and either require the students' participation or find ways to attract the great majority of students to volunteer." By 2003, about 90% of the ABA accredited law schools had some kind of organized pro bono program. Some even have mandatory pro bono requirements for graduation. These programs vary widely in scope and the level of participation across their student bodies. The clinical programs in some law schools have become among the largest public interest firms in the country. (A listing of law school programs has been collected and made available in the Directory of Law School Public Interest and Pro Bono Programs—www.abanet.org/legalservices/probono/law schools.)

Just as is the case with other nonprofit providers, many of these law school efforts form productive collaborations with law firms to address important issues that affect the underserved population. One example of this is a recent collaboration between DLA Piper and the Bluhm Legal Clinic at Northwestern Law School. With the financial support of DLA Piper, a faculty Fellow position was established to coordinate efforts to provide representation to children in delinquency and school expulsion matters. The Fellow is responsible for supervising Piper's young associates and Northwestern students in representation of young people in Juvenile Court in Chicago.

## Nonprofit Provider and Coordination Organizations

There has been tremendous growth in the last decade in the number of organized pro bono efforts based in non-LSC funded nonprofit organizations, and their contributions to the delivery system for legal services to the poor has been substantial. There are currently over 1,000 such programs across the country that serve the increasingly diverse legal needs of clients by focusing both on meeting the direct needs of individuals and addressing larger concerns of target groups through initiating systemic reform. Locating information on these provider entities is facilitated by several sources. The ABA's Standing Committee on Pro Bono and Public Service maintains a state-by-state listing of these programs on their website. Another source of such information is Pro Bono Net, which is a nonprofit organization headquartered in New York City. Its mission is to increase access to justice through innovative uses of technology and increased volunteer lawyer participation. Its website asserts that "there are now more than 25,000 registered users of the site—60% of these are volunteer lawyers from private law firms both large and small. 98 of the 100 largest firms in the country have volunteer lawyers using PBN." The Pro Bono Institute, a nonprofit organization housed at the Georgetown University Law Center, provides "support, guidance, training, resources and inspiration to major law firms, in-house corporate legal departments and public interest organizations seeking to expand and enhance access to justice for the poor and disadvantaged and promotes effective and productive partnerships among these groups."[11]

## Bar Associations

National, state, local, and specialty bar associations have long traditions of supporting efforts of the legal community to provide legal services to the poor and continue to have much to offer the delivery system for legal services to underserved communities. They have funded and supported the studies that identify legal needs and levels of pro bono support. They directly fund legal service efforts through contributions from their nonprofit foundations. Their referral networks and screening entities help direct individuals with legal needs to sources of assistance. Many bar associations support and encourage pro bono activities by providing resources such as malpractice coverage and training programs for members who wish to participate in these activities. CLE credit is offered in many instances as an additional incentive.

The ABA provides significant resources for lawyers interested in providing legal services to the poor. Initiated by ABA president Michael Greco, the Renaissance of Idealism in the Legal Profession project recently developed a Pro Bono and Public Service Best Practices Resource Guide that not only offers best practice statements for various legal practice settings, as noted above, but also provides access to examples of programs currently being undertaken by law firms, corporate counsel, government lawyers, and law schools that exemplify these ideals. The various Sections of the ABA also offer opportunities for lawyers seeking to make contributions of their time to pro bono efforts. Examples of these efforts include the Litigation Section's Litigation Assistance Partnership Project (LAPP) and the ABC Project sponsored by the Business Law Section. The website maintained by the Standing Committee on Pro Bono and Public Service offers, among other resources, a state-by-state pro bono program directory and information on pro bono program management and pro bono policies and rules.

## Conclusion

The need for the professional skills of the nation's lawyers by persons of limited means continues to grow. While lawyers across the country do make substantial contributions of their time to address the individual legal needs of persons of limited means and the issues critical to the situations in which these individuals find themselves, much more needs to be done. The landscape of delivery mechanisms for services to the poor has changed considerably in the last decade, but the profession writ large may not be aware of these changes and therefore may not be taking full advantage of the array of resources that have been designed to assist in the provision of pro bono services to those who so desperately need them.

The resources available for lawyers who wish to make a contribution of their professional expertise are substantial. Information can be obtained from a myriad of sources, including professional organizations and nonprofit provider entities. Incentives for participating in pro bono work extend beyond the sense of professional responsibility that every lawyer feels. They include the opportunity for professional development, for engaging with the communities in which one works and lives, and for improving the quality of one's professional life.

While lawyers may not find as much support as they would like within the organizations and entities in which they are employed for making contributions of their time to provide legal services to underserved and underrepresented individuals and entities, efforts to improve organizational levels of recognition are steadily increasing. It is becoming difficult to give credence to reasons offered for non-participation in pro bono activities other than the declaration that there is not enough time. If a lawyer wishes to participate in the efforts to provide pro bono legal services to individuals or to entities that address issues of importance to individuals of limited means, the opportunities are numerous and readily accessible.

## Some Informational On-Line Resources for Pro Bono Information

ABA Standing Committee on Pro Bono & Public Service (*www.abanet.org/legalservices/probono/home.html*)
ACCA (www.acca.com/infopaks/probono.html)
Corporate Pro Bono (www.cpbo.org)
Law firm websites
Law school websites
NALP Directory of Legal Employers (www.nalpdirectory.com)
Pro Bono Institute (www.probonoinst.org)
Pro Bono Net (www.probono.net)
State, local and specialty bar association websites

## Endnotes

1. Barbara Curran, *The Legal Needs of the Public: The Final Report of a National Survey* (1977).

2. *The Legal Safety Net: A Report on the Legal Needs of Low-Income Illinoisans* (2005), Executive Summary, 1–2.

3. Legal Services Corporation, *Documenting the Justice Gap in America: The Current Unmet Civil Legal Needs of Low-Income Americans 15* (2005).

4. *Id.*

5. Deborah Rhode, "Access to Justice: The Social Responsibility of Lawyers, Equal Justice Under the Law, Connecting Principle to Practice," 12 Wash. U. J.L. & Policy 47, 47 (2003).

6. Cummings, "The Politics of Pro Bono," 52 UCLA Law Review 5 (2004).

7. *Id.*, at 4.

8. ABA Model Rules of Professional Conduct, Rule 6.1, available at abanet.org/cpr/mrpc/rule_6_1.html.

9. Ann Southworth, Conservative Lawyers and the Contest Over the Meaning of "Public Interest Law,"in 52 UCLA L. Rev. 2005.

10. "The best practices in a government setting have, first and foremost, a policy adopted by the agency and/or its legal counsel component supporting its lawyers and in some cases, paralegals and staff, in their delivery of pro bono and/or public services. Once the buy-in exists at the highest levels, the lawyer is easily able to engage in various cases, projects or counseling including assisting low-income, disadvantaged individuals in various practice areas. The key to the success of these programs is an understanding of the ethical issues that might constrain the lawyer in certain areas, limitations on the use of government resources, and willingness to work in areas that are likely very different from the individual lawyer's practice area."(http:www.abanet .org/renaissance/bestpractices/government.html)

11. Pro Bono Institute webpage, www.probonoinst.org.

# CHAPTER 14

# Let's Start a Ripple: Building Diversity in the Legal Profession

**By: Kay H. Hodge**

## Introduction

Lawyers played a key role in shaping this nation. Lawyers drafted the Constitution and the Bill of Rights that define this democracy. Those founding documents promise equality, albeit an equality focused not on race, ethnicity or even gender, but religion. Many of the early settlers left Europe in search of freedom to worship without persecution. Today, genuine equality would encompass not only religion, but race, national origin, gender, age, disabilities and sexual orientation/sexual identity, as well. While all areas of diversity are important, this article will focus on the implications and challenges posed by the lack of racial and ethnic diversity within the legal profession.

Barely ten percent of the lawyers in this country belong to racial or ethnic minorities or are lawyers of color[1] while America's overall population is becoming increasingly diverse. As minority litigants are forced to navigate a justice system that is nearly all white, the shortage of minority lawyers has serious implications for the future of our democracy. When individuals of color see that the key players in the justice system, lawyers and judges, are white, they may question whether the system will treat them fairly. Yet public trust and confidence in our judicial system is essential to its survival and effectiveness in an increasingly pluralistic society. The viability of the justice system may depend on the legal profession's ability to increase diversity within its ranks.

Concern that a lack of diversity will fuel popular disillusionment with governmental institutions is not new. In an amicus brief filed with the U.S. Supreme Court in *Grutter v. Bollinger,* 539 U.S. 306 (2003), former high-ranking officers and civilian leaders of the various branches of the military related:

> The crisis that resulted in the integration of the officer corps is but a magnified reflection of circumstances in our nation's highly diverse society. In the 1960s and 1970s, the stark disparity between the racial composition of the rank and file and that of the officer corps fueled a breakdown of order that endangered the military's ability to fulfill its mission. That threat was so dangerous and unacceptable that it resulted in immediate and dramatic changes intended to restore minority enlisted ranks' confidence in the fairness and integrity of the institution. In a highly diverse society, the public, including minority citizens, must have confidence in the integrity of public institutions, particularly those educational institutions that provide the training, education and status necessary to achieve prosperity and power in America.

Brief at 28–29. Like the military, our justice system depends on the confidence of an increasingly diverse American population, which makes diversity within the profession an imperative.

Although law schools, bar associations, and legal employers regularly implement programs to enhance racial and ethnic diversity, attacking the issue in various ways, the results have not been satisfactory. There have been countless activities, programs and initiatives, but unfortunately, not much progress.

There is no silver bullet. If there were a clear solution to the lack of racial and ethnic diversity within the profession, there would be no need to write this article.

## The Facts

To put this article in context, some summary statistics about racial and ethnic diversity in this country's population, in the legal profession, and in other professions will be provided here. Statistics are not, and should not be, an end in themselves. They do, however, help us to visualize the extent of the problem by comparison with the increasing proportion of women in the legal profession and the representation of minorities in other professions.

The population of the United States is increasingly diverse. By 2004, one third of the American population was not white. The U.S. Census predicts that by 2050, 50.1% of the American population will be white and 49.9% will be minority (24.4% Hispanic, 14.6% Black/African American, 8.0% Asian, and 5.3% all others[2]).[3]

These statistics pose a particular challenge to the legal profession because the profession has been unable to match the current diversity of the population. Over the past 20 years, the diversity among lawyers and judges has grown but remains far short of the diversity of the population as a whole.

**LAWYER POPULATION U.S**

| | White | Black/African American | Hispanic | Asian | Native American | Other |
|---|---|---|---|---|---|---|
| 1980 | 502,456 | 14,839 | 9,287 | 3,776 | 1,158 | |
| | (95.7%) | (2.8%) | (1.7%) | (0.7%) | (0.2%) | |
| 1990 | 691,313 | 25,067 | 18,612 | 10,513 | 1,417 | |
| | (92.5%) | (3.6%) | (2.7%) | (1.5%) | (0.2%) | |
| 2000 | 776,625 | 34,610 | 28,630 | 22,320 | 4,540 | 4,395 |
| | (89.2%) | (4.5%) | (3.4%) | (2.9%) | (0.6%) | (0.6%) |

Source: U.S. Census

Although there is recognition that judges should reflect the diversity of the general population, the racial composition of judges does not reflect parity with the diversity in the general population.

## JUDGES U.S[4]

| | White | Black/African American | Hispanic | Asian | Native American |
|---|---|---|---|---|---|
| 1980 | 25,508 | 1,618 | 553 | 144 | 166 |
| | (92.5%) | (5.8%) | (2%) | (0.5%) | (0.6%) |
| 1990 | 28,527 | 2,253 | 1,098 | 332 | 184 |
| | (88%) | (7%) | (3.4%) | (1%) | (0.6%) |
| 2000 | 48,530 | 5,155 | 2,650 | 910 | 465 |
| | (89.2%) | (8.8%) | (4.5%) | (1.6%) | (0.8%) |

Source: U.S. Census

A comparison of the statistics for the general population, lawyers and judges in 2000 provides a clear picture of the disparities between and among groups.

## COMPARISON OF 2000 STATISTICS

| | White | Black/African American | Hispanic | Asian | Native American |
|---|---|---|---|---|---|
| General Population | 69.1% | 12.3% | 12.5% | 3.6% | 1% |
| Lawyers | 89.2% | 4.5% | 3.4% | 2.9% | 0.6% |
| Judges | 83.2% | 8.8% | 4.5% | 1.6% | 0.8% |

Source: U.S. Census

Unfortunately the current number of law students of color will not significantly change the minority composition of the overall lawyer population. The percentage of minority law students compared to white students has more than tripled in law schools accredited by the American Bar Association going from 5,568 or 6.1% in 1971–1972 to 29,768 or 21.2% in 2005–2006. However, in absolute numbers, only 9,568 minorities received J.D. degrees in 2004–2005. Hence, while law schools are admitting more minority students, the absolute number of minority lawyers entering the profession remains small.[5]

The increase in minority law students has lagged behind the increase in women law students. For example, in 1971–1972, 9.4% (8,567) of law students were women, and 5,568 or 6.1% were minority. The number of women attending law school rose steadily reaching 40% or 47,486 by 1985–1986 and has fluctuated between 40% and 50% in the last 20 years. In contrast, by 1985–1986 minority enrollment had only reached 12,357 or 10.4%, and the numbers did not reach 20.1% (25,266) until 1998–1999.

Moreover, there has been very little change in the percentage of minorities attending law school over the ensuing eight years with the highest minority enrollment achieved in 2005–2006 just 21.2% (29,768). In comparison to that of women, the increase in minority enrollment in law schools has been exceedingly slow.

The lack of minority representation within the legal profession is particularly troubling because we lag behind other professions in this area.

> In 2000, minorities made up 25.5 percent of the civilian labor force, including 20.8 percent of accountants and auditors, 23.1 percent of computer scientists, 24.6 percent of physicians and surgeons, and 18.2 percent of college and university teachers, compared to only 9.7 percent of lawyers... According to the Bureau of Labor Statistics, combined African American and Hispanic representation among U.S. professionals was 13.6 percent in 2002, compared to 7.7 percent among lawyers.[6]

Why does the legal profession lag behind others in diversifying its ranks? Why is the number of minority law students dropping? Perhaps, most importantly, what, if anything, should the profession do about it?

## Lawyers Must Advocate for the Education of Minority Children

To become a lawyer, a child must receive an education that provides a quality education with real and meaningful educational opportunities to develop an ability to read, write and think critically. Unfortunately, the educational opportunities available to many poor and minority children are often inadequate. We (majority and minority lawyers) must work together to ensure that all children are provided with real and meaningful educational opportunities. No child left behind must be more than a slogan—it must become reality.

How do we do it? We must marshal our considerable power as a profession to address this problem. Using our skills, we should begin advocating for a public policy that does not ignore educational problems and deficits, but begins to redress them. We must support after-school programs, like those of the Boys & Girls Clubs, that provide children with a safe place to do their homework, to be tutored and mentored, to make friends and to learn to be good citizens and leaders.

Too often, we (majority and minority lawyers) move to the suburbs to take care of our own children and then "forget" about the children left behind. We should serve on school boards and school committees. As Thurgood Marshall did 50 years ago, lawyers must step up and insist that our public education system educate minority children in a manner which makes college and law school a realistic possibility. When necessary, we should file law suits. Lawyers should not only work to ensure that the poor have food and shelter, but also that poor children are educated well. That work should address the institutional and systemic barriers to equal education. While *Brown v. Board of Education* eliminated "separate, but equal," the problem in many school systems today is that minority children may be attending the same schools as white children, but still are not being educated to fulfill their potential.

We should also get involved in schools and programs for our youth. Lawyers regardless of race or ethnicity must begin to focus on each student of color as an opportunity to advance the diversity ball. With minority students in elementary and secondary schools, after school programs, and colleges, we must plant the seed that they should consider becoming a lawyer. While a speech in a classroom may generate a spark of interest, we need to recognize that interest alone is not enough. Many students of color need our help to succeed academically so that becoming a lawyer is a possibility. It also means that lawyers should support with their time and charitable contributions the myriad programs that provide after-school programs to youth, such as the Boys & Girls Clubs, Scouts, Big Sister/Big Brother programs, and other youth programs, including sports programs. Take an interest in students of color and help to provide them with real opportunity.

### The Legal Profession Must Be a Profession We Want Our Children to Join

The statistics set forth above reveal that, despite the best efforts of law schools, bar associations, legal employers and individual lawyers, other professions appear to be doing a better job in increasing the presence of minorities among their ranks. Why is that?

Although the pipeline problem for the legal profession is often attributed to the fact that children and young adults living in urban areas are not being educated and are dropping out of school at alarming rates, problems with America's education system alone do not explain why the legal profession has failed to attract enough students of color to match the diversity achieved by other professions.

Some success by other professions may reflect aggressive programs working with diverse students at an early age, such as those developed by the engineering profession. I submit, however, that the legal profession has a far more basic problem. In the view of many, including many lawyers, the practice of law is not the "honorable profession" we thought we were joining. Instead, law has become a business and lawyers are viewed as just another cog in the wheel or another stop on the assembly line.

In a focus group held with undergraduate minority students from five colleges in western Massachusetts, to learn what they knew about our profession and whether they would consider going to law school, I was shocked to discover how little these students knew and understood about the role of lawyers in our democracy. In fact, the students had numerous negative impressions of lawyers derived from television and other reflections of popular culture. They thought lawyers were deceitful, liars, cheats and generally despicable. They drew a sharp contrast between doctors, who visited campus in pre-med programs, and lawyers, who never came to campus. While programs targeting elementary and high school students have been a major focus of many bar associations and firms, we must do a better job of educating college students, who are on the verge of choosing careers, about the many varied and valuable roles that lawyers play in our society.

Unhappy lawyers cannot promote this profession. Anecdotally, I have heard many lawyers confess that they would not want to see their children pursue law as a career. I have also heard young lawyers confess that if they had it to do over again, they would not necessarily choose law as their profession. Unless and until we are able to convince ourselves that this profession offers more than just a paycheck, we will have a difficult time selling it to others. We cannot expect that minority students, who are being courted by other professions and the world of finance and business, will be any less astute about our profession than their white counterparts.

What does the level of satisfaction within the profession have to do with diversity? It has everything to do with diversity. Young people, minority or majority, are equally discerning. You cannot expect a minority student to choose to join a profession that many majority lawyers would not want their own children to join. Similarly, you cannot expect that a minority student will be enthusiastic about a profession that many majority associates leave in large numbers.

In sum, we need to become the profession we thought we entered—one that we would want our own children to join.

## Lawyers Must Embrace Diversity

Lawyers must begin to recognize what many corporations have learned—that diversity has significant business advantages. Decisions made after consideration of diverse perspectives and opinions are qualitatively better than those based on only one point of view. Diverse enterprises are better able to identify and serve diverse customers and constituencies.

Corporations that have begun to experience benefits from diversity in their bottom lines want the same advantages in their legal representation and legal advice. Hence, many corporations include diversity among their expectations for outside law firms, requesting that diverse lawyers handle their legal matters and requiring that the law firms provide statistical reports on minority involvement in their cases. Corporations committed to diversity in their outside counsel are looking for results, not just efforts.

Law firms must begin demonstrating a commitment to diversity through the lawyers they hire, retain and promote. Because there are so few minority lawyers in firms, there is often no critical mass within the firm. This leaves the minority lawyer feeling isolated and discouraged in the face of an on-going exodus from firms to other legal and non-legal jobs. While no one should fault the minority lawyer who leaves a firm to pursue another opportunity, the departure of a minority lawyer frequently has more impact on a firm than the loss of a white lawyer because there are so few minorities at the firm. Low retention and promotion rates for minority lawyers discourage minority lawyers who remain at firms. Retention of lawyers requires an ongoing commitment to affording minority lawyers opportunities to succeed, which should make employment offers from outside the law firm relatively less attractive.

We need ongoing efforts to ensure that law firms recognize that diversity is not just about numbers, but is also about inclusion. Meaningful inclusion means examining compensation systems and other firm policies to ensure that minority lawyers are given a fair opportunity to benefit from the business they generate.

Minority lawyers are not window dressing. They add value to an enterprise with their diverse experiences and perspectives. Indeed, in this increasingly global economy, the ability of a law firm to offer lawyers to clients who are knowledgeable about the culture(s) and fluent in the language(s) of the firm's clients provides significant advantages.

Corporate counsel are becoming increasingly diverse and will continue to call for diversity in their legal representation. Firms willing to ensure an inclusive culture will likely flourish going forward. Those who are not willing to diversify will miss out on the opportunities and advantages that diversity provides.

## Steps Toward a More Diverse Profession

The challenges of increasing diversity within the legal profession are many. Real change will require real actions and continued vigilance to address the root causes of the legal profession's pipeline and diversity issues. General Colin Powell explained the military's approach to affirmative action by relating that: "In the military, we . . . used Affirmative Action to reach out to those who were qualified, but who were often overlooked or ignored as a result of indifference or inertia." (Commencement Address at Bowie State University, 142 Cong. Rec. S9311, S9312 (daily ed., July 31, 1996)). We in the legal profession can afford to do no less.

So what should we do? What works? Unfortunately, that question assumes that a cookbook is out there somewhere with the secret recipe. It would be great if there were such a book, but it does not exist. On the other hand, there are plenty of organizations that have taken the diversity challenge seriously and have made some substantial progress. Of course, every organization is different, and each culture requires solutions that fit that culture. One size clearly does not fit all. However, there are some common elements of all diversity efforts that are successful, or at least more successful than others.

**Walk the Walk.** If you want a diversity effort to be successful, it is essential that you demonstrate—not just talk about—diversity as a core value of the organization and inclusion as the norm, rather than the exception. Successful organizations have diverse people in all important parts of the organization, not just on the diversity committee. When diverse people observe other diverse people in places where important decisions are being made and important events are happening, they are more likely to feel included and pay more attention to what the organization is doing rather than wondering why no one like them is in charge.

One concrete way to demonstrate the organization's commitment is by making diversity one of the organization's strategic goals with metrics to measure achievement and success. By adopting metrics the organization is not only making a public commitment to diversity, but it is also saying to the world that achievement of the goal is important. In other words, it is actually evaluating progress.

Another way to demonstrate a commitment to diversity is to encourage discussion about diversity without shutting down questions and concerns. Too often it is impossible to gain the necessary acceptance of diversity because people are discouraged from talking about it out of a concern that what they may ask or what they may say will be politically incorrect. In those instances, the issue of diversity may be a stated goal, but the chance of meaningful change is often hindered by the lack of conversation and discussion of relevant issues. Commitment to diversity without essential dialogue is not likely to achieve meaningful change, or at least change at a reasonable pace. Having the dialogue may cause some discomfort, but is likely to result in overall success faster.

At the end of the day, each person must take personal responsibility for making the profession and our society more inclusive. It is not just a problem for those who are racial or ethnic minorities, but it is a problem for all of us.

**Be Welcoming and Inclusive.** Essential to any diversity program is being welcoming to those who do not share the characteristics of the majority. This includes everything from making appropriate introductions of new co-workers to ensuring that you make the effort to meet and greet new attendees at meetings or other social events. Being welcoming requires intention; it does not happen by chance. Both majority and minority lawyers must make the effort to ensure that new minority lawyers are welcomed by taking the time to get to know lawyers of color and to include them in all of the day-to-day events.

Most law firms, corporate law departments and legal organizations think that they are open, welcoming and inclusive. However, such opinions are often one-sided. How often do law firms, corporate law departments and other legal organizations ask those who are new or different whether they felt welcomed or felt included? I suspect that such introspection is rarer than it should be.

Active listening to what minority lawyers are saying about inclusion is an important element of any program that strives to be effective. In the drive towards diversity, silence is not necessarily golden. Organizations that succeed at diversity are tireless in getting real-time input from people of color on how the organization can improve. They also work hard to ensure that both minority and majority lawyers accept and support the implementation of the ideas that come out of those active listening sessions.

**Become a Mentor.** Whether you are a minority lawyer, you can, and should, help to mentor a minority law student or lawyer. Effective mentoring is taking the time to share what you know and who you know. It begins with being available and letting a law student or new minority lawyer watch you in different work and social settings. Many new lawyers, majority and minority, learn how to socialize with clients through observation—by accompanying a more experienced lawyer and his/her client to lunch or dinner, to a sporting event, golf outing or other function.

While many bar associations have organized mentoring programs, it is not essential that you participate in one of those programs. Many of the best mentoring relationships just happen because a more seasoned lawyer took the time to get to know a less experienced lawyer in his or her law firm or other professional setting. Make it a point to meet and get to know the new lawyers of color hired by your firm or corporation. If you practice in a smaller firm setting, take the time to get to know a minority lawyer you meet in court or at a closing.

Success in our profession regardless of your practice setting can be significantly influenced by who you know. Be willing to share your success and your stature by introducing your mentee to clients and professional colleagues. Share your contacts. Give advice and counsel to help your mentee learn and succeed.

**Create an Effective Diversity Committee.** Creating a diversity committee is a common first step of many organizations. However, a diversity committee should not just be for (and include only) people from minority groups. The committee must include individuals from all racial and ethnic groups and must include those from all strata of the organization including those with clout and status within the organization. Too often successful lawyers (minority and majority) are too busy to work on diversity initiatives. But diversity must be a priority on both an institutional and individual level.

The diversity committee must work to make the organization more inclusive by involving all of the stakeholders. The feeling that the committee is "preaching to the choir" is one of the fastest ways to ensure failure of the diversity initiative started with all of the right intentions. Successful organizations have active diversity committees that are pro-active on inclusion initiatives and populated with important players in the organization who are used to getting things done, and not wasting time. If the diversity committee is a working part of the organization with tasks, staffed with achievers, things will get done. As a wise friend of mine opined, the diversity committee cannot graduate from being the "choir" to being the "preacher," if people "with pull" are not engaged.

## Conclusion

Diversifying the legal profession is not just an issue for lawyers of color, but for the entire profession. Majority and minority lawyers alike have a stake in the preservation of our constitutional democracy and the third branch of the government to which we have all sworn allegiance. Frequently, we find that the increasingly diverse public fails to understand and appreciate our legal system and the role that lawyers play. This lack of understanding has fueled calls to change the justice system, often in the form of referenda which make the issue a subject for the ballot box.

We cannot effectively convince an increasingly diverse American public about the bona fides of the legal profession when we are 90% white. We must, therefore, demonstrate to young people of color that we are a profession that they should join. That will require a profession that is not only diverse, but welcoming. That also will require a profession that grapples with the difficult issues posed by diversity, including the sharing of finite opportunities. That will require minority and majority lawyers, and minority lawyers from different racial and ethnic groups, to work together.

We must challenge each other to keep working so that indifference and inertia do not block further progress. Regardless of where you practice, and even if you are no longer practicing, take personal responsibility for the way our profession, our justice system and our society address diversity. There is no excuse for doing nothing. Take the time to talk with a lawyer of color in your office who otherwise might not have received any mentoring today. Approve the request of a minority lawyer to attend a minority bar convention. Write a check that won't bankrupt you, but might mean some bright young person is able to attend law school. There are a host of other little things you can do to advance diversity.

In 1966, nearly thirty years before the fall of Apartheid, South African students heard Robert Kennedy proclaim:

> Some believe there is nothing one man or one woman can do against the enormous array of the world's ills. Yet many of the world's great movements of thought and action have flowed from the work of a single person. . . It is from numberless diverse acts of courage and belief that human history is shaped. Each time a person stands up for an ideal, or acts to improve the lot of others, or strikes out against injustice, he or she sends forth a tiny ripple of hope. And crossing each other from a million different centers of energy and daring, those ripples build a current that can sweep down the mightiest walls of oppression and resistance.

Start a ripple effect. Pay it forward. Invest in our future.

## Endnotes

1. The term "minority" and "of color" will be used throughout this paper interchangeably to refer to the following racial and ethnic groups: Black/African Americans, Hispanics, Asians, Native Americans/American Indians. The use of these terms is not intended to

ignore the fact that in some parts of the country whites comprise the minority, to ignore bi- and multi-racial individuals, or to ignore the fact that Hispanic encompasses many colors and ethnic groups. These terms are used solely for ease of expression.

2. This includes American Indian and Alaska Native alone, Native Hawaiian and Other Pacific Islander alone, and Two or More Races.

3. Source: U.S. Census Bureau, 2004, "U.S. Interim Projections by Age, Sex, Race, and Hispanic Origin." (http://www.census.gov/ipc/www/usinterimproj/).

4. On the federal bench, there are currently 837 active judges. Of this number, 679 or 81% are white, 89 or 11% are Black/African American, 60 or 7% are Hispanic, 7 or 1% are Asian, 2 or 0% are Arab American, and 0 are Native American/American Indian. Source: Alliance for Justice wesite at http://afj.org/judicial/judicial_selection_resources/selection_database/.

5. Source: ABA Section on Legal Education, http://www.ababet.org/legaled/statistics/stats.html1.

6. Chambliss, Elizabeth, Miles to Go: Progress of Minorities in the Legal Profession, ABA Commission on Racial and Ethnic Diversity in the Profession (December 2004) at 6 quoting statistics from U.S. Census Bureau, Census 2000 EEO Data Tool, http:// www.census/gov/eeo2000/index.html, and U.S. Census Bureau, Statistical Abstract of the United States, 2002 (2004) (Table 615), http://www.census.gov/prod/2004pubs/03statab/ labor.pdf.)

# CHAPTER 15

# Should We Mandate Doing Well by Doing Good?

**By Lawrance J. Fox***

I hold, right here in my hand, the legal profession's playbook. All on one sheet of paper—an insert to the AmLaw 100 issue of The American Lawyer[1]—it is all summed up, revealed in a stark fashion, the profession's bragging rights and the profession's shame.

Consider the listed achievements, beginning with law firm revenue-per-lawyer. The American law firm has broken through a barrier not unlike a three-minute, thirty-second mile. And it did it as if it were not there. Currently, there are four law firms with revenues of $1,000,000 per lawyer, and in the top 100 the revenue-per-lawyer averages $650,000. Just think what it takes to break that barrier, to achieve these results. You not only have to

---

**These remarks were inspired by the author's participation in the conference "Professional Challenges in Large Firm Practices," held on April 15, 2005, at Fordham University School of Law. Special thanks to Professor Bruce Green and the Stein Center for Law and Ethics at Fordham for their dedication to the ethics arena and thoughtful consideration of the important issues facing our profession.*

be charging a lofty hourly rate across an entire law firm, but you have to be generating an unfathomable number of hours. Finally, you have to convince clients that your lawyers are entitled to exalted rates not for a brilliant inspiration or a breakthrough idea, but for 2,000 or 2,500 or 3,000 hours per year spent sifting documents, digesting depositions, and right-clicking in front of a computer screen. What an achievement!

Next, consider a second metric, the most important of them all. What are the profits-per-partner of the top 100 law firms in America? For thirty-two of them that number exceeds $1,000,000. These are not the earnings of a couple of superstars or firm leaders, the greatest of the rainmakers. This figure represents an average across 100, 200, or in some cases, even 300 lawyers. An average!

Undoubtedly, firms play some games in trying to report higher figures. They do not count dollar partners whose incomes are lower. They also play with expenses. But even after these adjustments, the numbers are truly stunning. Where, I ask you, is it written that you can have a business where that many people make that much money each year? Yet that is the health and wealth of the great American law firm.

These statistics reflect real achievement. Moreover, I have no quarrel with well-paid lawyers. Indeed, I celebrate the economic success of this tier of the profession. I have been a happy beneficiary of this extraordinary turn of events. So what is the shame? You would think with such bounty, with such munificent wealth, with such financial achievement, the contribution of the lawyers at these firms—above all other lawyers in America—to pro bono services would also be measured by stratospheric statistics. They've got the talent, they've got the wherewithal, they've got the legions of lawyers, they could afford—each of these firm families—to have quite a few "priests." But, alas, in spite of the rhetoric, the metrics for pro bono tell a far different tale. Only forty-five of the *AmLaw* 200, less than one-quarter of these great firms, achieved fifty hours of pro bono services per lawyer in the most recent year. Only twenty-seven, just a little over ten percent, of them had more than half of their lawyers undertake any pro bono services at all. The most committed firm in the bottom fifty had less than fifteen hours of pro bono per lawyer. And seventeen firms were so embarrassed by their pro bono commitment, they refused to share pro bono statistics with

*The American Lawyer* at all, even though they proudly shared their income and revenue figures.

There are other apparent contradictions when examining the pro bono commitment of America's most financially successful firms. Look at some of the dismal statistics about the pro bono services offered by top law firms, and compare them with the literature these same firms send to law students; with the prominent pledges of commitments they make about their "commitment" to pro bono on their websites; and with the emphatic statements they undoubtedly make to inquiring law students about their fealty to their professional obligation to the poor.

A few examples will demonstrate the point. Just in the top five highest grossing law firms in America, an elite group indeed, we have three that rank either at or very near the one-hundred mark in pro bono commitment. Yet read what these firms say about their pro bono endeavors:

> All around the world '[the firm's] lawyers and professionals embrace opportunities to help others through pro bono legal services, community leadership, charitable giving and public service.
>
> As [the firm] moves into the 21st century, we do so with a renewed sense of commitment to the public good through pro bono service.
>
> The firm has a long tradition of providing pro bono services. The firm's pro bono policy strongly encourages all attorneys to devote time to pro bono legal matters, including legal assistance to the poor and to the charitable, community or other organizations that serve the indigent, who would otherwise be unable to afford legal representation.[2]

How can it be that so many firms talk the talk but do not walk the walk? How can such impoverished pro bono programs exist amidst the prosperity these firms so proudly share with The American Lawyer?

It is, quite simply, that prosperity and competition have created an environment that makes it less likely that firms will take a leadership role on legal services for the downtrodden. While their absolute profitability statistics look wonderful, for all but one of these firms, there is some firm ahead of them, and for most there are dozens. It is the relative standing of one firm over another that creates the dynamic. Those at the top of the food chain have the pressure to stay there because then they can hire lateral practices from those below. Those at the bottom, to keep their "underappreciated" top producers, must move up the profits-per-partner food chain to enhance their chances of retaining those colleagues with a wandering eye, and to snare new top producers as well. Unfortunately, it is not a surprise that a casualty of the brave new world of large firm economics is pro bono, a frill to which lip service can be paid, but no real commitment can be made if billable hours are to be enhanced. Even if there are lawyers in these firms truly dedicated to the cause, the resentment they face—whether spoken or simply thought—from those who have their eyes on the economic goals is palpable.

If we cannot harvest more pro bono work at the richest, most fertile firms in America, how can we ever expect to achieve what the preamble to our rules of professional conduct holds out as our obligation? How can we continue to proclaim that, "A lawyer should be mindful of . . . the fact that the poor . . . cannot afford adequate legal assistance. . . . Therefore all lawyers should devote professional time and resources and use civic influence to ensure equal access to our system of justice"?[3]

The answer, I believe, is mandatory pro bono. I know this is not a popular idea. It is not pro bono if it is mandated; lawyers should give from the heart, the critics say. It is involuntary servitude to force lawyers to give their time and thus violates the Thirteenth Amendment of the Constitution. Still others assert that these lawyers wouldn't be qualified to do the work and their resentment at being forced to do pro bono would only further diminish the quality of the services provided.

These arguments are time-honored and not without merit, but they are not all that persuasive. First, there are many lawyers—particularly at large law firms—who would love to be "forced" to do pro bono, because in their present practice setting they face hostility at the idea from those who "count the beans" and calculate one more pro bono hour as the equivalent of one less billable hour. Second, if we lawyers want to maintain our monopoly on legal services, we clearly have an obligation individually to meet the legal needs of the poor. Who else will do it? Third, the argument that these lawyers are unqualified to do pro bono work is disingenuous. Do any of these same lawyers, those who are so quick to feign lack of capability when importuned to undertake pro bono, ever turn down paying clients for the same reason? Of course not. Moreover, there are excellent training programs available to provide any competent lawyer with the necessary tools to enter the rewarding world of representing children in foster care or social security appellants or tenants about to be evicted or whatever matter these lawyers might take on for the otherwise unrepresented. Finally, even the most hardened lawyer would see resentment evaporate as soon as the lawyer was charged with representing a live human being in need. The concept of mandatory pro bono may generate resentment, but the encounters that lawyers have with clients—appreciative clients, who are in real need—would surely cure that problem.

We are proud of our rules of professional conduct. We believe they reflect what makes us special, not in the sense of entitlement, but in terms of our responsibilities. And every one of our rules speaks in mandatory terms. They tell lawyers what they shall do, with one exception. The only rule that is written in terms of "may" is Rule 6.1, the pro bono rule. One could argue, I suppose, that this would be okay if the profession were delivering in response to this hortatory command. But the profession is not delivering, even at its most highfalutin levels. Therefore, we should change the "should" to "shall" and mandate that lawyers provide the necessary services.

How we do it raises a catalogue of interesting questions. Should lawyers be able to buy out of the obligation, as prospective soldiers did in the Civil War? Should law firms be permitted to fulfill the obligations of individual lawyers collectively; for example, by having two hundred lawyers in a firm provide 10,000 hours of pro bono, allocated among them as they see fit? And what really counts as pro bono service? Such issues must be resolved once pro bono service is required. But those are details that can be worked out. First, we must establish the principle and now is the time to do it.

## Endnotes

1. At the time this lecture was given on April 15, 2005, the most recent *AmLaw* 100 was from 2004. All statistics contained herein refer to ***The AmLaw 100***, AM. LAW, July 2004.

2. These are real quotes on file with the author. Since this article is designed to encourage pro bono, no purpose would be served, in the author's view, by identifying the firms whose quotes are so instructive.

3. MODEL RULES OF PROF'L CONDUCT Preamble 6 (2005).

# CHAPTER 16

# The Statesman Lawyer: An Oxymoron?

**By Robert N. Sayler***

## I.

My adored, accomplished daughter asked me: "It is time for me to decide—law or a graduate science degree? Dad, you loved practicing law, but you seem skeptical these days. What is the matter? Would you be scared if I started out *now* as a lawyer?"

Here is the nub of it. If there is no room for my daughter as a stateswoman, starting at the bar in 2010, then I have to tell my daughter this: it was a noble calling but now go work on molecules or ocean fishery issues or struggles with terrorism. It's an answer I would dread giving.

But can that be? Is law at essence now about sharp elbows, back-biting, Attila run amuck, fundamentally reduced to head-spinning mergers, portable billings, lateral moves galore—not just a business, but closely approximating a franchise business, with mandatory hours quotas where quantity trumps quality and quality of life? Have the craftsmanship of the Statesman, the

**Much credit is owed to Professor Molly Bishop for thoughtful insights and edits.*

professionalism of the problem-solver, the personal rewards of doing good for the sake of doing good, aspirational goals always beckoning—have these ceased to call? If Statesmanship is lost in this profession, then we have forsaken too much to justify launching into fifty years of the emotional and physical drain the practice exacts. Take away the Statesmanship payback and the rewards of other livelihoods soar in comparison.

Not so fast. For the thesis here is that the statesman and stateswoman was always at the heart of the profession, that those seeing it the other way are wrong. We just need once again to be reminded of the power of Statemanship.

## II.

The definition of a lawyer-statesman is an elusive one. Dictionaries speak of politicians, not lawyers: sagacity, the adroit skill of a leader of nations. So what springs to mind for the *legal* statesperson? Objectively, surely a rule maven: rigorous follower, even crafter, of canons, rules, one who honors calls from bar and courts to improve the dispensation of justice. Ethics matter to this character. But other important qualities reach beyond: balance, calm, judgment, decency, fair play, word is bond, presence, aversion to bullying and cheap shots, a love and command of language. In Aristotelian talk, Ethos always. But a command of Pathos and Logos invariably right at hand to boot.

Sounds like something all lawyers should set out to be. But not so. Why in the world is that? Several reasons.

- The Statesman model is not systematically taught anywhere. Ethics courses abound and bar exams treat the subject; but no one does, or perhaps could, undertake a law school course on how to be an inspirational leader. Most of that is left to much later in law firm life.
- It is perhaps resisted by many as a role too difficult to achieve, and doesn't fit individual personalities or talents. It is like asking every person to be a good athlete. Statesmanship maybe perceived as a bastion of the privileged or the exclusive preserve of the well mannered.
- It is taught *against* in some quarters. Young lawyers in some firms are just following orders in rejecting it; it runs against the firm culture.

- It seems somewhere between counterintuitive to dead wrong to near unethical to some. In a 1987 *ABA Journal* article, Stephie Goldberg quoted a handful of practitioners claiming everything from "hardball is the rule in our Firm" to one "should take the most difficult position for your opponent you can and never back down" to lawyers who don't "pull out all the stops . . . don't love their client," to the "crime" is not being "over zealous, it is not being zealous enough." *Playing Hardball,* ABA Journal, July 1987.
- Consumers of our services sometimes demand the opposite of statesmanlike work—or some lawyers think they hear a clarion call to be the orneriest cuss on the block and these lawyers then think they are impressing clients with great flashes of breast-beating.

We need to deal in part with the easy seduction by what the author termed the Rambo approach nearly two decades ago in response to *Playing Hardball.* Sayler, *Rambo Litigation,* ABA Journal, March 1988.

A mini-epidemic of Ramboism had broken out. Name-calling was rampant, especially in some cities. Wars of nasty correspondence often wildly misrepresenting the substance of just-completed procedural phone calls were waged. Lengthy speaking objections at depositions; hard to fathom misconduct in discovery; intolerable sexist conduct—all were constantly reported. Polls showed that corporate clients perceived a sharp drop in lawyer professionalism. Courts were railing at the misbehavior; renowned court decisions in *Paramount, In Re Dondi,* and *Hanna* are representative. Sanctions were being imposed in record numbers.

Where in the world did this come from? Certainly not from any empirical evidence that a tough-guy approach to any aspect of lawyering—from litigation to mediation to deal making—produced better results; there was none. In the mediation, arbitration, and successful deal areas, the emphasis surely has been more on the win-win, fair play, accommodation side than shin-kicking. And trial advocacy training can be faulted for coming into full flower a bit tardily, but it has flourished in recent decades, where it was never instructed that Rambo techniques were either good ethics or, least of all, effective advocacy.

So where did this anti-statesman epidemic spring from? It probably grew from a mindset that Statesmanship is for wimps, that it helps you win if you make life miserable for your opponent, that civility ill-befits the warrior. So entire firms came to adopt this as their signature: We are tough, we are mean, we will leave you bloody, and it perforce has to follow that we will win by some inexorable law of the street.

The problem with all this, is that it is nuts. Rambos do not do better in court. They do not make better, faster, cheaper deals. They do not advance at a faster clip in the profession. They do not "love their clients" more than the rest of us. Rambo behavior is not even the law of the street, much less the law of the halls of justice.

## III.

In between the Rambo model and unvarnished Statesman craftsmanship there lies what most of us are most of the time, the perfectly competent attorney, be it deal maker or tax lawyer or litigator or whatever. The hallmarks of these lawyers are well known: hardworking, efficient, fair playing, ethical, caring of the profession, respectful of its values; these lawyers pay close attention to legal education, to self-improvement, and to the lessons taught by the best of the elders.

So are there still Statesmen in the profession and is it still worth aspiring to? There are statespeople aplenty, and always have been. And not just Jefferson and Lincoln and Marshall. Each of us can make a list of the most revered lawyers from our own firms or those we have watched argue great cases or heard about or read about. What the lawyers on our lists likely would have in common would be those earlier-listed attributes of Statesmanship: judgment, calm, problem-solving ability, an absence of acrimony and pettiness, a tendency to praise others and avoid limelight-hogging.

- In most of the great firms the statespeople have risen to lead the firms most of the time.
- Lawyers like John Doar, Burke Marshall, Dean Acheson, Vernon Jordan, Charlie Horsky, Lloyd Cutler, Chuck Ruff were all first-rank Statesman and were all sought by Presidents precisely because they were Statesmen.

- The list of great lawyer corporate presidents always includes Statesmen. Only recently the *New York Times* was making just that point about the seventeen-year tenure of the retiring, lawyer head of the National Football League, a tenure of unprecedented labor peace and other success that was Statesman-based.
- And it is impossible to talk about retiring Statesmen leaders without thinking of Sandra Day O'Connor, revered by so many precisely because of the Statesman qualities she possessed in record dimension.
- The Statesman approach is being urged in advocacy courses throughout the country in law schools and tutoring courses. And win-win and accommodation styles comfortable to the Statesman are being advocated in other problem-solving disciplines as well.

All of this means the Statesman role is alive and well in the law; there are many and they play an important role.

Statesmanship is not reserved for the few at the pinnacle, the stars at the top. It is attainable in stages right off and is a goal worth the quest. The reasons to have at it are powerful. They include these:

- Statesman lawyering is good (and, at its best, distinguished advocacy). Rooted in Aristotelian rhetoric, a first principle of persuasion in dealing with any audience is Ethos-manifesting good character. Trust me, therefore trust my cause. This holds with any audience: judge, jury, speech, opponent, opposite party in a deal, client. If an audience is lost at that level, nearly all is lost, nearly all the time. If a listener detects any sleaze or overstatement or misstatement, there goes the whole of the message—even if the rest of it is sound. The Statesman does not do that.
- To Ethos, Aristotle adds the sparing use of Pathos (emotion) and exciting the mind with reason, Logos. Thucydides, Demosthenes, and others stress restraint, judgment, and calm. These gods of rhetoric were all the forerunners of today's Statesman, the *opposite* of Rambos. They would do the old turn-over-in the grave bit at "in our firm hard ball is the rule" stuff. The reason for that reaction is that

the Rambo approach turns classical rhetoric teaching on its head. Ethos is a proxy for fair play, objectivity; it means that we can reason together, we can trust each other, and we can respect each other, even like each other. The railing, overstating, arrogant, cocky, sarcastic, mean advocate is communicating that whatever you think of the message of my words, they are coming through the filter of a moral character that may be flawed. Then the listener will at least footnote the message and probably reject it flat out. And if it goes on for hours or weeks, Rambo is a loser, while the Statesman cannot lose because listeners are thinking, I like and trust this presenter and, to take the simplest test, would like to go to dinner with him.

- Now on to Pathos. The Rambos will use emotion all wrong—they overuse it and distort it. The occasional and heartfelt use of emotion is fine. All great speakers have command of it, and invoke it sparingly when they feel it. "I have a dream" and "Ask not what your country can do for you" and "The only thing we have to fear is fear itself" moved us because these thoughts were both felt and said by Statesmen. But the Rambo will trot out emotional terms in a phony way, constantly, to pull at the heart strings. It will be obvious and it will enrage the listener and backfire.
- The teaching of the rhetorician on the effective use of *logos*—clear, simple, never misstated or overstated use of facts or logic—proves elusive to most Rambos. Aristotle was a great teacher and a believer in the persuasive force of logic, if kept sufficiently clear, to all manner of listeners. It was the reason he was so fond of the syllogism and enthymeme—they were so powerfully elegant and clear. Statesman gravitate to that approach. Rambos so often fall short.
- The Statesman is admired and never disliked by judges and juries. Ask judges who make no point more vigorously at ABA and judicial conferences. Ask jury consultants. Judges and juries often detest mean-spirited lawyers, especially in long trials. It is certain that *some* jurors will detest them in *every* case. That is a price way too steep to pay.

- The Statesman lawyer must to be more effective in getting better and faster results in making deals and achieving acceptable results in mediation and arbitration than the confrontational ones, the fight-pitchers, the lawyers that cannot be trusted. How could it be otherwise? That defies common experience.
- The Statesman lawyers tend to advance more certainly to leadership roles in their firms and professional organizations. Their judgment will be more trusted, especially if any possible trying times are foreseen, and they will not have engendered camps of foes along the way.
- If the Rambo aspires to a federal judgeship, a top government position, membership in the American College of Trial Lawyers, or other positions based in substantial part on canvassing other lawyers, including opposing or co-counsel—as it often is—her path will be blocked by a chorus of criticism of her style.
- The Statesman, at least nine times out of ten, will fare better in presentations to clients, especially at the highest level (such as Executive Committees or Board of Directors) where most members are not well known to the presenter. Do we sue or settle? Make the deal? These decision-makers seek balance, counsel, calm, judgment, presence, confidence; they crave the Statesman.

## IV.

Finally, here are few suggestions for the aspiring young Statesman lawyer:

- Pick mentors wisely. Every institution of size has Statespeople. Most have at least informal mentor programs. Pay rapt attention to their admired qualities. These are not patented.
- Some look down on active involvement in bar activity. They are wrong. It broadens horizons, exposes one to other bar leaders and judges from all over, as well as to pressing legal issues of the day. As a side benefit, it generates business. Get active. Join a committee as soon as possible.
- Oral advocacy skills are, if not critical to assuming the Statesman mantle, the next thing to it. Yet we are still

way behind in teaching them. Some law schools, many law filers, and outside programs are now offering excellent programs. Search them out.

- Look for pro bono work. It is a professional obligation. It is good for the soul. And it provides levels of responsibility that permit development of high-level Statesmanship skills at an earlier age than otherwise possible.
- Without making a pest of yourself, look for opportunities to be active in myriad ways in your firms or other organizations. Head up summer program committees, speak whenever possible at firm-wide or committee meetings, ask to have a role in mock trials held in the firm, offer to help organize firm retreats. Just start the process of having a leadership voice. As our first mentor Howard Westwood said to me and retired NFL Commissioner Paul Tagliabue on Day Two at our firm, "Never miss a chance to speak up when (1) you can claim it is your turn and (2) you damn well know what you're talking about."

* * * * * *

A last note returning to the start. Sharp practices. The business model. Hours quotas. Mergers galore. Portable billings. Loss of professionalism. Ramboisms. The task of the statesman lawyers is to see to it that the cherished values of the raised bar never give way to the drugstore model.

Statesmanship will not fade away. The chief reason is that the Statesman feels better about his profession and his profession then feels better about him. It is a role achievable in spurts at first and then you know it is why you became a lawyer.

# CHAPTER 17

# Service to the Bar

**By Robert Grey, Jr.**

As I considered this task, I went into my third-person mode and tried to consider the question, "Lawyers derive a great benefit from bar association work because . . . ?" But after considering that question, I realized that one's own personal experience is a far better beginning. I have had twenty-eight productive, enjoyable, and stimulating years with the greatest group of Americans that provides legal services to our country and to many abroad. The short answer is I am proud to be a lawyer because of you. How can a lawyer think of doing anything else when you are joined in debate with the likes of a Larry Fox, Estelle Rogers, or Dennis Archer?

"May we live in interesting times:" How true, as every aspect and fiber of this country is being tested to determine the extent of its commitment to govern and be governed under the rule of law. Bar associations serve as important platforms for lawyers, judges, law professors, students, and politicians who bear much of the burden and responsibility to promote the rule of law, protect the balance of powers and speak clearly about the legal challenges and opportunities as key leaders of our society and the free world. That in a nutshell is the reason for my 28 years of continuous active bar service.

My first job as a volunteer was to introduce the then-candidate for Lieutenant Governor of Virginia at the Old Dominion Bar (statewide mandatory bar) Annual Meeting. The die was cast when the scheduled presenter went AWOL and yours truly was the only one in the President's range of vision. From that introduction in 1978, the President of the Virginia State Bar Young Lawyers Conference asked me to head the committee on admissions to the bar and orientation. I thought it a great honor and huge responsibility at the time. I took the job very seriously and was sure to dot every "i" and cross every "t."

Our orientation for new admitees called upon the Chair of the Committee to moderate the swearing-in ceremony. The presidents of the Virginia State Bar and Virginia Bar Association, the Chief Justice of the Virginia Supreme Court, and the Virginia State Delegate to the American Bar Association were among the dignitaries in attendance. Four years later I was the first person of color to be President of the Virginia State Bar Young Lawyers Conference.

Holding that office accomplished a few things for me. I met and worked with my peers. I refined my leadership skills. I learned the importance of public service as a responsibility of lawyers to society. I started developing a wonderful network of friends in the profession.

The legal profession's long and important role as a major contributor to preserving and improving justice in our society is both impressive and honorable. To that end, many lawyers find great satisfaction and reward as active members of bar associations. Whether it is with a local, state, national, or specialty bar, working with other lawyers to improve the profession, the justice system, and themselves help make being a lawyer a worthwhile endeavor.

Fundamental to being a lawyer is seeing oneself as a citizen of one's community, state, and country and using one's special training to make meaningful contributions to the well-being of all. The pride and fulfillment lawyers enjoy from their contributions to charity and the profession are based on the time-honored tradition of leaving the institutions a better place than you found them.

The lawyer's role in our society has not changed in over 200 years. Lawyers have assumed the mantle of leadership in state, local, and national political elections. Many have served on the bench and still others have served as Presidents, Governors, and

Mayors. We all get a dose of advocacy training, both formally and informally. The intensive heavy training we get in analytical thinking and organizing information makes us uniquely suited to lead in this role. And in many cases, lawyers have been the change agents making our society more fair and more wholesome for future generations. The bedrock of a free and prosperous society is its ability to promote opportunity and equality for all its people. Combining a fierce independence with high ethical standards has made lawyers particularly suited to assume this role. Lawyers and judges are relied up on as the experts on the meaning of the Constitution, which our society has recognized as the basis for its democracy. The American system of justice is viewed by most other lawyers around the world as the gold standard. For good reason: We demonstrate a willingness to challenge the government intrusion up on Constitutional protections, to maintain an unbiased and fair judiciary free of corruption, and to establish rigorous standards for practice in the profession by both our law schools (in providing the essential education) and again by the courts' in establishing and implementing standards for licensure of lawyers in the various states.

These skills, professional requirements, and ethical obligations allow lawyers to make significant and thoughtful contributions to charitable and civic life in their respective communities. These pro bono activities are considered part of the lawyer's role in daily life. Lawyers fulfill these obligations by representing fellow citizens who are without means to defend or prosecute their claims or answer criminal charges against them. Lawyers serve on the governing boards or serve as legal counsel to charitable and civic organizations. To round out their volunteer commitment time, lawyers are among the most active in their professional organizations, evidenced by the fact that the American Bar Association is the largest professional organization in the world with over 400,000 members.

Why do lawyers contribute their time to the work of their professional organizations in such large numbers? In part, because we believe that it is an honor and a privilege to be the guardians of our legal system and of our Constitution. Equally important, lawyers believe firmly in an independent profession and judiciary with the highest ethical standards to promote the public trust, and a rigorous legal education, maintaining quality CLE training and skill development for life-long learning.

Lawyers also pursue bar activities to build a network of friends, colleagues, and mentors.

### The Network

Building a network of lifelong friends has to be one of the most rewarding aspects of participating in bar activities. The cast of characters one meets is spectacular, from thoughtful to irascible, from kind to tenacious, from global to parochial. It is a kaleidoscope of brilliant individuals, with polish and rough edges, all having multiple talents. Many lawyers have occupied strategic positions in government services and as thought leaders here and throughout the world. Our purpose is improving the profession and the justice system, at the same time learning from each other. Bar associations allow us to express ideas about the law with others who will give candid and critical assessments. Bar associations help us sharpen our advocacy skills without being litigators and to enhance our organizational skills without being transactional lawyers. The work we do in bar associations is critical to both the development of the profession and to fulfilling the lawyers' commitment to self-governance of our profession.

Bar associations expand our legal and social circles. The causes and contributions of our work enrich the lives of others, as they provide fulfillment and accomplishment to ourselves. Bar associations have become more diverse culturally and racially. This development alone requires us to appreciate our differences and benefit from the rich and varied experiences our diversity represents. Bar associations demonstrate the best and most challenging of group dynamics. The art of compromise and the skill of negotiation to achieve a collective good plays out in bar groups in towns, cities, states, and countries every day. Lawyers band together to add strength and meaning to their activities and message: a unified voice on fairness, equity, and civil liberties.

### Improving the Profession

Bar associations also provide a forum for discussion and work on the challenges and opportunities of the ever changing landscape of the profession. Consider the events of the early 1960s. The country was undergoing historical changes in an era when civil rights and social unrest topped the nation's agenda. President Kennedy and his administration were concerned with the lack of access to justice and legal representation that many in the nation were faced with. The Office of Equal Opportunity and the ABA engaged in a dialogue about different ways to address the deficiency. Consideration was given to an idea that the federal government should provide representation to the underserved, sending shock waves through the profession prompted by the fear that the bar's solo and small firms would be displaced with federal legal employees who would be in competition with the private sector lawyers.

The idea of federal lawyers doing civil legal work was considered a direct encroachment on the independence of the profession. It was Lewis Powell, Jr., then ABA president, who brokered the compromise. The solution would enable greater access for the underprivileged and it would maintain the independence of the lawyers performing the service. Under the compromise, Congress would appropriate funds to an independent corporation with oversight by a board of directors whose members would be appointed by the President of the United States. Thus was created in 1964 the Legal Services Corporation. To this day bar associations led by the American Bar Association are the primary advocates for the Legal Services Corporation and the congressional funding for it.

In 2006 I spent a day meeting with bar leaders of Bucharest, Romania. Fifteen years since emerging from communism, the legal profession there struggles to find a way to better serve its community and the profession. What was crystal clear is the universal attitude that it was important for lawyers to be the voice of the legal profession, and that the profession should not rely on the executive or legislative branches for the development of rules governing the practice of law, standards of legal education, and the ethical code for judges. This work must be done by lawyers. Bill Meyer, the first volunteer country director for CEELI, the American Bar Association's Central European initiative, was the moderator and I was a technical advisor. In a room of 25 to 30 advocates, government officials, prosecutors, and magistrates I witnessed the most vibrant debate and dialogue about the future of the Romanian legal profession. It was only the second time that all had convened to engage in such a discussion, part of the first effort to revamp the legal profession of a modern post-communist country trying to apply democratic principles.

The discussion was civil but sharp, diverse, and imaginative. There was conflict between those who wanted progress and those who wanted to cling to old ways. It reminded me of the ABA House of Delegates debates on multi-disciplinary practice. In the end all agreed that it was important to have an independent legal profession and that issues facing lawyers abroad were important to us in America.

What does it mean to be involved in the bar association? It means you care about a cause greater than yourself. It means using your learned and unique skills to give back to your profession and communities. It means making lifelong friends and gaining the respect and admiration of your colleagues. It means getting the heartwarming satisfaction that can only come from adding your voice to improving this country's administration of justice and defending the principles contained in the U.S. Constitution.

# PART VII

# Valediction

# CHAPTER 18

# The City Upon the Hill

**By Michael E. Tigar***

*. . . . a cruel and shallow money trench, a long plastic hallway where thieves and pimps run free, and good men die like dogs. There's also a negative side.*

Dr. Hunter S. Thompson wrote those words about "the music business." Many people think they apply as well to the practice of law.

You, reading this essay, may be pleased with your work-life in the legal profession, or if you are not yet a lawyer, with the prospect that lies ahead. You may be satisfied with what you understand to be the state of your profession. If so, perhaps you will not want to read on, although I hope you will. I have some ideas to share with you.

I am speaking to you: the associate who feels alienated, unfulfilled, anonymous; the partner who wonders what has become of her image of how law could be practiced at this time in her professional career; the law student who mournfully surveys the career services postings and wonders how he will pay the law

*Facts and figures in this essay were compiled by Jennifer Dodenhoff, a 2007 graduate of Washington College of Law.*

school debts and still make the difference that he came to law school to make. I am even speaking, perhaps in a more challenging way, to those who assume that the legal profession as a whole is irreversibly committed to law as a business, directed by those seeking financial rewards and on behalf of those who already have achieved them.

The book of which this essay is a part is built, to some extent, upon assumptions that I do not share. I understand that in the age of mega-firms, and the decline of personal relations in the practice of law, alienation and anonymity are inevitable. What sense of literary style, or self-expression, can one detect in a set of 100 interrogatories, ground out by an associate who must bill at least 2,500 hours per year in order to have any chance of making partner?

I reject the assumption that once upon a time there were lawyers who were public citizens as much as they were advocates and scriveners, but that today this public function is eclipsed by the way that law is now practiced. I reject the idea that "boutique" law firms are "outliers" in the profession. I remember and reiterate the story of James Otis, with whom John Adams and others litigated the illegality of British searches and seizures in 1761. Of Otis's advocacy, John Adams wrote, "then and there was the child independence born." I remember Andrew Hamilton's defense of the colonial newspaper editor John Peter Zenger, whose acquittal "was the morning star of that liberty which subsequently revolutionized America," according to Gouverneur Morris, who signed the Declaration of Independence. Right now, the same rights of privacy and free expression are under attack, and lawyers are called upon.

I accept the reality around us. Funding for legal services programs is unforgivably low. Public defender and appointed counsel systems are under financial and time pressures that make representation of the accused a cruel joke in many parts of the country. Congress has legislated limits on legal services offices that restrict the kinds of services that those lawyers can offer. Law firms are studying "business models" and "best practices" that tend to crowd out professional ideals such as pro bono service. Law graduates who can find jobs in the legal services sector will face more difficulty than their private practice peers in repaying law school debt, unless they are lucky enough to graduate from a law school that has a debt-forgiveness program.

Numbers tell a part of the story. Median law student educational debt increased by 59 percent between 1997 and 2000. In 2000, median law school debt was $84,400. In a survey of over 1000 law school graduates, 50 percent reported graduating from law school with $75,000 in debt while 20 percent carried debts of over $105,000. More than half of the survey participants had additional debt from their undergraduate education.

Among those respondents entering government work, 58 percent carried debts between $55,000 and $105,000. Lawyers entering public service positions were even more likely to carry high debt burdens: 64 percent of entering legal service attorneys; 61 percent of future public defenders, and 67 percent of future state or district attorneys completed law school with debts between $55,000 and $105,000. With a median debt amount of $84,400 for law school, the typical young attorney will spend approximately $950 per month to repay loans. A lawyer graduating with more than $100,000 in debt will make monthly payments of more than $1,000 per month. High debt loads compared to low salaries prevent many young attorneys from entering public service. Sixty-six percent of survey participants stated that law school debt kept them from considering a job in the public or government sector.

The median salary for first-year associates working in private practice ranged from $67,500 in firms of 2–25 attorneys to $125,000 in firms of more than 500 attorneys. The median first-year salary for survey participants was $100,000. In large urban areas, the median starting salary for first-year associates in large firms (over 251 attorneys) was $125,000.

In sharp contrast, the median starting salary in 2001 for attorneys entering public interest jobs was $35,000. Attorneys entering federal government jobs made a median salary of $45,000 while those working in state or local government earned a median income of $41,000.

I do not know of any study that has sought to correlate high debt rates, low public interest salaries, and access to legal representation for low-income populations. As a law teacher who also carries a heavy docket of pro bono cases, and as a participant in bar activities related to pro bono representation, I have plenty of anecdotal evidence. One can reasonably conclude that high law school debt combined with lower starting salaries prevent many young attorneys from entering public interest jobs. In turn, there are fewer qualified attorneys to serve low-income clients. According to a study conducted by the Legal Services Corporation, for every client who requested help from a legal services-grantee, one potential client was turned away due to lack of resources.

The number of attorneys providing legal services to low-income individuals is significantly lower than the number of attorneys for the general population. There is one legal aid attorney for every 6,861 low-income people while in the general population, the ratio of attorneys is approximately one for every 525 people. The general population has 13 times more attorneys providing it with civil legal services than the low-income population, and this figure does not take account of the skewing effect of private attorney service for wealthier individuals and entities versus that for middle-income people.

Some people look at these numbers and events and describe them in the passive voice, as though impersonal forces have wrought inevitable changes in the way we must live our professional lives. I regard this way of seeing things as disempowering, in any context.

Ascribing to "the bar" or "the profession" a personality portrays events that happen to people "naturally occurring," rather than the predictable, controllable results of individual and group action. The focus on "the bar" helps to generate a feeling of powerlessness among those not in positions of power. A commentator in the French newspaper *Liberation,* speaking of a scandalous recent case, notes that the wrongful detention and conviction of defendants is characterized by the government and media as a "judicial catastrophe" as though it were an act of god or a natural disaster, without intentionality. From there comes a fatalistic attitude preached by the powerful in the form "hey, that's the way it is, you better get used to it," and by the powerless as "well I guess I better go along in order to get along."

Look around you. The ABA Litigation Section conducted two informal polls in 2005. In one survey, 48% of lawyers reported that, in their firms, they are encouraged to take on pro bono work and given credit for it. 12% say they are encouraged to do pro bono work but not given credit for it. 40% say they are neither encouraged nor given credit. In another survey, 79% said that their current practice did not match the expectations they had in law school, while 21% said that it did. Apparently, most of the 79% felt tyrannized by the billable hour and chagrined that the ideals that led them to enter the profession had escaped them.

I pause here to note one comment from the pro bono survey, "Pro bono is worthless and a waste of time. It is also economically inefficient." That view has been expressed by those who say that the poor's legal problems are best handled by lawyers who only make $40,000 a year, and that wealthier, higher-paid lawyers who want to help should send money to legal services programs. I don't expect to convince anybody who shares that view. If you think poor people's problems are less important because their lawyers don't get paid as much, or that private lawyers helping poor people wastes time, then your view of the profession seems wedded to a financial calculus. Or maybe you are locked into a certain way of practicing law and are happy where you are. A little later, I will analyze this view that poor people's problems are fundamentally different from those that rich people have.

Several years ago, I was appointed by the court to represent a criminal defendant in a complex case that promised to present challenging issues and to require a significant time commitment. I asked a partner in a major law firm to join me in the case. This lawyer declined, saying that the firm could not accept this lawyer's participation because the Criminal Justice Act fee of $90 per hour (actually $60 per hour on a current basis and then $30 per hour additional when the case is over), was simply not enough compensation. That is, the firm and this lawyer would not accept the overall diminution of firm revenues involved in becoming counsel in such a case. Yet, this was the sort of case that would and should call out the very best legal thinking and legal work of which the profession is capable.

Of course, for every such tale there are stories of lawyers in private practice accepting major challenges in pro bono and appointed cases. However, you and I know that there are considerable financial and career disincentives to that kind of practice.

I speak now of what you have seen with your eyes and experienced in your work. Law firm partners are merging, forming multi-city and multi-country entities that defy any effort to create meaningful personal relations among those who work for the same entity. With impersonality come partner decisions to focus on profitability and productivity. Young lawyers report billable-hour expectations of 2,000, 2,500, even 3,000 hours if one expects to "make partner." Given such expectations, the lawyers in the 12% who can do pro bono but don't get credit for it are under imposed pressure little different from that experienced by the 40% who are neither encouraged nor given credit.

I don't think you can have what one may properly call a "life" in an environment that imposes workloads such as those experienced by young lawyers today. And to the extent that the partners—driven by the desire for financial reward, by peer pressure or whatever—work in that mode, the same observation goes as well. I repeat, if this is your schedule and you are happy with it, fine. But the Litigation Section informal survey suggests you are in the minority. So if you share with me, at the least, a sense of unease at the way things are for you and your profession, what shall we do about it?

First, we must have confidence in our own sense of what justice is about. At a minimum, justice requires that access to the forums where rights and obligations are determined be open to all on some reasonable basis. This thought is captured, to a great extent, by the mission statement of Washington College of Law, where I teach: "Engaging the Community, the Nation and the World through Legal Education. This mission is grounded in three main ideas: law should be based on values of human dignity and respect; law represents an interaction between people and their environments; and law schools have a critical role to play in teaching students to shape their world."

The values of human dignity and respect cannot exist in conditions of gross inequality. They cannot exist when powerful leaders feel free to deny that fundamental norms prohibiting aggressive war, torture, and accountability do not apply to them. They cannot exist when the working conditions of a profession assertedly based on justice actively discourage concern with whether and how justice is achieved.

You may not share all of my views. You may define and express your sense of unease differently. No matter. Indeed, the search for meaning, though it inevitably takes place in a social context, is always personal. Ten years ago, I wrote:

> I will try to derive truths from the past and present, and from a sense of responsibility to those who will come after, but I am making decisions for myself and not as an apostle

of others or with a claim to lead. If the ideas appeal to you, there is plenty of work to do and all are welcome.

The sense of hesitation, and of personal quest, is also evoked by [the late Jacques] Derrida in his lectures. He begins [in *Spectres de Marx*] with a translated passage from the first act of Hamlet. Hamlet sees the spirit of his father, and learns how and why his father was murdered. "The time is out of joint," Hamlet says, "O curs'ed spite, That ever I was born to set it right!"

Derrida conjures with the spirit, and with various translations, of this passage to show us that thinking of justice drops us into the stream of history, the flow from past to future. In the past are the events that put time "off its hinges," or that "turn the world upside down." But to say that things are "wrong" implies that from that same past there is some idea of how things are "right-side up," or "on their hinges." This past-given sense, which is encompassed in an ideology that we can study and know, is not simply about carpentry or gravity. It is about subjective but verifiable principles of human flourishing.

And then in the present is our action, which tends into the future, towards the "set it right." To make a personal commitment to that path is not to pretend to be Prince of Denmark. It is simply to have understood the text in a certain way, and to have drawn from it certain lessons—as well as certain warnings about excessive or obsessive commitment.

This last observation is important. If the time is out of joint, the remedy is surely not to swing off one's own hinges, to become "unhinged." "And what if excessive love bewildered them till they died," Yeats wrote of the Easter martyrs, and again warned us that "Too long a sacrifice can make a stone of the heart." But the dangers are not, for me, a reason not to step into the stream.

These thoughts lead to the second point. As your sense of unease, of the time being out of joint, is personal to you, so must be your response to it. That response must not only address the conditions you find troubling, but your role in working to change those conditions. There is always an integral relationship between the task and the doer, and doing changes the doer as well as the object or event on which work is being done. This is but an instance of Heisenberg's principle that the act of observing or measuring changes the object being measured, for the process is interactive.

And so, the Prince of Denmark and Yeats's heroes ought better to have said, as in the phrase Derrida attributes to his anonymous questioner, *"Je voudrais apprendre à vivre enfin."* Finally, I want to learn how to live. In typical Derrida fashion, he has chosen a verb—*apprendre*—that can mean to learn, or to teach, thus acknowledging that the public side of our "living" provides an example to those who hear of or see us. When you are seen to take action, you begin to build your own "city upon a hill." That image comes from George Winthrop's eponymous book, written in 1630, setting out his hopes for the New World.

It is of course possible to seek and to influence change at the cost of one's own sanity and stability. Hamlet certainly found that to be so. Struggles against injustice sometimes, perhaps too often, consume the strugglers, who do not survive to see any meaningful change. We can try to avoid any such extreme personal outcome. To begin, let us see if we can learn how to live, in the fullest meaning of that verb. In this essay, I describe two paths to your own "city upon a hill."

Learning to live must begin with candid appreciation of one's current situation. If you are an associate in a mega-firm with mega-billables demanded of you, you are in fact a wage worker whose asserted professional status is being used chimerically. The firm's business model is in fact little different from what you would find in a profit-centered entity that markets petroleum products or makes automobiles. The analogy has some painful parallels—the corporations engaged in those activities are notoriously unsettling their workers' lives in order to maximize profit.

Your personal response can take many forms, depending on where you live, the kind of law you practice, and your tolerance for risk. Look outside. There are jobs in legal services and public defender offices. There are jobs that are nominally "non-lawyer" but for which you are well-suited. For example, in many communities there are substantial numbers of immigrants from Latin America. In response to the legal, family, political, and social problems that these immigrants face, there are now nonprofit social service agencies. In Chatham County, North Carolina, just south of Raleigh-Durham-Chapel Hill, the Vinculo Hispanico has an executive director who is paid $45,000 per year. That position is, at this writing, vacant, as are similar positions in other counties. If you worked at that job for three years, you would develop a network of relationships that would permit you to set up your own law practice or join a small law office.

There are other avenues out of your law firm. Every month, the District of Columbia bar counselor talks to five or six people about setting up in solo practice. Twenty years ago, solo practice involved higher overheads than it does today. You needed square feet for a library; today we go online more often. Today, there is word processing and other software that lets you do more of your own work. You can make a contract with an office-sharing company. In sum, you keep a higher percentage of what you take in. You might, in short, do the arithmetic and decide you will join the large plurality of American lawyers who are in solo and small firm practice. In 2000, 74% of the approximately 900,000 attorneys in the United States were working in private practice. Of those in private practice, 48% were solo practitioners; 15% worked in firms of 2–5 attorneys; 7% in firms of 6–10 attorneys; 6% in firms of 11–20 attorneys; 6% in firms of 21 to 50 attorneys; 4% in firms of 50 to 100 attorneys; and 14% in firms of 101 or more attorneys. These numbers give you an idea of the possibilities.

These examples are ways of changing your life by getting up and going someplace else. Of course, you are never locked in to an option you have chosen. I know one lawyer who started out in a large firm, decided that the culture there was not for him, and went to the public defender. He had fun there, trying cases and learning the litigator's craft. A partner at a small litigation firm saw him working, and so hired this young lawyer. The young lawyer became a partner in the litigation firm, but after a few years yearned for a life with more public service and fewer long trips to distant trials. So he became a judge. The point here is not that everyone can become a judge, but that there are so many paths open in this profession of ours. Realizing that there are one, two, many paths open to you is the first step in your personal liberation.

Let us visit another possible path. You may decide not to leave your law firm. You may be a partner there, or on your way to becoming one. Influencing the culture of a law firm is a worthy challenge. The process is, I think, more difficult in this time of the mega-firm, and even more so if a firm has become "national." The Los Angeles office of a multi-city firm is but one outpost, and decisions about firm culture are more difficult to influence. Nonetheless, there are success stories out there. A vocal group of young partners and associates can make themselves heard.

You can begin right now to organize your workplace, with two interconnected goals in mind. One goal is to make working conditions better. The related goal is to rededicate the law firm to the important goals of our profession.

Who are your allies in this endeavor? You can seek support among young partners and associates. You can use your membership in bar groups to spread your message, seeking like-minded people in other law firms and in other parts of the profession. Look around for senior people who may share your values and goals. For example, many large firms have been hiring big litigation names as lateral entry partners or "of counsel" lawyers. These lawyers include those who have made a name in public service or in law teaching. They add luster to a firm's reputation, and help it to attract business. They may be willing to add their clout to your efforts.

Before taking your organizing too far down the road, you should define your goals. If you don't know where you are going, it is hard to know when you have arrived. What is it about the practice of this profession that drew you to it, and that you feel is now missing. What does professional satisfaction look like, for you?

Your list might include some or all of the following. First, you want to litigate, not just sit in the office and push litigation paper. You are, in some measure, a warrior. You also want time to reflect on what you are doing, where you have been, and where you are going. Billable-hour expectations of more than, say, 1,800 per year, make that goal impossible. Long workdays that stretch into the night corrode your relationships with family and friends. You have seen your colleagues cope with such pressures in harmful ways that may include substance abuse. After all, the adrenalin rush that fuels the litigator's spirit can also lead him or her to compulsive, addictive, and ultimately destructive behaviors.

You may want your professional life to be about justice. If you are in private practice, you must pay the bills or contribute to doing so. I have been a partner in two law firms at different times, and have maintained a private practice of law in one form or another for forty years. It costs a certain fixed amount to put the key in the office door every day, to see that everybody inside is paid, and to pay all the vendors who are providing you goods and services. In the nature of law practice, the best-paying clients are in the private sector. Court-appointed work can pay your overhead in a small or solo practice, but few if any larger firms subsist by that means alone.

Inevitably, therefore, you will represent clients with whose social agenda you may disagree. As in any litigation practice, if you cannot find a level of generality with which to accept and defend your clients' goals, you have to move on to some other setting. This issue is by no means unique to large firm practice. If you are a public defender, you probably do not support murder, or theft, or drug dealing. Rather, you justify your noble role in the practice of law because you are defending the most important line the law can draw—between human freedom and the state-sponsored violence of incarceration and even death. That line involves defense of the idea of reasonable doubt and the obligation of government to respect fundamental procedural rights.

Your private-sector clients are also seeking to vindicate their claims for justice through procedural and substantive rules of law. You must, in order to stay sane, be able to accept the range of results for which your clients are contending. It may be that you will tell the leaders of your law firm that there are certain kinds of cases on which you will prefer not to work. That is a permissible position, for nobody is entitled to your legal services except the client to whose case you are appointed by a court.

But let us assume that you have made peace with your firm's client base. You still want a significant role in seeking justice and professional fulfillment, as well as a workplace that respects your need to have a life – to learn how to live. I believe that you can and should have all that, and that it is in your law firm's and their clients' best interest to join you and your colleagues in that quest.

Yes, your law firm's best interest. In a labor dispute, which is what we are talking about here, it is often wise to tell management how the workers' proposals can help the company achieve sensible goals. A blunt formulation, of course, is "either you agree to some of this or we shut this place down." Gentler ways of seeing change are also possible.

Some years ago, I represented flight attendant labor organizations. Airline travel is a service industry in which customers have choices. Good labor relations translate into good attitudes towards work and towards customers. It is in management's interest to agree to flight attendant demands for good working conditions.

Can this sort of analysis work in the law firm setting? I think so. This book of essays is by and for litigators, so let's talk about some ways that litigation law firms, or even litigation "departments," might respond to the issues we are discussing. From discussing ways of seeing our work, we can consider ways of changing how we are being told to do it.

First, litigation costs too damn much because many law firms do it grossly inefficiently. Many of these inefficiencies arise from and are abetted by discovery abuse, loose pleading, and the problems of an underfunded system for administering what is called justice. Litigation done sloppily costs too much in part because clients will pay for it and there is little incentive to achieve maximum efficiency. I have done side-by-side comparisons that make this point. Consider a major white-collar crime investigation in which one or more defendants or targets are represented by a large law firm and others by boutique firms or even solo practitioners. All the lawyers do their job in their usual ways, and a large law firm operates at a much higher cost than the other firms in the case. One should also observe the distressing number of instances in which large law firms encourage their lawyers to "churn" hours, and are caught inflating their bills.

I have been appointed counsel in huge criminal cases involving thousands of potential witnesses and millions of pages of discovery. I have made budgets and hired staff. From this experience, I have achieved my point of view, which you may call my prejudices if you like.

In our white-collar case example, the small-firm lawyers take home more money than the large-firm lawyers because they have a smaller staff. In the appointed case example, we all get paid less than in a retained case.

So the first lesson of firm organization is either to have fewer people doing the work or to pay them less. I am not in favor of layoffs, and you needn't be either. So we need to face a major cause and consequence of litigation costing too much. The partners are making way too much money, and in many firms so are the associates. That's right, too much. The disparity between public sector/public interest employment and private practice compensation has widened considerably in the past thirty years. While it is true that young lawyers today have amounts of law school debt that are greater than ever, this mound of debt cannot alone justify the starting salaries that have for some time been standard in large firm hiring.

I know, this thought of less compensation may be galling to you. I tell you, however, that "learning how to live, finally" will probably involve asking first about maximizing your sense of personal accomplishment in your profession and only then considering how to maximize your income. Money is deceptive. It is a universal commodity. Subject only to a few legal limits, you can set a price on anything. In law school courses, we are taught about the cost-benefit calculation. How much should "the system" spend to guarantee a certain level of reliability? Remember the due process cases about pre-judgment seizure of household goods? Mrs. Fuentes's stove may not be worth much, certainly not as much as it costs to get a judicial order before seizing it, but without her stove she cannot cook dinner for her family.

And even those attachment/garnishment cases deceive us, because they deal with commodities that do have a monetary value. Have you ever been to a family court, where decisions about the well-being of children are made every day? There are many able, caring family court judges, but they almost all share one problem: They and their court staffs are overburdened and underfunded, as they struggle with a docket on which three-quarters of the litigants are without counsel. You could help cure those problems with money, but money would never be the measure of success. That is the nature of our profession, and I mean by the part of our profession that represents people in disputes and seeks to get justice for them.

The first step in your campaign is to recognize that meaningful change may require that everybody take home a little less money, or more broadly that money cannot be the measure of professional satisfaction. A law firm that seeks to maximize "profitability" and "productivity" as its principal goals will inevitably be a bad place to work, unsuited to developing a sense of professionalism. You will not, in such a place, learn how to live.

Thinking of "best practices" in terms other than per-partner compensation leads to better law practice and better client service, in addition to serving the workers' professional and personal goals. If your goals are to learn your profession and feel good about what you accomplish, you can find ways to do these things. If you are a young lawyer, you cannot expect to have a major responsibility in a mega-case. The skills to run such a case, and to do the "stand up" work, come with experience. If you do not have that experience, you probably want to acquire it. So one issue for your firm is organizing cases to see that young lawyers—and paralegals and others involved in the work—are meaningful participants who have a view of the entire case. Too many large litigation firms compartmentalize work and responsibility, and deprive young lawyers of the opportunity to participate in decisions in ways that help them learn. Even in the biggest case, young lawyers can learn their craft by taking depositions and performing other litigation-related tasks.

I have been lead counsel in complex civil and criminal litigation. A team, or holistic, approach that involves younger lawyers and paraprofessionals in the entire process gives better and more efficient client service. Such an approach contributes to professional development of all the participants. Therefore, your organizing effort in your firm can focus on "best practices" that are not profitability markers but rather enhance the quality of your work-life.

I understand that even relatively experienced lawyers in large firm practice may not have the opportunity to gain trial skills. The ABA Section of Litigation has sponsored valuable research into why the civil jury trial has been vanishing, and what must be done to make it less of an endangered species. On the criminal side, a congeries of problems make it hard for a defendant to get a fair trial. The system is organized around plea bargains made by often inadequate counsel.

These broader problems are a part of the malaise that affects your own situation. Unless you and others address them, they will become increasingly obdurate structural barriers to professional satisfaction. The profession as a whole, and you with it, are devalued by institutional pressures that deprive people of the chance to have their cases tried.

You can address the "vanishing trial" issue in a personal or firm setting, as part of your campaign to change the way you practice law. A client is a client. That is, listening to somebody's story and seeing how it can be a "story," in the sense of which trial lawyers speak when talking about the theory of a case, is at the heart of good lawyering. Learning to listen, and to translate a personal history into "law's story," requires practice as well as education and compassion.

A motion is a motion. Legal analysis is legal analysis. Some arrogant people say that the legal problems of the poor are so different from the high-flying kind of law they practice that poor people are best consigned to legal services lawyers. It is true that each field of law has principles and procedures unique to it, and that the adequate lawyer must take care to know those. However, in every case I begin by going back to what I learned in the first year of law school. That first-year curriculum is designed to teach you two sets of skills. The first is to ground you in the basic substantive elements of our legal system—contracts, torts, property, procedure, criminal law, and perhaps a couple of others. The second is to instill a way of seeing, which is best termed deconstruction. In every case that has ever come my way, I have reverted to the basic substantive elements that lurk in its legal structure, and to this deconstructive way of seeing.

A trial is a trial. We argue the legal issues, we present and cross-examine the witnesses. We argue to the deciders, judge, or jury.

In sum, it is wrong and silly to imagine that poor people have special types of poor people problems that are not worth the time of big-time lawyers. Beyond this, such a view rests on the demonstrably false assumption, discussed above, that justice can be understood solely or mainly as a cost-benefit calculus of dollars.

If you agree with what I am saying, then you and your firm need to talk about getting you and your colleagues into court. You gain invaluable experience. You may work with legal services or public interest lawyers who have insights to share. You learn how your decisions work out in the contest of litigation. Your firm gains prestige from the public perception that it cares about justice. Your firm gains because you are happier worker.

You are also a more productive worker because you are learning your craft in ways that being sixth chair in a complex civil case cannot ever teach you.

And what about this "vanishing trial" issue? One way to stop trials from vanishing is to see that people are not priced out of the trial market. Shouldering the litigation load for legal services, civil rights, pro bono, public defender, and other such programs is the most direct and effective way to revive the endangered trial species.

You and your firm, if you prefer, can also find complex pro bono litigation. Under federal law, legal services offices are precluded from bringing class actions and other types of impact litigation. This prohibition sweeps broadly across federally funded programs. Even offices that do not labor under a formal prohibition may not have the resources to do big cases. The ABA Litigation Assistance Partnership Project matches law firms with the skills to take on complex cases with pro bono projects that need those resources. Major law firms have taken on post-conviction representation of death row inmates, and have even sent their lawyers to work with capital case trial defense teams. They have become involved in representing detainees and torture victims.

If you want to make specific proposals about how your firm can put its lawyers into pro bono service, you must do research. It is not difficult to find community organizations that are sources of good cases. Some of these organizations are designed around litigation: defender services and the ACLU are examples. Others serve client communities that inevitably present legal problems.

As you think about pro bono and public service activity, you will quickly see that taking on a "small" criminal case and taking it to trial or settlement may require you to spend dozens of hours. A 75-hour-per-lawyer-per-year pro bono commitment is, realistically, meaningless if your objective is to have lawyers do the work in a way that serves the client and the lawyers' own professional advancement.

If this part of the analysis makes sense, you can now see a set of interrelated demands around which to organize. The firm should revise its compensation goals downward, to allow for significant pro bono involvement by partners and associates, who will use firm resources. The firm should recognize that its lawyers' professional development is well-served by significant pro bono involvement. The firm should recognize that excessive billable hour expectations may erode the quality of work, and certainly erode the quality of life of all concerned. The firm should adopt a team approach to litigation. All of these approaches are today being taken by law firms. In legal newspapers and magazines, you can find out which firms are using which strategies. You can join bar groups and committees and get their newsletters. You can see which firms and which lawyers receive public recognition for public service, and point to them as examples of good publicity for your firm.

In this brief essay, I have sketched just two paths you might take. As I was finishing writing, I read of Betty Friedan's death. She wrote "The Feminine Mystique" in 1963. Her book, and her championing women's rights, helped to start a movement that changed the face of many American institutions, including the legal profession. I graduated from law school in 1966, and in our class of 313 were six women. Today half of the law students, and 30.2% of practicing lawyers, are women. As I read the obituary articles, I was reminded of the opening words of Betty Friedan's book. She said in her preface:

> Gradually, without seeing it clearly for quite a while, I came to realize that something is very wrong with the way American women are trying to live their lives today.

I think that the same thing can be said, and is being felt, about what has happened to a great deal of law practice. I take the 79% figure in the Litigation Section informal poll as some proof of this assertion. But as we look back these more than forty years at what movements for change have done, there is reason not to despair.

Learn to live, first by understanding, then by expressing, and at last—*enfin*—by joining with others to redeem the promise that this justice-seeking profession is supposed to keep. And in that process, keep your own promises, to yourself and those close to you.

# INDEX


## A

ABC Project (ABA), 233
Adams, John, 274
advertising, by lawyers, 5
Affirmative Action, 245
after-school programs, for children, 242
"After the JD" (American Bar Foundation), 57, 59, 61, 62–63
Alston & Bird, 36, 38–39
  communication at, 73–74
  community service of, 77
  culture of fairness at, 72–73
  on *Fortune* "100 Best Places to Work" list, 71–72
  hiring practices, 75–76
  social events at, 81
  work-life balance at, 78–79, 80
American Bar Association. *See also* bar associations; Model Rules of Professional Conduct (ABA)
  *ABA Journal*, 259
  Central European initiative of, 269–270
  importance of service to, 265–270
  Litigation Assistance Partnership Project, 288
  on pro bono work, 230–231, 232, 233, 276–277
  Raise the Bar Project, 28, 53, 63–64, 70, 82–83, 100, 201–202
American Bar Foundation
  "After the JD," 57, 59, 61, 62–63
  on pro bono work, 222–223, 225–227
  "Report on Pro Bono Work of American Lawyers," 226–227, 228–229
American Corporate Counsel (ACCA), 230
*American Lawyer*, 5, 47
  AmLaw 100, 34–37, 45, 187, 251
  AmLaw 200, 27, 34–37, 42, 47–51, 252–253
  on pro bono work, 226
Americans United for Life Legal Defense Foundation, 223
Andrews Kurth, 36
appointed counsel system, 274, 277. *See also* pro bono work
Aristotle, 258, 261–262
Arnold & Porter, 49, 116
  communication at, 74
  community service of, 78
  on *Fortune* "100 Best Places to Work List," 71–72
  hiring practices, 76
  work-life balance at, 79–80
associates. *See also* mentoring
  effect of leverage on, 45
  perspective of, 90–95
  Project for Attorney Retention, 118, 124 126
  respect for, 164
  values conveyed to, 57–58
Association of the Bar of the City of New York, 178
attrition. *See* retention, of new hires

## B

Baggott, Horace W., Jr., 138
Baggott, James C., 138, 139
Baggott, James H., 138
Baggott, Roland W., 138
Baggott, Thomas M., 138
Baker, Botts, 36, 49
Baker & McKenzie, 48
Balanced Hours Coordinator position, 130
balanced hours programs, 113. *See also* work-life balance
  defined, 114
  developing, 127–128
  implementing, 128–130

balanced hours programs, *continued*
need for, 114–121
part-time status *vs.*, 114, 121–124
Project for Attorney Retention (PAR) usability test, 118, 124–126
reinforcing, 130–131
"banking" time, 19
bar associations, 25. *See also individual names of associations*
core professional values and role of, 63–64
for development, 202, 211–212
importance of service to, 265–270
involvement in, and statesmanship, 263
mentoring programs, 174–175, 178–179
pro bono work by, 232–233
*Bates v. Arizona*, 5
Bell Boyd, 36
benchmarking, 81–83
Benton, Cathy, 71, 72–73, 75
Bernthal, Rick, 194
"100 Best Places to Work" *(Fortune)*, 71–72
Beyond Ethics Project (ABA Litigation Section), 62–63
billable hours, 6–13, 61, 104, 148—149. *See also* compensation; law firm size
arguments for, 27–28
average increase in, 6
bonuses, 16, 20–22, 187–188
credit for pro bono work, 78
distortive effect of, 17–19
expectations of associates, 277–278
fee arrangement flexibility, 156–157
generating new business, 26–27
history of, 15–17
non-billable activities, 22–26
providing "credit" for training, 203
Raise the Bar Project and, 28
Bingham McCutchen, 48
Bluhm Legal Clinic (Northwestern Law School), 231
Boies Schiller, 47
bonuses, 16, 20–22, 187–188. *See also* compensation; performance
Brian, Brad, 82–83
Brill, Steve, 5
*Brown v. Board of Education*, 242
business practice firms, 34. *See also* law firm size

## C

Cadwalader, 47
Cahill Gordon, 35, 47, 49
Caldwell & Moore, 20–22, 103–104
California Women Lawyers, 174
Call to Action, 176
career satisfaction, 146
balanced hours programs for, 120–121
career advice for lawyers' children, 1–5, 242–244, 257
diversity of legal profession and, 243–244
enacting change, 279–282
expectations for law career and, 87–90, 95–101
flexibility and, 155–156
fulfillment and, 90–95
geographical factors and, 62
income correlation to, 57–58
increased leverage and, 42–46
law firm size and, 40–42
setting goals for change, 282–289
case assignments
better assignments as reward, 191–193
mentoring and, 170–171, 177–178
"shadowing" by young lawyers on, 206–210
workload, 129–130, 188–189, 191–193
Center for Individual Rights, 223
Chapman and Cutler, 49
charitable activities. *See* pro bono work
Christopher Commission, 172
civic/community service, 25, 76–78, 241–242. *See also* diversity; pro bono work

Cleary Gottlieb, 48
CLE credits, for pro bono work, 219, 233
client service
  balanced hours programs and, 117–118
  diversity demanded by clients, 175–176
  effect of leverage on, 46–47
  law firm size and, 42
  lawyers directed by clients, 161–164
  for poor clients, 276–277, 280–281, 288–289
  values of clients and, 62–63
Clinton, Bill, 230
communication, in work environment, 73–74
compensation, 61–62, 104. *See also* billable hours; law firm size
  alternative forms of recognition, 80
  appointed counsel, 274, 277
  in balanced hours programs, 128
  better case assignments as reward, 191–193
  bonuses, 16, 20–22, 187–188
  career satisfaction correlation to, 57–58
  excessive levels of, 285–286
  firm leverage and, 46–47
  part-time policies and, 136 n50
  public service *vs.* private practice, 275–276
  starting salaries, 184–185
  tying to performance, 184–188
consultants, management, 64–65
core professional values. *See* ethics
corporate counsel, 42, 46–47
  core values and, 62–64
  diversity and, 245
  perspective of, 87–90, 109, 151–154
  pro bono work encouraged by, 229
  willingness to work with part-time attorneys, 118
corporate firms, 34. *See also* law firm size
Corporate Pro Bono Infopack (ACCA), 230
corporations, expectations for diversity by, 244–245. *See also* corporate counsel
Covey, Stephen, 196
Covington & Burling, 49
Cravath, 35, 47
Criminal Justice Act fees, 277
C-SPAN, 90
Cummings, Scott, 221
Curran, Barbara, 219–220

## D

Davis Polk, 35, 48
Debevoise, 35, 48
Deloitte & Touche USA LLP, 115
Derrida, Jacques, 279–280
Deutsch, David, 147–148
development, of young lawyers, 199–200, 212–213. *See also* mentoring; training
  bar association programs for, 211–212
  case assignments and, 206–210
  "development plans" for each associate, 209–210
  feedback for, 204–206
  mentoring for, 210–211
  need for, 200–201
  as part of firm's culture, 201–202
  training and, 202–204
Dick, Francis, 139
Dickstein, Shapiro, Morin & Oshinsky, 187
Dinovitzer, Ronit, 57
*Directory of Legal Employers* (NALP), 227
diversity, 115–116, 118–119, 237–239, 248–250. *See also* balanced hours programs
  commitment to, 244–245
  committees for, 248
  education of minority children and, 241–242
  of judge population, 240
  of law student population, 242–244
  of lawyer population, 238, 239
  sexual orientation, 76

diversity, *continued*
strategies for increasing, in legal profession, 245–248
women lawyer population and, 171–173, 240–241, 289
DLA Piper Rudnick, 184, 231
*Documenting the Justice Gap* (Legal Service Corporation), 221
Doody, Margaret, 142
*Doonesbury* (Trudeau), 101

## E

education of minority children, 241–242
Emanuel, Quinn, 195
Emerick, Darrin, 71, 73, 74, 77, 80, 81
Ernst & Young, 115
ethics
associates' view of, 57–58
bar association role and, 63–64
Beyond Ethics Project (ABA Litigation Section), 62–63
of billable hours, 17
client service and, 62–63
core professional values and, 55
leadership and, 54–56
management consultants and, 53–54, 64–66
of partners, 56–57
recruiting process and, 59–60
work-life balance and, 60–62
ethnic diversity. *See* diversity
Ethos, 258, 261
evaluation, 204–206
expenses, as incentive, 188–189

## F

fairness, as law firm culture, 72–73
family leave, 61
"family responsibilities discrimination," 134 n39
fee arrangements, flexibility in, 156–157. *See also* billable hours
fee collection process, 12
feedback, 204–206
*Feminine Mystique, The* (Friedan), 289
"50 Top Women to Watch" *(Wall Street Journal)*, 175–176
Fisch, Alan, 196–197
*Fortune*, 71–72, 193–194
Friedan, Betty, 289
Frisch, John, 195
Fulbright, 36

## G

Garth, Bryant G., 57
gender diversity. *See* balanced hours programs; diversity
geographical factors, career satisfaction and, 62
Georgetown University Law Center, 232
Gibson Dunn, 36, 48
Gilson, Ronald, 57
Glincher, Andrew, 74
Goldberg, Stephie, 259
government lawyers, pro bono work by, 230–231
Greco, Michael, 233
Greene, Andra, 70
Greer, David, 155
*Grutter v. Bollinger*, 238
Guberman, Ross, 197

## H

Hamilton, Andrew, 274
Henderson, William, 56–57
Hibey, Jim, 190–191
hiring practices, 74–76. *See also* career satisfaction
honesty in, 103–109
recruitment, 42–43, 59–60, 105, 116–117
in solo practice, 157
Holland & Knight, 48
home offices, for associates, 189

## I

Illinois, legal needs studies, 220, 221
image of legal profession, 12–13
diversity and, 243–244
respect among lawyers, 162–164
tracking billable hours and, 17
immigrants, as clients, 280–281
insurance industry, 160–161
Irell & Manella, 48, 49

## J

Jenner & Block, 49, 109
Johnson, Ben F., III, 72, 73, 77
Jones Day, 48
judges, diversity of, 240
justice, as career goal, 283–289

## K

Kadish, Marc, 227
Kennedy, J.F., 269
Kennedy, Robert, 249
Kilpatrick Stockton, 36
King & Spalding, 36, 77
Kirkland & Ellis, 36, 48

## L

Latham & Watkins, 36, 48, 194
law firm size, 33–34. *See also* solo practice
  client service and, 42
  core professional values and, 55
  growth in, and leverage, 34–36
  increased leverage and working conditions, 42–46
  lower leverage and client service, 46–47
  management layers and, 40–42
  mentoring and, 170–171
  pro bono work and, 228–230
  professional/financial success in small firms, 47–51
  reasons for growth in, 37–39
  working conditions and, 40–42
law review, 143–144
law schools
  career expectations of law students, 87–90, 95–101, 108, 158–160
  competitiveness in, 142–144
  curriculum, 287
  diversity of students in, 242–244
  enrollment fluctuation, 38–39, 43, 159
  placement by, 60
  pro bono work by, 219, 229–230, 231
  student debt, 274–275
lawyer population. *See* diversity
Lawyers Alliance (New York), 229
leadership. *See also* diversity
  commitment to balanced hours programs, 129–130
  commitment to diversity by, 246
  ethics and, 54–56
  importance of bar service and, 266
  management layers and, 40–42
  statesmanship and, 264
  values conveyed by, 54–56
*Learning to Serve* (AALS Commission on Pro Bono and Public Service Opportunities), 231
legal aid, 220, 276
legal citation, 144
*Legal Needs of the Public, The* (Curran), 219–220
legal needs studies, 218–223
Legal Services Corporation, 219, 220, 221, 269, 276
Lerman, Lisa, 27
leverage, 106. *See also* partners
  effect on working conditions, 42–46
  growth in law firm size and, 34–36
  Profitability Per Partner and, 45, 47–51
  reasons for increase in, 37–39
liberal arts education, 142
*Liberation*, 276
Litigation Assistance Partnership Project (LAPP) (ABA), 233
Logos, 261–262
Louisiana, law school graduates in, 159
LSAT, 43

## M

Madrid, Linda, 117–118
malpractice, 41
Marshall, Thurgood, 242
*Martindale-Hubbell Law Directory*, 34
Massachusetts Women's Bar Association, 126
Mayer, Brown, Rowe & Maw, 227
McKee Nelson, 48, 49
meals, as incentive, 188–189

mentoring, 70, 210–211. *See also* diversity
activities for, 172–173
choosing a mentor, 173–174
diversity in legal profession and, 247–248
law firm commitment to, 176–179
matching services for, 174–175
statesmanship and, 263
for women and minorities, 167–181
*Metropolitan Counsel*, 74
Meyer, Bill, 269
Microsoft, 196–197
Milbank Tweed, 35, 48
Miles & Stockbridge, 195
minorities. *See* diversity
Minority Counsel Program, 175
Mnookin, Robert H., 57
Model Rules of Professional Conduct (ABA). *See also* American Bar Association
on case withdrawal, 153–154
on conflict of interest, 10
Model Rules of Professional
on fees, 9
on pro bono work, 222–223, 225–226, 255
moot court, 143–144
morale. *See* career satisfaction
Morris, Gouverneur, 274
Morrison & Foerster
community service of, 78
culture of fairness at, 72–73
on *Fortune* "100 Best Places to Work List," 71–72
hiring practices, 75–76
social events at, 81
motivation, 183–184
better assignments for, 191–193
expenses for nights/weekends and, 188–189
sense of purpose and, 193–197
through good work relationships, 189–191
tying compensation to performance for, 184–188
Munger Tolles, 48, 49

**N**

Nath, Bernard, 7
National Football League, 261
*National Law Journal*, 61
new business generation, 26–27, 106
balanced hours programs and, 119
in solo practice, 157
"New York model," 184
*New York Times*, 261
Nixon Peabody, 74, 76, 77–78, 79, 81
nonprofits, 90–95, 229–230, 232
Northwestern Law School, 231

**O**

O'Connor, Sandra Day, 261
Office of Equal Opportunity, 269
O'Melveny, 36
open-door policies, 73–74
Operation Greylord, 4
oral advocacy skills, 263–264
Orange County Bar Association, 202, 211–212
Otis, James, 274
out-of-court settlements, 11, 13, 149–150, 286–288
overhead expenses, law firm size and, 41–42

**P**

Pacific Legal Foundation, 223
Pantaleo, Peter, 184
partners, 6
attainability of partnership, 105–109
commitment to balanced hours programs, 129–130
downgraded status of, 44, 106–107
lateral moves between firms, 107–108
management layers and, 40–42
participation in training by, 203–204
Profitability Per Partner, 45, 47–51, 106, 107, 109, 252–255
status of, 44–45
two-tier partnerships, 44, 56–57
values conveyed by, 56–57
women and minorities as, 171–173

part-time policies, 80
balanced hours programs *vs.*, 114, 121–124
compensation and, 136n50
corporate counsel and, 118
"schedule creep" and, 121–123, 125
stigma of part-time status, 121, 123–124
Pathos, 261–262
Patterson Belknap, 35
Paul Weiss, 47
performance
bonuses for, 16, 20–22, 187–188
recognition for, 80
tying compensation to, 184–188
Perkins Coie
communication at, 74
community service of, 77
culture of fairness at, 72–73
on *Fortune* "100 Best Places to Work List," 71–72
social events at, 81
work-life balance at, 79
"Pig Case," 147–148
"Playing Hardball" *(ABA Journal)*, 259
plea bargains, 286–288. *See also* out-of-court settlements
Powell, Colin, 245
Powell, Lewis, Jr., 269
Powell Goldstein, 36
"Pro Bono and Public Service Best Practices Resource Guide" (Renaissance of Idealism in the Legal Profession), 233
*Pro Bono Directory* (Vault), 227
Pro Bono Institute, 226, 230, 232
Pro Bono Net, 232
pro bono work, 7–13, 217–218, 233–235, 267. *See also* civic/community service
bar association support of, 232–233
core professional values and, 59
by corporate counsel, 228–230
demand for, 218–220
for development of young lawyers, 208–210
by government lawyers, 230–231
law firm culture and, 224–228
by law schools, 219, 231
nonprofit providers, 232
on-line resources, 234
poor clients needs and, 276–277, 280–281, 288–289
*pro bono publico*, defined, 217
as professional development, 288–289
profitability of law firms and, 251–255
statesmanship and, 264
supply of, 221–223
types of, 223–224
views against, 276–277
Profitability Per Partner (PPP), 45, 47–51, 106, 107, 109, 252–255
Project for Attorney Retention (PAR), 118, 124–126, 178
promotion
balanced hours programs and, 126, 128
lockstep system of, 184–188
mentoring and, 170–171
public defenders, 274

## Q

Quinn Emanuel, 18, 19

## R

racial diversity. *See* diversity
Raise the Bar Project, 28, 53, 63–64, 70, 100
on benchmarking, 82–83
on development as part of firm's culture, 201–202
recruitment. *See* hiring practices
Renaissance of Idealism in the Legal Profession project, 233
"Report on Pro Bono Work of American Lawyers" (ABA), 226–227, 228–229
retention, of new hires, 28, 40–42, 60, 98, 115, 164. *See also* balanced hours programs; development, of young lawyers
balanced hours programs and, 119–120, 126
discovering reasons for attrition, 178–179

retention, of new hires, *continued*
  mentoring for, 169–171
  Project for Attorney Retention (PAR), 118, 124–126, 178
revenue-per-lawyer, 251–252. *See also* Profitability Per Partner (PPP)
Rhode, Deborah, 220
Rice, Walter H., 144
risk management
  balanced hours programs and, 120
  malpractice and, 41
Robbins Kaplan, 49
role models. *See* mentoring
Romania, 269–270
Ropes & Gray, 48, 49

## S

Sandman, James, 80, 116
San Francisco Bar Association, 178
"schedule creep," 121–123, 125
Schulte Roth, 48
*Seven Habits of Highly Effective People, The* (Covey), 196
sexual orientation, 76
"shadowing," 206–210
Shearman, Sterling & Wright, 34, 35
Simpson, William, 76
Simpson Thacher, 35, 47
size of firms. *See* law firm size
Skadden Arps, 35, 48
social events, 80–81
solo practice. *See also* law firm size
  as alternative to large law firms, 281
  number of practitioners in, 281
  perspective of, 154–164
Solovy, Jerry, 7–8
Sonnenschein Nath & Rosenthal, 7
statesmanship, 257–258
  attainment of, 263–264
  attributes of, 260–263
  defined, 258–260
Strook Stroock, 35
substance abuse, by litigators, 282
Sullivan & Cromwell, 35, 47
summer associate positions, 104, 105
Sutherland, 36

## T

tenure, of partners, 106–107
Thompson, Hunter S., 273
Thompson, Knight, 36
time accounting, 17–19. *See also* billable hours
  integrity in, 160–161
  by sole practitioners, 157–158
  strategies used for, 151
training, 43. *See also* development, of young lawyers
  balanced hours programs and, 129
  core professional values and, 55
  feedback and evaluation, 204–206
  formal methods of, 202–204
Trudeau, Garry, 101
Trueheart, Harry P., 76

## V

values. *See* ethics
Valuskas, Anton, 4
Vinson Elkins, 36, 49

## W

Wachtell, 47, 48, 49
*Wall Street Journal*, 175–176, 227
Washington College of Law, 278
Weil Gotshal, 35, 48
Westwood, Howard, 264
White & Case, 35, 48
Williams & Connelly, 49
Willkie Farr, 48
Winston Strawn, 36
Winthrop, George, 280
Women Lawyers of Los Angeles, 174
work environment, 69–72
  benchmarking and, 81–83
  civic/community service and, 76–78
  communication in, 73–74
  culture of fairness in, 72–73
  development as part of firm's culture, 202–204
  diversity in work relationships, 246–247
  fostering good work relationships, 40–42, 189–191

hiring practices and, 74–76
work-life balance and, 78–81
work-life balance, 21–22, 25–26, 78–81, 278. *See also* balanced hours programs; career satisfaction
non-equity lawyer categories and, 44
values of firm and, 60–62
workload. *See also* case assignments
for balanced hours programs, 129–130
monitoring, 191–193
motivation and, 188–189

**Z**

Zenger, John Peter, 274